DI002715

edited by

David Martin

Volume 20   Issue 4   Winter 2012

Published in cooperation with:

WriteLife, LLC
2323 S. 171 St.
Omaha, NE 68130

www.writelife.com

Fine Lines, Inc.
PO Box 241713
Omaha, NE 68124

www.finelines.org

Printed in the United States of America

Cover Photo Credits

Front Cover: "The Sky's the Limit"
© Leonardo Roberto Caucino

Back Cover: "Winter Road Trees"
© Kim Justus

ISBN 978 1 60808 050 2

ISSN 1523-5211

First Edition

About *Fine Lines*

Fines Lines is published by Fine Lines, Inc., a 501(c) 3 non-profit corporation. Publishing services are provided by WriteLife, LLC, a non-traditional book publisher. David Martin is the managing editor. In this quarterly publication, we share poetry and prose by writers of all ages in an attempt to add clarity and passion to our lives. Support is provided through donations, all of which are tax deductible. Join us in creating the lives we desire through the written word.

Composition is hard work. We celebrate its rewards in each issue. Share this publication with others who love creativity. We encourage authors and artists of all ages. Our national mailing list reaches every state. Increased literacy and effective, creative communication is critical for all.

Fines Lines editors believe writing of life's experiences brings order to chaos, beauty to existence, and celebrations to the mysterious. We encourage readers to respond to the ideas expressed by our authors. Letters to the editor may be printed in future issues after editing for length and clarity. Reader feedback is important to us. We support writers and artists with hope and direction. Write on.

Donations

Contributions are tax deductible. When you support *Fines Lines*, four perfect bound journals will be delivered to your front door. Frequently, we send an e-letter with *Fines Lines* news, upcoming events, and the inside scoop on special issues.

In addition, we provide hundreds of copies to students who have no means to buy the journals. You will add to their literacy, too.

We offer two methods of payment for your *Fines Lines* donations:

- U.S. residents should make checks payable to *Fines Lines* for $50. Schools and libraries in the U.S. should send $40. Those living outside the U.S. must send their checks for U.S. $60. Please include your name, address, and email with your payment and send to:

  Fines Lines Journal
  PO Box 241713
  Omaha, NE 68124

- We also accept credit card payments via PayPal on the *Fines Lines* Web Site: www.finelines.org

Submissions

- We accept email, file attachments, CDs formatted in MS Word for

PCs, and laser-printed hard copies.

- Editors reply when writing is accepted for publication, if a stamped, self-addressed envelope or email address is provided.

- Submissions must not include overt abuse, sexuality, profanity, drugs, alcohol or violence.

- Do not send "class projects." Teachers may copy *Fines Lines* issues for their classes and submit student work for publication when they act as sponsors.

- Address changes and correspondence should be sent to *Fines Lines*.

Robert W. Service, the great Canadian/Yukon poet:
"Imagination is a gift from the Gods.
If granted, one need not search for stories.
There is romance in every face."

Contents

Essays & Art

After 20 Years:
Fine Lines Celebrates the "Best of the Best"

David Martin

This winter 2011 issue of *Fine Lines* (20.4) is our "Best of the Best" publication, which celebrates 20 years of sharing "fine lines" of writing by young authors of all ages. Our Special Editors went through every back issue we have printed since 1992 and pulled out what they felt were the best articles and poems that we sent to our readers. This subjective evaluation centered on each writing's focus, message, and impact. One of our editors' favorite quotations which they used to select the submissions to print in our four books per year for the past two decades was by Bill Wheeler: "Good writing is clear thinking made visible."

Since 1991, *Fine Lines* has provided a place where creative writers can share their written ideas with others. Our journal is dedicated to the writing development of all its members. What started out as a journal writing project in one classroom in one high school is now a fifty-state network of authors who love the written word.

Fine Lines incorporated on May 8, 2000. Our IRS standing is a 501 (c) 3 non-profit organization. Through 2012, we have printed nearly 7,000 articles and poems by almost 3,500 authors. Submissions have been received from more than 30 foreign countries and 47 states in the USA. We estimate the number of our readers exceeds 10,000 people. The first issue was only 4 pages long, and it allowed students an opportunity to show others outside their classrooms the results of "clear thinking made visible." Now, each of the four quarterly journals is 300 pages of fiction, nonfiction, and poetry written by students, teachers, and community members of all ages.

We receive prose articles of medium length, reflective essays on widely diverse topics, authors' life experiences, what individuals learn through the writing process, and poetry in all forms. We have published writers from as far away as the Alsatian Islands, Azerbaijan, Australia, Barbados, Canada, China, Denmark, Dubai, England, Germany, India, Iraq, Ireland, Israel, Italy, Japan, Jordan, Kazakhstan, Malaysia, Poland, Russia, Scotland, Sicily, Sierra Leone, Sri Lanka, Sweden, Switzerland, Thailand, Togo, Turkey, United Arab Emirates, and a US Navy aircraft carrier in the South Pacific. How cool is that?

Writers of all ages and occupations are encouraged to submit to *Fine Lines*. We have printed poetry by a 7-year-old third grader and several pieces by a 94-year-old great, great grandmother. We have printed the work of students, teachers, professors, farmers, janitors, doctors, lawyers, ministers, truck drivers, nurses, and scientists. If you want to read interesting and controversial ideas, *Fine Lines* is for you. Send us a submission of your writing in the near future. You might become a published author, too.

Fine Lines is devoted to writing across the curriculum. We hope to provide insights for writers of all interests, encourage discussion of composition in ways that cut across content areas, and publish contributions by all members of the writing community. We welcome articles on all topics of interest to our readers. Our editors encourage a variety of approaches, methodologies, and styles. We accept articles and practical submissions that describe innovative approaches to life's challenges. We are glad to receive work encouraging stimulating dialog that crosses traditional rhetorical and disciplinary boundaries, forms, and roles. The views expressed in *Fine Lines* are solely those of the authors. Therefore, *Fine Lines* does not represent any author's point of view, politically or religiously. Our purpose is to be a vehicle of fine writing for all serious thinkers.

Submissions must be sent via email file attachments using Microsoft Word, CD disks, or laser-quality hard copies. If replies are requested, authors must include a self-addressed, stamped envelope, or mention this in the email submission. All submissions must use the MLA format. Please include a one paragraph autobiographical statement and a digital, head-shoulder photo.

Fine Lines has held twelve continuous creative writing summer camps. Our week-long "campers" range in age from 7 to 75, and every session is filled with comedy, art, dance, music, history, and composition. We are hard at work developing the summer camps for next summer! Check our website for more details.

Our archived volumes 1.1 (1992) - 20.4 (2011) may be purchased. Contact us at fine-lines@cox.net for prices, mailing costs, questions, comments, concerns, and letters to the editor. Remember, if it is not written down, it did not happen.

Write on,
David Martin
Managing Editor

P.S. I am always amazed how many people say they like what we do and are moved by our humble attempts to help others develop their interests and abilities to write and communicate more effectively. Many say they see the world in a better light after they read *Fine Lines*.

It would mean a lot to us if you would become involved in our writing network. Is that possible? We hope you will send us some of your writing and support others just like you who value effective and moving communication. Wouldn't it be wonderful if you became a *Fine Lines* representative in your school and community? I know you could help us make a difference.

We do hope you join our mailing list. Stay in touch. Please send us your snail mail address, too. Go to www.finelines.org, and see more of what we are up to these days. I could see you becoming a representative where you live. Our non-profit organization has no employees or paid staff, and we rely on voluntary contributions from interested writers like you. It is fun. We help "young writers of all ages" develop their craft. We meet writers from all over the world, and we improve our own work. Write back to the email address shown at the top of this page, if you have any questions.

The Loss of Spirit

Summer 2002

Kathryn Aagesen

 "Do you know what I like best about you, Kathryn?"

Oh great. This should be rich. I'm just casually chatting with this girl in one of my classes. We are not exactly friends. It's not that I don't like her. She is a sweet girl, but she irritates me, slightly, because she doesn't strike me as a thinker. She is cute, popular, and perky, but something tells me she hasn't really developed a mind of her own, yet. I don't hold this against her. Lemmings are everywhere in high school. She just does what the crowd does, and this is why I am a little skittish about hearing what she likes "best" about me. Here it comes.

"You don't care what everyone thinks about you. You are just yourself. You don't care what people think!"

Now, I know Miss Jane Q. Public High School meant this as a compliment, but I was somewhat insulted. What she said kept ringing in my ears all day.

"You just don't care, care, care, care."

I do care. I am cautious about my actions. Sometimes, I have to alter my behavior so people will think I'm normal. My personality is overwhelming at first. I admit I get a little out of control, sometimes. I get riled up. I'll yell in a crude, Cockney accent. The very timid and shy might be a bit taken aback. That is the way I am, but I care enough to want people who are around me to feel comfortable and safe, so I'll tame myself down when I need to. I don't change myself, ever. If people think I'm nuts, so be it. What can I do? People are entitled to their opinions, but if a person genuinely does not like me because our personalities don't coincide, my feelings are hurt. I care plenty! I care if my hair looks nice. I care if my lipstick is smudged.

"You just don't care!"

What was that supposed to mean? If I'm the way I am and I can still carry myself with some degree of pride, then I just must not "care" what other people think? Like I'm the weirdo who everyone thinks is weird but should be commended because she "Just doesn't care!" How dare she say that I don't care what everyone thinks of me, but I do care what a selected few people think of me. Sure, I don't care what all the shallow girls in school think of me. If I don't think too highly of a person, I really couldn't give a rat's eye what they think of me.

If I really don't respect someone at all for a reason I feel strongly about, then I would almost rather that they not like me. I'd feel better about myself knowing that I don't appeal to the really ignorant, mean spirited, shallow people. I don't understand how I give off the "I don't care" vibe. I am not so completely detached. It matters to me. I may not be anything like the typical student, but that doesn't mean I have to belong somewhere. If I can't fit into any label, then give me my own, but don't just assume that because I'm not in a group with a bunch of clones that I don't fit in anywhere!

"You just don't care what everyone thinks about you!"

So, that makes me paranoid. Is this true! Is the general consensus about me, that I'm nuts? Does she know what everyone thinks? Maybe she knows something I don't know.

Ha, Ha!

I can't get bent out of shape about this. The only reason she said this was because she is the teen queen and repressed. Either she is vacant or has no mind of her own. Only a repressed person would say that, poor girl. I forget to think of all the other people who try really hard to be well dressed and popular. I honestly think I got the popularity thing out of my system in the sixth grade. I am concerned not with my school, its student council members, or its most elite people. I focus on my life, my own goals, my close friends, my family, and my own well-being. Isn't that the way it should be?

I see the people in school who go with the flow. They do what everyone else does. They wear what everyone else wears. Lemmings, lemmings, lemmings! They are sheep! I don't have a major problem with those types, really, because they come with the package at high school. I want to shake them, sometimes, but the majority of them are nice people. Even though half of the things coming out of their mouths are disingenuous, they don't know they are being insincere. I should be admired for not caring. Not like it takes any strength, but maybe for girls like the one in my class, it does. The thought of being different and friendless sounds cold and lonely. It's funny how some people will try so hard to fit in and be liked. They build up more walls that trap them inside. When a person lobbies to be popular, then she can't ever go back. She will always have to be on her toes; careful, politically correct, and sweet, even when she doesn't feel like being sweet. I say, let it be. I say, STOP trying to be socially acceptable.

I want to make my own rules. How bothersome to take everybody else into consideration when I speak, dress, and make plans. I am not a misfit, but I celebrate my differences. People should rejoice in what makes them different and not try to diminish the traits of their personalities. The code is dumb! Not that I know the code, but I'm sure it includes smiling until your cheeks ache, doing whatever it is the crowd does, and never voicing my opinions in the terrifying fear that I will be ostracized. No thanks.

The problem is people like the Prom King and Queen types are going to realize too late that popularity doesn't matter when they get old. It doesn't matter what they wear, what they say, or how pretty they are. All of the old school codes are lost. They will recognize too late that all they take with them is the beauty and depth of their spirit, and what a sad day that will be.

I don't care, I'm happy with my spirit.

> ### *"Look with thine ears."*
> - Shakespeare

What Really Matters

Autumn 2003

Alina Banasyak

I grew up in a lovely town in the Ukraine. I lived there until I was sixteen. Both of my parents were successful business people, and there was nothing that I could not get if I wanted to. My life was filled with fun, many wonderful friends, and the freedom to do anything I wished, but this was not enough. I thought I was the unhappiest person in the world. I did not have any specific dreams or goals, but I wanted a brand new life away from my country.

One day Mother told me she was seeing an American, and there appeared hope. A "Land of Opportunities" might become my home, my new beginning, my other ambition. Every day I went to bed and imagined living in the United States with a happy home, a good school, and a different environment. There was nothing more exciting to me then.

It took nine hard months just to get a "Go ahead" from the American Immigration Agency. Mom and I had to pass full medical exams and many interviews just to get into the United States. It seemed as though we were trying to get into the White House. Finally, the door was opened, and it was time to leave home. That whole process was such hard work. On the day of our departure, I was as happy as if I had won the lottery. After a 72-hour trip, we arrived at the Omaha Eppley Airfield.

From that day on, my illusions started to fall apart. I saw the truth, and I saw the reality. It dawned on me that nothing I saw here was like the American movies I watched in the Ukraine. Everyone is not rich and happy, and fewer are even content with their lives.

Now, I could have either felt sorry for myself and turned mad at the world, or I could try to make something out of my situation. It is not the country, the government, or our wealth that makes a difference, it is the individual and the people around us. Even though my journey was everything I did not want it to be, I have found myself here, and I have discovered what really matters in this world.

The time has come, and we are on the threshold of choosing careers. This choice will affect our future, just as much as choosing a person to share it with will.

I would like to share with you what I learned from being in America. No matter how much others enjoy doing their work, this does not mean that we will enjoy doing the same thing, as we are all different. Every one of us is unique, and it is very important to remember that. As Joseph Conrad wrote in *The Heart of Darkness*, it is through doing work that we can truly find ourselves. What we see others do is nothing but mere show. Life is what we make of it, not what we expect it to be.

For the entire senior class of 2003, I want to thank those who devoted their lives to teaching us. The extent of our gratefulness to you is unlimited, as teachers you committed yourselves to passing on not only what is required by the state curriculum, but also your own experiences, knowledge, and wisdom. Your job is building the foundation to the future house of America's professionals. I cannot imagine anything nobler than that. I would also like to thank everyone who works at Central High for the care, concern, and support we have received over these past four years. Your jobs do not go unnoticed!

Of course, we also thank our dear parents! We could not have accomplished our goals without you! Thank You!

The Greatest Music in the World

Winter 1999

Josh Bieber

To most, music is for hearing and enjoying. In the car, in the kitchen, or in a darkened room waiting for sleep to come, people listen to their music of choice. Music helps people feel good when they are sad, and it heightens their happiness when they are already happy. It has been said that music can soothe even the savage beast. From the dawn of humanity, music has been a refuge for us in its various forms and styles.

To me, music is not something merely to experience from the outside. Music is blood and bone, sweat of labors unknowable, tears and laughter, triumph and despair. Music is not just a collection of sounds arranged in a pleasing way. Music is a part of the universe that has been transformed by the musician into something almost indescribably beautiful. A good song will bring the musician skin to skin with the ultimate reality. I have heard God speak through the notes of a guitar.

A tree falls. Men turn the tree into lumber. The right lumber, in the right hands, is molded into the body of a guitar. This guitar is unlike any other guitar ever made. It is different because every artisan is different from the next, and every artisan changes from moment to moment, like a song getting better with time and effort. Iron is changed into steel and wound into guitar strings The guitar and its strings meet and become one.

A child is born, unlike any other child, because all children are different. He learns to feel love and pain. The child learns to listen to life instead of watching it. A lifetime of memories are saved in the dark recesses of the mind. These memories will undergo a transformation from mere events to powerful symbols and cries heard in the wilderness. He and the guitar become one.

His fingers touch the strings and set them vibrating, sending sound waves into the air. He fills his lungs and lets them relax, making vibrations with his vocal chords. He loses himself, at first in the song, and then in the joy of being in the song. The world whispers the right notes to play and sing, and he responds. As the song builds, his happiness spills over into it, and it is possible to hear his happiness. Not in the words he uses, but in the

27

way he uses them and the notes they are sung on, is his joy apparent. The singer and the song become one.

There is a moment in all great songs where it is impossible to tell the difference between the musician and the music he makes. In this moment, the barriers between an individual and the universe in which he exists seem to grow paper thin. I do not know what Christ or Buddha said concerning music, but I do know that, if salvation exists, it is hidden somewhere between the notes of an octave. I also know that I am one of the acolytes of this salvation, and I count myself fortunate to be such. There have been moments where I have found myself onstage, striking out the chords to a song, and catching a glimpse of that ultimate knowledge. I know that if I could write music that even poorly described part of that experience, it would be the greatest music in the world.

See No Anvil :: Raleigh Wilkerson

I Like to Invest in People

May 1993

Kay Bret

What would I write today? Would I write of my family – the wonders of them or the problems? Would I write of my health and the frustration and anxiety of the diagnosis given to me this week? Or would I write of the people who touch my life and make a difference!

I like to invest in people, special people, those who are honest, work hard, and truly care about others (children and adults) and care about trying to make the world a better place! We may not make huge changes, but even a pebble thrown into the water makes movement farther out. That is how I like to look at life. Those I encourage or help will carry the word on to help others slay their dragons!

How many lives do we touch in a day? Was it a positive or negative touch? How easy it is to smile and say, "Hello," than scowl and groan! Doom and gloom is not my bag. We all have choices with our lives and the problems or challenges that are given us. I truly believe each trial is a learning experience. I have to look hard and search deeply, at times, to learn each lesson and grow, but with God's help and my friends, I know I can do it. It's possible, I am sure. I've done it! A divorce, the death of my parents with cancer three months apart, and psychological problems with my youngest daughter, all of these made me feel I'm a better person for living through these experiences!

We all need a hug, one that says, "Oh, I'm glad to see you," or one that says, "I'm sorry, I know you hurt, just know I care." Sincerity seems to be a rare commodity. If I don't really mean it, I don't say it!

I am convinced writing really helps sort out our values and know ourselves. It allows me to know if I control my feelings or if I let people and surroundings dictate my attitude!

We have to be a friend to have a friend. It's like marriage. It takes work on both sides. How many friends, not acquaintances, do we have in a lifetime? I've found death and divorce certainly clarify that issue, and isn't that a shame? When we most need support, hugs, and reassurance, many people scatter in the breeze. Few stay to hold our hands or offer their shoulders and hugs!

Those who are there through the good and bad times are worth more than diamonds and gold. Money does not buy true friends. Life experiences and walking together day by day are the materials of which true friends are created. They help me see the dragons and help me slay them!

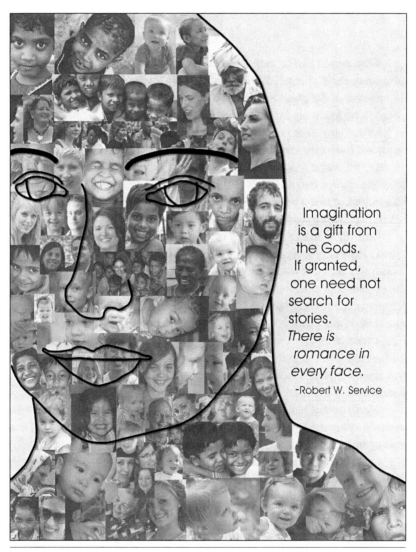

Imagination is a gift from the Gods. If granted, one need not search for stories. *There is romance in every face.*
-Robert W. Service

Humanity :: Anna Schmidt

My American Hero

Summer 1996

Meghan Brune

Caring, teaching, helping, and sharing. What does it take to be a hero? People have their own ideas about this because we all have different needs and wants. There are all kinds of heroes, one for almost everything you can think of. One that stands forward in my mind is a lady that changed my life like no one else, and she does this every day. It isn't a one time occurrence. It is her job.

Mrs. Fleming at Oakdale Elementary School in District 66, Omaha, NE, my sixth grade teacher, was a very special person, especially for me. From the day I entered her classroom to the minute I graduated and moved on to middle school, I was treated with respect and understanding. This treatment made me want to make her proud and to do the best I could. The great thing about her was that this feeling she could give to others was not just for one, but for anyone and everyone she met.

Often kids at this age are considered wild, impolite, and immature. For this reason, they are treated as lower than adults and as not having thoughts or feelings of real value. My sixth grade teacher saw through the preconceived ideas of all of us. When she looked at us, it was like she realized that she had the most precious gold in the world, not yet polished to its full potential. She knew that her students were talented in one way or another, and by the time we moved on, she let us all shine in our own ways.

Learning can be a hard thing to do, if it is not taught in an interesting way that holds everyone's attention. My teacher had all kinds of methods of teaching, and I can tell you that all of us had a raise in our grades when we found ourselves learning and remembering. She also had all kinds of anecdotes about her family, friends, and past students. She was always sharing her life with us and making us feel like we were a part of it, which we definitely were.

I remember how she used to put in so many hours after school, before school, and during school with me, helping me do special projects and to talk about things that I was working on or could use some help on. Another thing she did was spend many hours on plays and musicals. My class very

31

much enjoyed these, and she always went further to include us all in some way; be it the acting, lighting, scenery, or directing; we all fit in, always. Through it all, she was patient, yet strong, giving us someone to have fun with and respect.

Heroes can be anywhere, anytime. Unexpected or expected. My sixth grade teacher was a hero every day of the week, cheering us on to succeed. I admire her for her strength, love, and caring. She is my American hero.

"It is better to know some of the questions than all of the answers."

– James Thurber, American humorist, 1894-1961

A Missouri Wild Flower

Spring 1992

Evetta Brunk

When I was a little girl living on a farm in Missouri, I roamed the hills and pastures each day, growing as a wildflower might, each New Year blossoming in a new field further and further away from the house, independent and sturdy. It was in these days I learned the meaning of awareness and appreciation of what is really important to me in life. In the midst of trees and fields and hills, I developed a desire for choosing the road not taken that has stayed with me my entire life. The weedy, overgrown paths led me to new adventures, explorations of nature so deep they became indelible in my mind. Here was my solitude, my place of worship, my field of dreams. Here I found myself.

Since those days, I have chosen a few wrong paths and many right ones. Some might say I had to choose the wrong ones, occasionally, in order to learn. Perhaps, that is true. If so, I had many opportunities to learn, but old habits die hard, and I still yearn for the road not taken, despite some hard knocks I received in doing so since my days of innocence. When I find myself lost in a jungle of materialism, conformity, and hopelessness, my salvation is nonconformity, getting off that beaten path I somehow wandered onto, returning to the familiar realm of balance I knew once before.

That balance is the thing I search for. I want to be able to follow that path in my new "modern" existence without affecting others in my life, negatively. I want to journey down new avenues of self-discovery each day, knowing I will never find all the answers, but relishing the search. Some of those answers still lie in the woods, in the energy that abounds there that gives me strength and inner peace. There I shall wander and think and dream, like I did as a child, and find some of life's answers and more of myself.

The Yom Hashoah Memorial Service

Summer 1995

Carolyn Bullard

I have been silenced. I just attended a Yom Hashoah Service at Temple Israel, Omaha, Nebraska. This Holocaust Memorial service was in so many ways unexplainable. I was on the verge of weeping so many times during the service. As strange as it may seem, I felt so alone, because those at the synagogue whose past was a part of the horrible Holocaust of World War II did not cry. Their blank stares filled the temple; a million ghosts surfaced, assured never to be forgotten.

They did not cry, yet I weep. I have a deep admiration and respect for the Jewish people. The suffering inflicted upon them seems to have caused calluses. That is why I weep. I do not live with the constant reminder of a tragic past. As I continue to contemplate, I believe that, indeed, I should.

I remember the words of John Donne:

"No man is an island, entire of itself;
every man is a piece of the continent, a part of the main;
if a clod be washed away by the sea,
Europe is the less, as well as if a promontory were,
as well as if a manor of thy friends or of thine own were;
any man's death diminishes me,
because I am involved in mankind, and therefore
never send to know for whom the bell tolls;
it tolls for thee."

With this thought, I realize that a clod did fall from Europe in World War II. It fell from the world; therefore, the world's responsibility is to mourn.

The Yom Hashoah Service was taken from *The Six Days of Destruction: Meditations toward Hope* by Elie Wiesel and Robert H. Friedlander. I once read a book by Wiesel, who is a survivor of the Holocaust and is now a professor at a school in the East. *Night* is an honest account of his experiences living in a ghetto, then the Auschwitz concentration camp, where he lost all his family members.

There was a poem used in the service by Dan Pagis. I don't know the title, but it haunts me still.

"written in pencil on the sealed railway car: here in this carload, i, eve, with abel, my son. If you see my other son, cain, son of man, tell him I ..."

That was it. There were so many whose sentences were left unfinished. "Tell him i ..."

After the main worship service finished, a few members of the Omaha Symphony played some pieces by composers who died in the holocaust. They were beautiful.

One song, in particular, was really disturbing to me. It was a duo for violin and cello by Gideon Klein. There was a note in the program that this movement was unfinished. As I slipped to the back of my program to read further about the life of Mr. Klein, it became obvious to me why the piece was unfinished.

The original copy of the music was hand dated "6 November 1941." In December, 1941, he was taken to the Theresienstadt Concentration Camp. When the music was played and then abruptly stopped, abnormally ended, the room was filled with a powerful silence.

"tell him i ..."

I Will Try to Write Beauty

Summer 2010

Stu Burns

I will try to write beauty and abandon the depths of hate and rage, because their ebony pits have tempted me long enough. I will put down the mirror of death, since its reflection will catch up to me in its own time, and turn away from the ugliness of my life. It was made to be forgotten, not preserved.

I will try to write beauty and reach to touch the wings of angels, feel their feathers of air, be swept away in their wake, bask in their wind, ascend in their virtue, and strain to see the spectrum glittering vaguely in the crystal. I will trace its patterns on my retinas, dance them through my brain, envelop myself in their glow, and shine with the light of a diadem.

I will try to write beauty, embrace the little children, not damn their joy with my pathetic sorrow, drink in the colors of the great painters, bow to the portraits that my hand could never create, absorb the love wrung from their pain, and lie prostrate before the Earth. Her organic breath will run through my blood. My mind will be lost to her depth, and I will finally tire of listless words.

The Fairy Tales of Oscar Wilde

Spring 2003

Rachel Danford

I have been told about the first day my parents brought my older brother home from the hospital after he was born. They propped him up in a corner of the couch and read to him.

My mom claims that reading to a newborn is difficult because his attention span isn't very long. She says that Andrew, my older brother, could only listen to a page of *The Little Engine That Could* before losing interest. So, she would read the words "Chug, chug, chug," show Andrew the picture on that page, and then stop for the day. I'm not exactly certain how she could tell he was no longer interested in the book, perhaps he fell asleep, but she was persistent and continued to read to him every day for the next fourteen years. Later, when my parents brought Chris, my twin brother, and me home from the hospital we joined these regular reading sessions. Eventually, even my younger sister listened to a story every night.

I'm not sure what my favorite book was. Anything adventuresome written by Robert Louis Stevenson: *Kidnapped*, *The Black Arrow*, *Treasure Island*, etc., was always welcome. That's not to say I didn't enjoy the more sensitive books such as *Black Beauty*, *Little Women*, *A Little Princess*, and *The Secret Garden*. Maybe, I just liked books that made my brothers whine and complain. To make up for my girly books, my mom read just about every Jules Verne novel ever written. I didn't complain about these novels like my brothers did about mine, because I actually liked *Twenty-thousand Leagues Under the Sea*, *Around the World in Eighty Days*, *The Mysterious Island*, *Journey to the Center of the Earth* and all the others I cannot think of. I enjoyed everyone of them.

A great many books may be read in the course of fourteen years if a chapter is read every night, and some books took less time than that. For example, my mom finished *The Rhyme of the Ancient   Mariner* in one night. Add to that, the sum of books I have read on my own, and the result is quite a large number. I hope it is now apparent how difficult it was for me to decide upon a single book and call it my "best friend," or rather the one that has most significantly affected my life. No such book exists. I have never found a book that has absolutely no appeal to it, or at least one that does not have a lesson for me, even if it is only to teach me how not to write. So, why, when I have read so many books, and have been   affected deeply by essentially all of them, did I decide to write about *The Fairy Tales of Oscar Wilde*?

My parents gave me the book, *The Fairy Tales of Oscar Wilde*, on my ninth birthday. At first I didn't pay much attention to my book. It annoyed me a little how my mom could not come up with any more interesting presents than books (she gave one to me every year for my birthday and Christmas). The truth was I really wanted a television for my room. I'm a little ashamed to say that now, when I have found out how much I actually love books, and how extremely valuable they are. Still, I was annoyed then, so I just glanced at the cover, saw nothing more than it was green with a picture on it, and went to open my next present. I don't even remember reading the title.

Later, when my mom began to read the book at our nightly sessions, I was immediately turned off by the boring introduction. It had far too many complicated words for a nine year old. Perhaps, if I had been a little older and listened to anything beyond the long, complicated, flowery tone of the introduction, I would have found something to interest me. After all, Oscar Wilde was not a boring guy. He was actually imprisoned for homosexuality in 1895 and led a very flamboyant life. This was all in the introduction, of course, but as a nine-year-old, I heard these words without listening to the meaning. I wasn't too excited about my book and was too tired to give much thought to the first fairy tale, "The Happy Prince." In the end, what first made me fall in love with *The Fairy Tales of Oscar Wilde*, shameful as it is, were the pictures.

The "green book with a picture on the front" is in all honesty the most aesthetically pleasing work of literature I have ever owned. Now that I look back, I have no idea how I missed the beautiful cover on my book after I unwrapped it. It is a deep, green marble floor with golden peacock feathers inlaid in the stone. When I tilt the book, the peacock feathers shimmer in the light. On the front, in the same shimmery gold as the feathers are the words *The Fairy Tales of Oscar Wilde*, and in a picture under the title stands a golden statue of a prince overlooking the countryside. A little swallow flies up to greet him. This is a scene from the first fairy tale, "The Happy Prince." Scrolls of color crawl up the edge of every page and fantastical pictures accompany each story. When I saw these pictures, I could not help but feel affection and interest for my book.

My mom did not buy the book solely for its illustrations though. In fact, she bought it because my grandma read one of the fairy tales to her when she was younger. The version of "The Selfish Giant" my grandma read her had absolutely no illustrations whatsoever. My mom told me that she had to envision the exquisite garden of the giant entirely in her imagination. It was one of her favorite stories as a child, and that, I believe, is why she got me the book for my birthday.

The next night, I paid more attention to the fairy tale. My mom read "The Nightingale and the Rose." The nightingale gives her life to magically grow a white rose, so that a young student can charm his sweetheart into dancing with him. The little bird hears the young student pining away for his sweetheart and decides to sacrifice herself for the sake of true love. In the end, the nightingale is dead, and the sweetheart throws the white rose into the gutter. The young student is perplexed by his sweetheart's actions, so he decides to give up on love and study philosophy and metaphysics. The nightingale dies for what she imagines to be the epitome of true love, which turns out only to be an illusion.

When my mom finished reading, I was shocked. I had never before heard and understood a story where the hero and/or heroine did not triumph in the end. Never had the hero died! Then, after I was tucked into bed, the shock wore off, and I felt like crying. It seemed so frivolous for a beautiful creature such as the nightingale to die for two ungrateful, foolish people. They didn't even know about the sacrifice she made so that they might be happy. At that time, I saw nothing but hopelessness in the fairy tales. It was not until much later that I realized how beautiful they really were.

Everyone of the tales has a bittersweet touch of love to it. The evils of the world, selfishness, pride, and ignorance, destroy the beauty of compassion, righteousness, and love. These evils are nonchalant about love and beauty. They waste it without a thought because, wealthy as they are, they can always buy more to amuse themselves. They forget beauty and love as soon as they see them. I felt so frustrated when I first heard the fairy tales. The aloof and the proud who destroyed simple beauty did not receive any sort of retribution, not even guilt about what they did. In the very least, the villains should have felt guilty, but they didn't. They were not true villains in the way that they were purposely doing an evil to someone. They were just rich, self-absorbed people who cared nothing for anyone or anything besides themselves. To me, the villains in Oscar Wilde's fairy tales are the most diabolical the world of literature has ever seen.

At the end of each tale, nothing emotionally beautiful is meant for the world. The world is for the villains, but love finds its place in Heaven among God and the angels. Many times the hero/heroine will sacrifice all he or she has for the sake of love and die. They are then taken to Heaven where there is a place for love. This is a sad triumph.

I think these fairy tales showed me that things do not always turn out to be "happily ever after," but there is beauty to be found in everything in this world, even if it is bittersweet. Not everything in life is sad and bittersweet, but this book opened my eyes to those things that were not quite perfect. In the end, I found comfort that God made them right. I would only expect such stories from a man who had the view in life that, "We are all in the gutter, but some of us are looking at the stars."

I love this book for its bittersweet, enchanting fairy tales. I love it for its beautiful cover and pictures. I love this book, because it has meaningful lessons to teach.

> ### *"Humans need beauty."*
> – Richard Yatzeck

Voice

Winter 2003

Deb Derrick

 It scared me, the first time someone called me a writer.

See, you're fakin' it, showing up at that writer's conference. You aren't a writer yet, just a "wannabe." You figure if you rub enough elbows with real writers, maybe you'll turn into one.

She comes up to you on the sidewalk after the conference. You make small talk. You tell her why you're there.

"Ohhh, you're a writer," she says. She says it with such awe. Your head spins, and you shudder inside. You're too astonished to deny it, but you can't stop thinking about it.

A writer? Yeah. That's who you are. A writer. Not what you do but who you are.

You always knew you were a writer. You just tucked it away cuz life got in the way. Being a writer, see, explains a lot of things. Like why you always feel left behind and out of sync with everyone else. Why you daydream a lot. Why you lose yourself in a good book. And all you want to do is write, when everyone wants you to do something else.

You wear retro clothes with fringes and laced up boots. You take your journal everywhere and write down random thoughts at odd hours.

However, you aren't really a writer. You haven't found your voice yet. Words don't come out right. They don't sound like you. Don't sound like they do in your head when you string 'em together and set 'em to music. But you keep writing. Lots of garbage comes out. Once in a while, something good happens. A real nugget. Must have been someone else who wrote those words.

Why can't you write like Terry Tempest Williams or Sandra Cisneros? Raw, powerful prose. Distilled and synthesized to the bare truth. Full of passion and energy.

Trouble is you haven't suffered enough. Haven't had that many wild adventures, either. There was that time you and your girlfriend were going to fly down to Mexico, lie on the beach, and write a steamy romance novel, but that was just talk ya know, just like your sex life.

See, sometimes that wise-crackin', gum chewing voice just sneaks out. But that's not you. Sounds too New Yawkish. You're from the Midwest, way too repressed.

You keep writing. Your voice still doesn't sound right. There's that schmaltzy, sentimental voice that oozes all over the page. The intellectual voice, oh, so ivory towerish, writing about things you don't know much about. You are a writer, aren't you? And they do pay you for it. You actually make a living doing this stuff.

If only you could find your real voice. The one that jumps off the page, clutches at your throat, and starts singing loudly when everyone else wants to shut you up. And when you read it, you start singing, too. That voice.

Ten Gears and Thirty Years

Autumn 1998

Ray Dewaele

Since the summer of 1968, thirty years have drifted in like so many banks of fog. Looking back on those days on our Iowa farm when I was 15, the view of the world was as narrow as our 30-inch rows of corn and soybeans. There was a light at the end of this tunnel, and it was reachable by bicycle.

First, it was a one speed, replaced after literally thousands of gravel road miles by a trim English three speed. Due to the fact that all of my friends lived miles away, I found that I became faster and faster. Stallone had a crusty old trainer named Mickey to train him in the movie *Rocky*. I had Duchess.

Duchess was the neighbor's German Shepherd. In addition to having the sprinting speed of a cheetah, she was famous around the county for having the ability to puncture car tires with her canine teeth. There's nothing to develop one's adrenaline gland and leg muscles like a hundred pounds of teeth rising from a ditch, then inches away from your back tire.

On a Sunday excursion to town, I saw him. Most vehicles for some reason are "she's." This one was as much a "he" as the Black Stallion. There in the window of the Schwinn shop was the metal-flake, brown Continental. It could be had for the king's ransom of $89.00. It was an amazing creation with drop handlebars and ten gleaming gears.

It took awhile, but finally, I had enough money to purchase "him." With this increased capability, my clandestine trips became longer and longer. I remember once my mother's best friend, Lois, saw me about ten miles away in forbidden territory, town. I arrived home, soaked in sweat, before the phone rang. Mom informed Lois that she must have been seeing things because I was at home.

I found that I could out run the man at the tollbooth and slip into Omaha and get a glimpse of a teeming metropolis. Interstate fences and railroad trestles were no match for the two of us. I had a taste of the forbidden fruit, and I wanted more.

I wore out three such bikes. I pedaled out of '68 and into '69. I watched from a distance as race riots raged, Woodstock played, and Armstrong's footprints appeared on the moon. We were at the first Earth Day and commuted to college. Even my new car took a backseat to my two-wheeled friend. Those were hostile days for cyclists. I dodged flying bottles and exploding M-80's. I was run off the road numerous times and chased by carloads of toothless migrants fresh from the movie *Deliverance*.

Once, a mile out of Crescent, Iowa, I heard a pack of Harleys closing in on me. Much to my dismay, I discovered they were Hell's Angels. One was having engine trouble and asked for directions to the nearest garage. When my instructions with two turns proved too difficult for him to remember, he ordered me to lead the way. I road into town like Marlon Brando in *The Wild Bunch*. It was perfect timing because a group of my friends were clustered on the bridge. With a cool wave, I acknowledged their astonished presence as we rode "the outlaw trail."

College came and went, and the trips I plotted on maps failed to materialize. One day while reading *Bicycling* magazine, I saw hidden in an article a paragraph that mentioned the world's highest paved road that snaked up Mt. Evans in Colorado, so, I loaded up the forty-one pound Continental on my bike rack and headed west. Just outside Denver, I took the Idaho Springs exit. I parked, unloaded my gear, and began the twenty-six mile climb from 7,000 to 14,260 feet.

I was okay for the first twenty miles, but then as I left the tree line and rose through the clouds and startled some mountain goats, I knew I was in trouble. The final six miles were incredibly steep with many switchbacks, and the only way to the top was in little segments. I would lock on to a distant crack in the pavement and will myself to get that far, then pick the next landmark. Hours later, when I ran out of road to climb, I savored the sweet realization that if I could do this I could do anything.

The descent was well worth the climb. Leaning into the curves without guard rails for protection, the wind blew tears from my eyes, as I exceeded 50 mph on some of the longer sections.

In my mid-twenties, I decided it was time to see how good I really was. I purchased a new, handmade English racing bike and began competing. Without my teammates and a sponsorship, I found my way to the state championship road race. After being battered by several riders from the national team and 126 miles later, I rolled across the finish line. Although I completed the trip in the top third of the field, I learned the difference between good and great bicycle riding when I saw true excellence pull away from me.

My black Raleigh still hangs in the garage. Occasionally, I dust it off and attempt some of the old routes. It seems a bit more sluggish than in years past, or perhaps, the hills have continued to grow. I know it can't be me.

Sometimes, when the wind is right, I can hear the call of Mt. Evans beckoning me. I now have a rakish mountain bike with hopefully enough gears to negate the accumulating years. Someday, soon, I'll pack it in the family sedan and head west again, back in time to an era when the sunlight danced at the end of the corn rows, and Duchess searched for prey.

Elie Wiesel: A Lifetime of Sacrifice
Autumn 1999

Mike Dropinski

Eliezer Wiesel led a life as normal as many other young Jewish children. Growing up in a small town in Romania, his world revolved around family, community, and God. Then his family, community, and faith were destroyed upon the displacement of his village in 1944. Wiesel's accounts of hatred, racism, and genocide come from first hand experience. This is a very special man with sacrifices to prove it.

One of the most powerful and renowned passages in Holocaust literature, his first book, *Night*, records the inclusive experience of the Jews. "Never shall I forget that night, the first night in camp, which has turned my life into one long night, seven times cursed and seven times sealed. Never shall I forget the smoke. Never shall I forget the little faces of the children, whose bodies I saw turned into wreaths of smoke beneath a silent blue sky. Never shall I forget those flames which consumed my faith forever. Never shall I forget that nocturnal silence which deprived me, for all eternity, of the desire to live. Never shall I forget those moments which murdered my God and my soul and turned my dreams into dust. Never shall I forget these things, even if I am condemned to live as long as God himself. Never."

Wiesel was lucky enough to survive the concentration camps at Auschwitz, Buna, Buchenwald, and Gleiwitz, although they left deep scars in his heart and memories he will never forget. During his stay at the concentration camps, he viewed suffering and sacrifice on a daily basis: people beaten, tortured, and killed in the gas chambers at Auschwitz. On his arrival, his father and he were together, but they were separated from his mother and his sisters and never saw them again.

Elie managed to remain with his father for the next year, as they were almost worked to death, shuttled from camp to camp on foot or in open cattle cars in driving snow storms without food, proper shoes, or clothing. He had to watch his dad die a slow painful death from dysentery, starvation, exhaustion, and exposure. After being freed from the camps in 1945, he spent a few years in a French orphanage, since he was only sixteen, but he lived a life that was more than any could have even imagined.

For ten years, he observed a self-imposed vow of silence and wrote nothing about his wartime experience. It was not until 1956, at the urging of a Catholic writer, Francois Mauriac, that he sat down and began to write his account of the Holocaust in Yiddish. It was 900 pages in length.

Later in 1956, while in New York covering the United Nations as a reporter, he was struck by a taxi cab. His injuries confined him to a wheelchair for almost a year. Shortly after that, he decided to become an American citizen. A question asked of Mr. Wiesel during an interview was, "What people were important to you? Who influenced you? Who inspired you?"

His answer was, "My father taught me how to reason, how to reach my mind. My soul belonged to my grandfather and mother. They influenced me profoundly to this day. When I write, I have the feeling, literally and physically, that one of them is behind my back, looking over my shoulder and reading what I am writing. I'm terribly afraid of their judgment."

The Holocaust was much more than sacrifice, more than mass killings of millions of innocent people at death and labor camps. He sees the Holocaust and Auschwitz as "not only the failure of two thousand years of Christian civilization, but also the defeat of the intellectual who wants to find the meaning with a capital "M" in History." One lesson of his writing teaches us to "distinguish between what we need to understand and what we should not attempt."

In 1986 Elie Wiesel was awarded the Nobel Peace Prize. There is not a more deserving person for this award.

"Let us remember,
let us remember the heroes of Warsaw,
the martyrs of Treblinka,
the children of Auschwitz.

They fought alone,
but they did not die alone,
for something in all of us
died with them."

Teaching and Story Telling

Autumn 1993

Rebecca Fahrlander, PhD

As an undergraduate, I was a philosophy major, and I've always been fascinated by the existential issues of life, i.e., Why are we here? What gives our lives meaning? Where are we going? How do we focus and develop our lives so that we make them fulfilling, unique, and interesting journeys? How do we remember to live each day as if it were our last, and yet, as though we will live to be 100? How do we make life a work of art?

After watching a Sam Keen interview a couple of years ago and reading his book, *Your Mythic Journey,* my latent interest in all these issues once again rose to the surface, and I felt compelled to develop a course/workshop on the topic. The non-credit course that I developed and taught at the University of Nebraska at Omaha's College of Continuing Studies last fall was targeted at those individuals whom Keen would call the "multi-born," that is those who constantly search, passing through many ups and downs, many transitions in life, usually experiencing a radical rebirth at mid-life. The "multi-born" are constantly on a journey, questioning, seeking, and learning.

I began the course as a very brief two-session program and viewed it very much as a seminar or consciousness-raising session "a la the 1970s." It was an opportunity for like-minded people to congregate, share ideas and questions and discover more about themselves and where they were going. I called the course "Telling Your Own Story: A Journey of Self-Exploration."

We include a combination of discussions, reading, and in-class exercises. The students explored their own stories and mythic journeys, examined role expectations that influenced who they were, learned to apply self-exploration principles to contemporary life experiences, such as plateauing on a job, and learned how to use their personal stories to empower themselves for the future.

As any professor knows, each group of people who make up a class is a unique gestalt with dynamics of its own. I found that a majority of the individuals in this class shared an interest in writing. Because of this, the course moved in its own direction to incorporate more storytelling and writing. Students wrote story segments and shared some of their own life stories with the class. As it turned out, the two-session format was too short, and the class members felt they had only begun to re-examine their life stories.

Some members of the class wanted to continue to meet after the end of the actual course. Consequently, I lengthened the course to four sessions for the fall. The topic of this course and the informal consciousness-raising format meant that there really would never be an "end" or true sense of closure. I considered the class a success if most of the individuals felt they re-examined aspects of their lives and would continue the journey of self-exploration on their own through writing.

> *"It's one thing to feel that you are on the right path, but it's another to think that yours is the only path."*
>
> - Paulo Coelho, novelist

Mood

Summer 1999

Molly Fairchild

Julia Cameron admits that she also has not been in the mood to write. The author explains that one does not have to be in the mood. Ms. Cameron compares being in the mood to write for the writer, as to being in the mood to make love for the lover in a committed relationship; sometimes, it just takes a first "caress" to get started, a very interesting metaphor, indeed!

The author loves e-mail, because it allows the writer to be intimate, yet informal. E-mail is "nonauthoritarian" and "naughty," like "passing notes in school." A good observation, I think.

To make writing more convenient for a writer, it cannot be a "big deal." The author suggests using bribes when motivation to write is difficult: a reward system, such as allowing oneself to watch a particular television program after writing for twenty minutes. She suggests breaking down writing into workable blocks of time, so writing can more easily become a daily ritual.

The author reminisces about her mother, who with seven children took the time to write daily. Evidently, Ms. Cameron's mother provided the excellent example that Ms. Ueland speaks of in her book, *If You Want to Write*. Her mother grabbed tidbits of time to write throughout her day without making a production of her writing, providing an excellent example

Final :: Eddith Buis

to Ms. Cameron as she grew up.

A friend of the author's, who is a swimmer, carries a notebook to the beach. He swims to keep physically fit, and writes to be mentally fit. He never waits for the "mood," but plunges into each endeavor. He uses his writing to get into "right thinking," which is the result of writing when you think you are not in the right mood, but tired, cranky, or angry.

Regine was a stubborn writer-friend. She wanted to write only when she felt in the right mood to write well. This sounded logical to me, as I read Regine's story, until the author pointed out that writing should be like a permanent friend with good and bad days. She encouraged Regine to spend time with her writer, as in the "artist dates," we read about in Cameron's book, *The Artist's Way*. The author suggests Regine get to know the writer in all of her moods and just write.

"Watch your thoughts; they become words.
Watch your words; they become actions.
Watch your actions; they become habits.
Watch your habits; they become character.
Watch your character; it becomes your destiny."

\- Patrick Overton

My Paper Friend

Summer 1996

Mary Filkins

I have been blessed with many good friends over the years. Some have come, and some have gone. They fade in and out of my memory. Some are easier to share life's ups and downs with. Some are not very good at listening, but there is nothing they would not do for me. I am fortunate to have one friend who has always been there.

This friend is very different, for we do not verbally exchange conversation. We just stare at each other. During the very best times and struggling with the very worst times, this friend never missed a moment, a feeling, a tear, or a laugh. I experienced death, marriage, childbirth, illness, and divorce with this friend. We have a bond that is unbreakable. No matter how much time passes between visits, we reunite and never miss a beat, without speaking a word.

There is a trust that exists between us like I never had with any other friend. I am not afraid to show my true colors because I know my friend will not judge me. This friend can see me at my best, and at my worst; no boundaries will be violated.

I confided in my friend when I first met my husband. My friend was elated when we married. I agonized with my friend when our marriage was on shaky ground. I rejoiced with my friend when I was pregnant. I cried with my friend when I gave birth to my son. I ached with my friend when my mother was sick. I struggled with my friend when I went through my divorce. My friend never left my side. When I displayed ugly, deep-seated anger, my friend walked the road by my side, never leaving me alone.

How can I repay a friend of such magnitude? How do I express appreciation, so this friend knows how much I care? The best way, I discovered, is to keep the friendship active and alive. I call on my friend quite often, and when I get misguided, my friend calls on me, reeling me back in like a fish on a hook. Sometimes, I don't realize what pulls me. I turn around and see that familiar acquaintance. With open arms, I welcome my friend back into my life, and we spend hours catching up with each other.

I am proud to have this relationship and like to share it with other people. You are capable of this friendship, but there are a few steps you must take beforehand. First, you must buy a notebook, acquire a writing tool, and keep a journal. Secondly, you have to believe in the endless love of the friendship. Soon, you will discover a special friend on the pages laid out before your eyes. Over the years I have discovered how my journal bridges my thoughts and actions. I have survived some pretty steep valleys and treacherous roads, reaching the other side as a more refined and positive person, thanks to my journal.

1996 Forest Tunnel :: Dana Damewood

Nahualli

(In Mexico, native people use this word to mean a person who can take the form of an animal. In the United States, the Navajo have a similar term that means "skin walker.")

Summer 2011

Marcia Calhoun Forecki

I say that no one on earth is more free than an old woman. I enjoy my free life, although I may still be a married woman. *Dios sabe.* Maybe my husband is dead somewhere. Many nights, I burned a black candle so the spirits would come and put an end to Rigoberto. Then, I heard that a woman he was living with cracked his head with a big spoon. Let him live.

Why would I move to town? My house is here. I earned this house, every stick. See that oven outside. *Puro ladrillo.* All bricks and cement. I should know. We carried every brick up this mountain on our backs. Berto found them. Where? At the mine, where else? They had great stacks of them. On that stove, I made a mountain of tortillas. I kept chickens and goats. We fed the miners. Berto sold the tamales, beans, and tortillas to the miners. I grew my own chiles, *tomatillos*, onions. I made cheese from my goats' milk. The miners loved my food. They preferred it to what the company offered them. Beans in cans. Tomatoes in cans. Bread like old tree bark.

No, I didn't go down to the mine. The boys carried the food down. The boys? There are always boys around. They spring from the ground; they fall from the trees. How do I know? This is a poor country. The people use every scrap and thread. They patch and mend and dig through garbage to survive. See my roof? There and there? See how I patch the holes? I cut open the plastic water bottles the miners throw down. Then, I hammer them flat and nail them over the hole. *Oye*. If I live long enough, maybe the whole ceiling will be *pura plástica*, and I'll be able to see the stars when I lie in my bed alone. Cast off plastic bottles are everywhere in this country. Boys, too.

We covered the walls of my house with mud, adobe. My house is on the mountain and of the mountain. Rigoberto left, and I stayed. A woman can always find another husband, if she isn't too particular, but a house is not so easy to come by. Anyway, if I go, the mountain will take back the house I stole from it. Wind will blow off the roof, even my plastic patches. Then, rain will wash off the paint and adobe. The cold will crack the bricks, and the house will fall down. The mountain will devour it. So, I keep the mud patched and painted. The paint came from the mine, of course. I like this color, the yellow of the *jícama* on my walls.

The natives call the mine a wound, a cut to the heart of the land. They believe some day, unless the wound was closed and left to heal, the land will die. The plants, the animals and the people will all die. Then, the spirits of the dead ones will rise out of the cracks in the dead earth and hover over the bare hills. Their tears will water the land, and the birds will return, and the rich forest will grow again.

The Spanish say they discovered our country, but Mexico was never lost, until they came. Now, the land is scarred and mutilated. Her wealth is stolen. Her children hide themselves in the forests, as if they were the great green skirts of our mothers and grandmothers. What was done was done, but that's when it started. The rape of the land, the murder of the people. It started back then and led, one death after another, to my boy and *los chingados* who killed him.

He wasn't my boy. *No mi hijo*. He showed up one day, carried a plate of sweet tamales down the mountain to Rigoberto. The boy said his father called him "*el Otro*." Imagine a father calling his own son such a name. "The other one." The bastard used to present his children as "my two daughters and the other one." He said his father was more interested in the girls because they could bring home rich husbands. The old man hoped his daughters would make life easy for him, no doubt. The boy was baptized Juan or Jesus. They all are, even the lost ones. Maybe, he was *el Otro*. He belonged as much to the world of the spirit as he did to this one.

Let me tell you about the mine. A company from Scotland owns the mine at the bottom of the hills. They built good roads from the coast to the edge of the forest to bring in their diggers, trucks, and guns. The company is called CSSA *Cobre Selvático S.A.* The government says that all companies are to be owned more than half by *mexicanos.* Of course, that's all on paper. The foreign companies get some Mexican to sign a paper that he is the owner, or his company is the owner. Paper tears; it burns. You wipe your ass with it. That's how much the national ownership means. Did you see the sign in front of the office? (CSSA) *Chinga a los Sonorenses y a Sus Abuelos. ¡Ay!*

The natives tried to chase away the miners. For years and years, they fought the mining company the best they could. They set fires to the sheds of tools and equipment. They stole tools, punctured tires on trucks. Once a couple of boys dumped a bag of snakes into the office of one of the big bosses. They broke the window with a brick, and then one climbed on another's shoulders, and they tossed in the bag of snakes.

For the white *patrón* of the mine, that was too much. He had his mine police find the boys. The mine police were no more than black-capped guerillas he hired right out of prison. Someone in the governor's office let the *patrón* take his pick of wife-murderers and kidnappers. It didn't matter that their sentences still had years to go. The governor was paid; the warden was paid; and the guards were paid. CSSA gave its mine police arms and equipment better than the army had. So, after the snake incident, the mine police caught the boys by bribes, blows, and bullets, as they say. They tied the boys with primer cord inside two giant tires, the kind the biggest earth diggers use. They drove the boys into the forest and carried them in the tires to the edge of their village. Then, they set fire to the primer cord and rolled the tires right into the center of the village. Men and women were burned trying to free their boys from the burning tires. The boys were well roasted by the time the wires were cut with knives and axes.

When the mine police caught the boys, the state police watched. One took pictures of the burning tires. A woman in a village nearby used to recount that her husband said he knew where the pictures were for sale, but they are both gone now.

Rigoberto was always jealous. He acted like he was my owner, not my husband. I was his business. Without my tamales he had nothing to sell. Nothing he could make was worth selling. When he went to town for sacks of rice and beans, he always cut a small branch from one of the trees. Can you guess why? He swept the dirt on the path behind him, so he could see any footprints made on the path while he was gone. *Tonto Berto.* To track my lover, he should have swept the sky.

Boys don't remain boys forever. *El Otro* grew up quickly living in these hills. He belonged to no one. He wasn't native or *gachupín* or white. After his father threw him away, I think he just wanted to be free and unconnected. To fly. And he did fly. Oh yes, believe it. There are creatures that cross over between human and animal, whenever they like. They are called *Nahualli*. Stupid gringos, digging out the gold and silver from this country. The real treasure is in the people of the mountains and the forests. They know more about the world than all the scientists and engineers who ever looked at a handful of dirt. *¡Ay!* They know what it's made of, this land and this people, but they don't know what they know. Why? They never asked. Never wanted to know the native's magic. Gold and silver, gold and silver. They all have rocks in their heads. *¡Ja!* Rocks for hearts, most of them.

El Otro started coming to visit me when he was about 15 or 16. *¡Que hombre!* Rigoberto sweeping the dirt path. My lover came in through the window and never touched the ground. He came as a beautiful bird. The *guaca maya*. So many colors. And the tail. The *guaca maya* has a very long tail. Maybe that's why *el Otro* chose it for his other self.

My young lover came to me from out of a rainbow. I'm telling you that's how it looked to me. That long, curved tail, with so many colors grew bigger as he flew closer to my house on the mountain. He was inside my house without touching Berto's swept path. The young man learned the secret of how to change himself from a man to a bird from the natives in the forest.

Why did they share such a sacred secret with an outsider? Because they saw the strength and the beauty in him. His face was so calm. Berto said, when *el Otro* was carrying tamales from my kitchen to the miners, the boy had no expression on his face. Berto said it was because the boy was dull and slow. *¡Idiota!* My lover always wore an expression; he wore the face of *la tranquilidad*. Peace with all the world. He flew high and saw far with bird's eyes. A bird sees the slightest move of a mouse or a lizard from high above it. *El Otro* saw the way my chest heaved in longing for him when he sat high in the trees waiting for Berto to sweep the mountain path. He saw into the distance, too. My lover told me he saw men cut deeper into the earth for the last grain of gold dust. He saw the mountain gutted and useless. No men or women were left to cry for the violation of their ancient mother earth.

My young lover's touch on my skin was delicate, like a feather. I had chills as in a fever. His powerful legs never tired. A man needs strong legs to make love. When we had both spent ourselves, *el Otro* covered us with a colorful feather blanket of his own wings. Then, as I slept, he lifted himself from me and left on the wind.

Yes, I'm still awake. An old woman can close her eyes from time to time, can't she? These days, I see more clearly with my eyes closed. That is, I see more clearly what I want to see: the memories in my mind. I don't need eyes to see those, do I? Anyway, some of my memories are too *caliente* to tell.

One day, before the rains started, the natives stole a CSSA gasoline truck. They drove it into the forest. They hid the truck somewhere and waited. Not for long, they waited. The Manager General lifted his finger, and the state police came. The Army sent men, too. Hundreds of armed men filled our tiny village. The mine police put on their black caps, and they all marched into the forest. We heard the guns for two days and a night. The soldiers found the truck and drove it into the center of the *indígena* village. Every house, every garden, every animal was massacred. Nothing was left bigger than a matchstick. The *indígenas* were gone, of course. They fled higher up the hills, deeper into the trees. The soldiers and the police told the Manager General that many of the natives had been defeated, finally.

That's when the Governor ordered the state police to surround the native village. Death danced that night. The natives shot back at the police. The captain ordered the entire village to be destroyed. The President himself warned the natives that the army would come in big tanks. There were no tanks on the roads, only bodies thrown by the side of the road by police in pickup trucks. Then, the President himself talked to the people on the radio. He declared a "Day without Guns." The government promised to give amnesty to those who turned in their weapons. So, the "Day without Guns" ended, and the night of fire began. I looked toward the top of the mountain, and just at the edge, where the mountain meets the sky, there was a glow. It came from the fire on the other side.

When morning finally came, more bodies were thrown onto the road from pickup trucks. A solemn service was held in the cathedral in the capital. Then, trucks with big shovels came, at midnight, to pick up the corpses from the road and dropped them into other trucks. The next day, the miners were ordered back to work. They passed down the road where blood filled every little hole and crack. The radio played music and ads for soap. Some of the miners were sent out to cut back the trees and brush from the road for security reasons. Under the mountain, the digging started again.

One night soon after, *el Otro* visited me. He did not come for love but asked me to make him sweet tamales. I shaped the *masa* slowly, not wanting my young lover to leave. He was quiet, wearing his expression of peace.

That night, or maybe it was the next, the Manager General was killed. He was locked in his office, with guards outside his door. No one came in. It was a hot night, and the Manager General opened a little window, hoping for a breeze.

The guards heard the sound of a gun in the office. When they blundered their way inside, the Manager General was dead in his chair. One of the guards must have been startled by the gust stirred up by the wings of a *guaca maya*, trapped in the office. He picked up the pistol that lay next to the dead *patrón* and shot the bird. When the state police came, later that morning, a young man was lying on the office floor, shot through the breast.

The Governor came to our little mountain. He made a speech, and the owner of the mine made a speech. Then, the men climbed back into the mountain. The digging has continued every day since then. I hear the mountain moan and gasp, sometimes. Killing a mountain is slow business, even with dynamite and big machines. Now, I'm finished talking. I'll mix the *masa* for sweet tamales and eat.

A Dragon Slayer

Winter 1994

Kirsten Furlong

Sometimes, I feel as though I have a wonderful vision when I write in my journal. This vision allows me to see inside of people. To me, ugliness on the inside is hard to conceal; it always seeps onto the surface of things. Often, I see people with anger, hatred, and indifference boiling underneath, distorting their faces and furrowing their brows. The more I write about people or characters, the more of them I see.

Is it possible that I misinterpret? I've been told that I've make some people uncomfortable upon meeting them for the first time. Some cannot handle my silences when I write. Only few understand their value. Words are wonderful, but only when used properly. Too many times, they are wasted as time-fillers and silence-chasers. When I say something, I want my words to be worth being said. When I write, I want my ideas to be worth the effort!

Since I began writing in my journal, I learned that I like to write. I never thought this before. In fact, if someone asked me how I felt about writing before this semester, I would say, "I hate it!" I am very curious about how this journal will now affect my attitude toward writing in other classes. Will it be easier for me? I believe that it will.

I also know that I will continue my journal on a regular basis. There are classes that I have taken in college, in which, I could not come up with one practical thing that I learned. Learning to keep a journal is not only a good learning experience for writing, but it has a positive impact on one's life, or it did on mine! Before keeping a journal, I never saw writing as an enjoyable and creative activity. It was more of a task. Now that I am "enlightened," I will continue to enjoy my new creations with words.

The Three-Legged Stool

Summer 2005

Stephen Gehring

A month or so ago at my men's group, I discussed a process from my spiritual practice involving a three-legged stool. The legs of the stool were study, service, and meditation.

Study involves something inspirational and uplifting. The intention is to prepare the mind and the subconscious mind for meditation and growth.

Service involves the spontaneous effect of soul contact. Our personality deals with our selfish desires, compared to service, which is soul work. In this service, we need to be handless, and we need not cause suffering. We also must have a willingness to let others serve as they deem best. Service is a joyful expression of the soul. It does provide a "feel-good" in the heart.

Meditation is our attempt to be consciously in touch with our higher Self/God. As a discipline, we need to sit for 10-20 minutes a day, concentrating our higher mind. Another view is that meditation is a dialogue with God where we speak, and then we listen. It is an invoking and evoking process.

The three-legged stool is undoubtedly based upon sustenance offered to the practitioner of Buddhism, called the triple treasure: Buddha, Dharma, and Sanghi.

Sustenance comes from the Buddha. His awakening represents the potential for the awakening in each of us. Dharma represents the internal truth and the teachings that can bring liberation. The Sanghi is the community of awakened beings and all who practice the Dharma. Buddha would equate to meditation, Dharma to study, and Sanghi to service. These latter thoughts are derived from a wonderful book by Jack Kornfield, entitled *After the Ecstacy, the Laundry*.

A Long Love Affair

Spring 2002

Lawrence J. (Larry) Geisler

I cannot remember when I was not in love with language.
Circumstances in my early life generated the love affair. In August, I turned five, and later that month I started in first grade in a country school less than a half-mile from my home. I did not know that there was such a thing as kindergarten until years later.

Born in 1933 in the midst of Depression years, my home's reading materials were limited to Montgomery Ward, poultry catalogs, and the *Des Moines Tribune*, which was delivered daily in our rural mailbox. Television was unheard of, and radio use was limited to news broadcasts and markets. I distinctly recall that I could read the daily newspaper before I went to school.

My father was an Austrian-Czech immigrant who spoke two languages, and that in itself made him special. Neighborhood dads couldn't do that. One winter when my paternal grandmother who spoke only a very broken English stayed with us, my fascination with the sound of language reached new heights. She said strange things such as, "I'm an old lady, and pretty soon I will go died." She spent her days and evenings crocheting large spools of thread into doilies and dresser scarves. My Irish mother purchased crocheting manuals for her, and Grandma insisted that I read the manuals to her. My life was strange. I was drilled in phonics in the daytime and read crocheting manuals at night. It was some time before I realized that my grandmother had no need for my reading recitations, because she could make patterns by looking at the pictures in the manual. Apparently, she just wanted to hear me read in what must have been to her a strange language.

Foreign was the "f-word" in our home. The only time I ever heard it was when a car salesman brought out a new Chevrolet and made a comment to my father about these "damned foreign cars." I knew immediately that he had said a bad word, and we would not be getting a new car. When he left, my father made some remark to my mother about "a very stupid man." The power of language became evident early in my life.

As a ten-year-old sixth grader, I won the county oral reading contest, defeating more than a dozen eighth-graders. When the parish priest read about my victory in the newspaper, he asked me to read the Gospel describing the crucifixion of Jesus Christ on Good Friday. At that time, translations contained the sentence, "It is consummated," uttered by Jesus at his death. I recall that I asked the priest what consummated meant, and his reply was "Never mind," and he merely reinforced the pronunciation of the word. I delivered it accurately from the pulpit twenty minutes later. I never could find the word in the dictionary available in the rural school.

I was confused much of the time by what I read in the newspapers. I recall reading about pilgrims at Bethlehem at Christmas time, but my teacher had presented pilgrims with white collars and long blue coats as Thanksgiving coloring assignments. Once I came across the phrase "a body of water" in a school book and asked my brother, 15 years older than I, what it meant. He said that your body is "your arms and your legs," and for several nights after that I dreamed of being filled with water.

Penmanship was stressed in the country school, but I didn't know that writing was something different until I reached high school. That experience brought into my life people with college degrees who caused me to discover double negatives and tense in verbs. Writing assignments were called "themes," and each week we struggled to turn in some written piece of experience. My sophomore year brought a dynamo teacher of English, who not only taught us case in pronouns but also read brilliantly aloud. I was nearly paralyzed when he finished reading Edgar Allan Poe's "The Raven." He was a better reader than I. I started writing skits for pep meetings, and long before I finished high school, I had come to realize that even people who spoke English often sounded very different from one another. The vocabulary and grammar of my English teacher was far more elevated than what I heard daily in the rural area where I lived. My awareness-level must have been rising at a terrific speed.

After graduating from high school, I got a job in an office where my elderly boss, a Grinnell College graduate, could spot a misspelled word like blood on the snow. He appreciated my literacy and soon turned over routine letters for me to compose. His only requirement was that if he signed the letter, it had to be perfect. When he retired, I went to college.

Turning in immaculately groomed compositions in an Honors English class at Creighton University held no great difficulty for me. Satisfying the Jesuit professor was another matter. One of my first compositions came back with "*post hoc, ergo propter hoc*" written in red across the entire front page. My spelling and syntax may have approached perfection, but my logic apparently left great room for improvement. I recall his mentioning a "one-and-one-half negative," such as, "I cannot help but think" instead of "I cannot help thinking" and was startled in years to come to hear United States senators and television anchor people make the error that the Jesuit had scorned. If high school had laundered my usage, college cloroxed it.

I wrote an article in my senior year that was published in a Nebraska education periodical, and I placed in a national Jesuit essay contest. Writing had become a means of communication; whereby, I could reach large numbers of people. I found that thrilling.

One of my life's most inspirational people, a man named Dr. Edward O'Connor, appeared in my junior year. He, along with the nurturing influence of my student-teaching supervisor, the late Gunnar Horn, led me to believe that the language I so loved should become my life's work. Teaching it became almost an obsession. Following graduation, I joined Mr. Horn and the staff at Benson High School in Omaha where alert and sometimes sophisticated students responded eagerly to my attempts to make language meaningful. It was challenging stuff. Never having read "The Lady of the Lake" before, I taught it with three students in the room who had lived in Scotland! The memory of my outstanding high school teacher caused me to do more and more reading aloud in the classroom.

In years to come, I returned to my native Iowa and taught at Marshalltown High School for 25 years. Armed with state-of-the-art teaching methods I had learned in Omaha, I took the school by storm. The principal told me in early October that his telephone was ringing "off the wall" with requests from parents to get their kids into my classroom.

I was thrilled in a grocery store aisle when a Marshalltown mother told me that her son had raved about my reading of Poe's great bird poem. Not feeling well one afternoon, I made a 4:30 doctor's appointment. When I gave the receptionist my name, she said, " I know exactly who you are. Our one-and-one-half-negatives are corrected every night at the supper table." I froze with embarrassment. The kindly woman stood, touched my arm, and said, "My husband and I are behind you 100 percent. Keep up the good work. The doctor will see you shortly."

Not long afterward, I was named the language arts administrator in grades 7 through 12, but every year I taught at least three classes. Some parents even complained about my promotion, claiming that effective teachers should stay in the classroom full time. I learned much from the 30 or more teachers of English that I supervised each year and later spoke at national conventions where my audiences where keenly knowledgeable of nominative and accusative case in pronouns. I wrote long reports of the thirteen national conventions I attended, part of the reciprocity for the *carte blanche* trips the Marshalltown Schools underwrote. The reports went out to all teachers of English and to all administrators in the school system. I learned also that five-figure, frontline speakers at national conventions did not start speeches with such staid remarks as "Ladies and Gentlemen." Comprehensive reports of the year's accomplishments, often thousands of words, went to the members of the school board each year before my extended contract was considered complete, and the oral presentation I made to the board highlighted those accomplishments.

For years, I wrote daily in a journal, mostly of joys and anxieties that filled my life. One summer I decided to read the many spiral notebooks that I had filled. It was mostly dull prose, but I was able to see how insights had developed in my thinking, how ideas had changed in my mind, and even to some extent how I had gained in self-awareness from this daily activity.

All the rewriting and writing-as-a-process ideas from the Iowa Writing Program struck me as an exploration of the obvious, even though the program caused some teachers of English to discover the joy of writing from the experiences of their own lives. Usually, their previous writing consisted only of term papers demanded in college courses. Most of my rewriting has always been done in a churning mental process long before I set pen to paper. It seems to me that each person has to accept the method of his own soul. Experiences in standup storytelling made me even more aware that what the storyteller omits is just as important as what details he selects.

Writing has also been a great means of connecting otherwise unrelated experiences. Having written many radio and newspaper ads for political candidates, I had all the right ammunition to load an application for competitive summer institutes in civic writing at Harvard University. Such questions as, "Describe how an interest in government has been manifested in your daily life" left me worrying about the word-length limitations rather than the content of my answer. The only Iowan to qualify, I reveled in the three summers at Harvard which moved me from participant to teaching staff. The exciting interchanges in the workshops and the powerful speakers with backgrounds in government and national issues challenged me to transfer this new experience into meaningful high school writing assignments in civic education.

I tried teaching some college classes after I took early retirement. The challenge of teaching some kind of delivery of graceful prose to adults was enlightening. I tried reading passages from highly effective literature aloud. Many of the college students had read very little. I read aloud Margaret Mitchell's description of the Tarleton twins, passages from John Steinbeck's *The Grapes of Wrath*, some samples of Robert Frost's poetry, and Harper

Lee's description of Macomb, Alabama. I thought I saw some improvement in delivery. I also learned that it is not easy for an adult to learn to hear himself or herself write. It became increasingly evident to me that the sound of language is important in written discourse.

As a school administrator, my Creighton minor in journalism was invaluable. I could write news stories of activities in our English department, which the local daily newspaper published unedited. Other administrators couldn't do that. I read hundreds of application letters for teaching positions and struggled to find the person behind the often-predictable words. I recall that one afternoon I read the sentence "From the *Des Moines Register*, I have learned of a position in your English Department" 47 times. The sentence itself is all right, but no human being should be subjected to reading it that many times.

After 25 years in the Marshalltown School System, I elected early retirement which offered a "parachute" that allowed me to return to the country home where I had been born and reared. The parachute may not have been golden, but it was a bright color. Language became my only hobby. Leading discussion sessions over literary classics in the Churdan, Iowa, library has brought a *Des Moines Register* feature writer to the sessions. Writing is a daily part of my life. Sending and receiving real mail, handwritten notes and letters, has always seemed to me to be a classy activity. It's a rare day that I don't write at least one. I often write newspaper features which a Yale PhD does not edit. My attempts to deliver writing in fiction are commonly interrupted by the urge to publicize some event that I would like others to read about in a newspaper. I've given workshops for adults to learn to read scripture more effectively aloud in churches. Too often the phone rings, and the caller wants me to read poetry or otherwise entertain some group of people. As mortality becomes more difficult to ignore, writing becomes the communication skill which seems to have any chance of a lasting legacy.

I'm often reminded of the immortal words of Alexander Pope: "True ease in writing comes from art, not chance, as those move easiest who have learned to dance."

My Temple

Summer 1996

Dinah Gomez

 Some people say the body is the temple of the soul. Mine seems more like a used car lot. It is full of parts that might be useful, but none of them really fit. I want to trade this chassis in for a sportier model.

This may seem like a personal subject, but many females are taught that we should look like the models out of *Vogue*. That is a hard subject to ignore. Personally, I would like to forget my body altogether. I live so much out of my head that I feel like my body is something to tote my brain around in.

My body has always betrayed me. It seems to do the most inappropriate things at the wrong time. I have a right foot that can find any crack in the sidewalk and send me into the most graceful swan dive ever seen. My right shoulder will often miss a doorway by half an inch, and my left heel is always getting stuck in something, causing bodily whiplash on a number of occasions. Grace just doesn't fit into my vocabulary.

The reason for this confession is that I want to make friends with the part of me from the neck down. I want to call a truce. It was not always kind to me, but Lord knows I was not good to it either. I have over fed it, under fed it, left it in the sun too long, kept it up late at night, and tried to see just how far I could push it before it said, "Enough!"

My body deserves better than this. I deserve better than this. I would like to know how it feels to walk for several miles and not need a cab ride home. I would like to swim laps without fear of drowning. I would like to go on a twenty mile bike ride and not be hospitalized because of it. I have no desire to look like Christy Brinkley. I am happy with my looks just the way they are, but I hate limiting myself in any way, and not taking care of my body is limiting my capabilities. "Did you hear that down there?"

"Yes, tomorrow, we'll go for a walk, but you trip me just once, and ..."

Lessons from the Campfire

Spring 1996

Gregory L. "Woody" Gruber

Recently I was privileged to take part in a Vigil Honor weekend with the Boy Scouts. Having been chosen by my peers to receive this honor, I loaded my backpack and headed out to Camp Cedars, Iowa, on a cool, crisp November morning. Much of the impressive ceremony is private, but I am able to share from my scribbled notes some of what I learned from my sojourn alone in the woods.

Part of the experience was maintaining my campfire, in solitary silence, throughout the night. I left my watch behind, took a book of earth meditations, and settled in a remote location in the woods for the duration. The vigil was physically demanding, but by rotating tasks – gather firewood, tend fire, rest and meditate, gather again – I found a balance of activity that made the night fairly enjoyable.

The following are axioms, truths which I learned from the fire, as recorded in my rough notes (on the back of an envelope). After each I have added my thoughts since then on each particular topic.

"Build your fire carefully to sufficient level of flame, so you can work awhile by the light you produce." Many times in life we are tempted, by need or procrastination, to just "throw something together" and then sit back, hoping it will work well enough to meet the need. Half-hearted and ill-conceived efforts yield poor results. We cannot see much by limited, insufficient light – you must have enough to work by. To truly be prepared, good planning is a must.

"There is a cost to everything done well; every fire requires some kind of fuel." You cannot live by good intentions, high hopes, or love alone without some kind of action to bring the experience to life. Regardless of the process, resources must be invested. Sacrifices and decisions will be made, exchanges take place. Wood is consumed to provide me with light, heat, and emotional comfort. Valuable elements like gold and silver are subjected to intense heat, and must be refined from ore, released and molded for our use. In any process, the key consideration is finding, mixing, and putting together the right stuff, and achieving a consistent balance of the elements involved. You must commit resources of proper type and caliber to produce quality results.

"It is sometimes better to add small fuel – by little things gathered many great things have been achieved." This truth requires of us skill, patience, and insight. You don't start bonfires with logs. Tinder, kindling, fuel – and someone there to nurture each piece into the whole. There has to be a plan, goal, direction, and harmony in the assembly effort. Consider that every human person has the potential to exponentially affect the world by each small act, once properly combined with others. The power of any group is limited only by the degree of willingness its individual members hold towards applying themselves by the amount of oxygen allowed into the mix. A haphazard thrust of material can smother a young, tender flame. Build slowly, with purpose, keeping your eyes on your goals and your dreams alive in your heart.

"To find sufficient fuel, you must travel the entire circle around your fire." Sometimes the solution to a challenge seems simple, or found near at hand. Most of the time you must search, seek out the right resources, and in the needed quantities. Occasionally we need to travel further, reach higher, and search more fervently for the answers we need to sustain us through some pretty dark nights. Ground already traveled may yield treasure we missed, or did not recognize, on an earlier pass by. Don't discount people, sources, or solutions that don't seem to apply right now; they may be needed in some future situation or endeavor. The width of your circle may be defined by needs presented, known resources available, and limited only by your own imagination and willingness to apply yourself. The world is full of answers waiting for someone to ask the questions.

"Some fuels, like people, burn very bright for awhile – but because they are of limited substance, they soon go out. Learn instead from the coals." Accept your own limitations, once you discover them, and find peace. Be wary of those people who cannot perform as advertised. Don't get hung up when someone or something does not live up to your expectations. Have a backup plan when things fail, as some surely will. The lesson of the coal is that substance, not appearance, is the key thing. Coals burn hotly, deeply, and consistently. You cook with coals, not flames. We all need coals of the spirit to create true substance in our lives. A single coal, shared from our fire can enlighten, kindle, and inflame the hearts of others, illuminate the world.

"Gathering fuel may be necessary, and even fun – but don't neglect time to sit and watch the fire burn, enjoy its glory." Sometimes we need to lighten up, relax, slow down, or draw back far enough from the fire to see how it is really going. View the whole forest. Do not be such a work nut that you expend ourselves completely without enjoying the process. Creative beings, humans are designed to work and build, but also with an innate need to derive satisfaction from the fruits of our labors. A good balanced approach appreciates the whole work, process and product alike, thus finding joy in our accomplishment. We can and should discover and savor the good in what we're doing. We achieve greatness in life by the accumulative blessings of all those ordinary good works we have given ourselves to performing. In giving to our fires, we should also make time to receive the benefits available there for us.

My vigil in the woods was a genuine night of blessing for me. It is my sincere wish that these few embers from my notes would spark in my gentle readers some glow of understanding, illuminate coals of wisdom, and bring joy into your soul. When next you have occasion to camp, may you enjoy your own lessons from the fire, too!

> ## *"Words are the petals of poems."*
> - Karen O'Leary

List of Book Truths

Autumn 1996

Robert Hamm

The Proper Study of Mankind Is Books.

Books We Must Have though We Lack Bread.

The True University of These Days Is a Collection of Books.

No Furniture Is so Charming as Books.

Books Are Often Wiser Than Their Readers.

Beware the Man of One Book.

A Man Who Can Read Books and Does Not Has No Advantage Over a Man Who Cannot Read.

All the Glory of the World Would Be Lost in Oblivion unless God Had Provided Mortals with the Remedy of Books.

Wear the Old Coat and Buy the New Book.

Butterflies and Traffic Lights

Spring 1994

Mindy Hauptman

Life is a jigsaw puzzle that always has a piece missing. The accomplishment of finishing the puzzle would make "life" much easier for us all. Other people want to ask whether the meaning of life would be the same for them, if it was answered. Our goals in life would most likely be changed, if the answers were known. Not very many people would buy a puzzle, if it was already put together, and it is doubtful people would want life structured with the same concept.

In the story "The Butterfly and the Traffic Light," by Cynthia Ozick, Fishbein, the main character, tries to decide the best solution for the meaning of life. Fishbein compares life to the significance of a street. Throughout the story, the street represents life and the bends and turns it makes. The street does not tell a person what is around the corner, just like life does not predict the future. A street is not a smooth surface where a person riding or walking on it can glide like going down a slide. A street has bumps formed by travelers. In the same respect, life has its many trials creating the people we are from one day to the next. The street is just a guide, and how it is traveled is up to the traveler. There are no written rules on how to get down the street, just like there is not a book about life.

Fishbein compares the importance of instant beauty to livelihood. The butterfly is a beautiful creature, which once was not noticed before its transformation. The caterpillar, who works diligently to make food and create a cocoon for its future, is not noticed because of its ugliness. People have to look at other qualities of this creature to find its beauty.

This is also true for people and their vanities. For some, beauty is only shell deep like the butterfly, and for others it is found by getting to know the person. The caterpillar and the "not so pretty" people find life to be more challenging. They also have much more livelihood than the butterfly and the "pretty" people. The butterfly represents the instant gratification people look for in life. Others forget to look beneath the surface to find out not everyone has a beautiful face.

The traffic light represents the constant stability people need in life.

Although Fishbein is discontented with the sight of traffic lights, he is reminded of life's need for simple repetitions to keep its routine. "Why do we have to do it this way, and who made the rules?" people often say. They do not think where this world would be without the rules. Humans are programmed to do certain tasks each day without thinking about the reasons for doing them. The world would be a chaotic mess if it were not for "traffic lights" to direct us. They are a reminder of the needs each individual has. People need direction to accomplish their goals in life.

People experience, at one time or another, a passion to just be here and not to think about the "what ifs" or "how did it happen" in life. Humans find themselves tempted with instant gratification. Most people do things in a practical way. The people who choose the "beautiful" route find they only have to do what others did in the first place. There is no way to just throw the puzzle on the table and expect the pieces to fall into place. A puzzle takes time to solve, just as life takes years to discover all its mysteries. Life is full of many thoughts and treasures. People lack meaning in life when they do not consider where these wonders will take them.

Fine Lines Summer Camp :: David Martin

73

Giving Birth to a Novel

Spring 2003

Anna Henkens-Schmidt

It doesn't require monthly check-ins at the clinic, and you won't have to buy a two-year supply of diapers. However, writing a novel is like childbirth in many ways. It requires careful planning, daily attention, and a desire to create a piece of you that will be left behind.

I have made several attempts throughout my writing career to sit down and compose a full-length novel. The first times at the computer were exciting ones, as my ideas spilled onto the keyboard. Like many other amateur novel writers that I've talked to, my once exciting ideas soon became boring. Half finished novels cluttered my hard drive.

There had to be some way to keep motivated; otherwise, John Grisham and Danielle Steel wouldn't be household names. I had an idea for a story that formulated for several months. I was scared to actually start writing the novel. I worried that I would lose interest half way through, and a great idea would be lost.

That's when I devised a formula for writing novels: become acquainted with your plot, understand your characters, take one day at a time, edit twice, then edit thrice. Using these four easy steps, I completed a 286-page novel in four months.

To write a novel you will need old magazines, pictures, an idea, an imagination, writing tools, and an objective friend.

You cannot begin a novel before you know how it is going to end. Many writers become discouraged half way through their work, because they have no idea where their plot is going. Before the writing process begins, the writer should make an outline of the idea, including both major and minor events.

Keep in mind that the outline isn't written in concrete. Once you begin writing, you may realize that not every idea will work. However, you will have a game plan to follow. You won't find yourself lost for ideas because they will already be formulated on your outline.

When the rough draft of your outline is complete, read over your ideas with an objective friend. Find out if some of your ideas seem out of context and ask for advice on how to change them. Is your idea believable? Does it have excitement? Though it might be difficult to hear criticism before you even begin writing, it is better than being forced to rewrite the whole novel after you finished.

It is vital for the writer to understand the characters in the novel. This may seem like a common sense statement, but if you don't understand your characters, who will? You should know more about them than you will ever write about them.

There is no right or wrong way to choose the stars of your novel. It starts by picking up old magazines. I thumb through the pages until I find the face that I've been looking for. When I am secure in my decision, I cut out the picture and begin a character catalogue. Remember that the character is what will make your novel come alive, so make careful decisions with each aspect of the character.

Included in your character catalogue should be your character's name, address, social security number, and a complete outline of everything the character likes, dislikes, past childhood experiences, motives, and whatever else you can possibly think of. Who cares if your reader will never need to know that your character craves melted cheese over carrot sticks on weekends? The more real you make the character seem, the easier it will be to make the character seem authentic to the reader.

A novel is something you must devote time to each and every day. It's not a good idea to sit down and write twenty pages one day, and then not work on it for a week. You have to keep the novel fresh in your mind. Set a goal each day, and accomplish it. Tell yourself, "I'm going to write five pages a day." Sometimes, write more; never write less.

There will be days when you feel uninspired. Work through your downtimes. Your inspiration will return if you keep encouraging yourself. If you give up when you don't feel like writing, you will keep putting it off until your idea becomes wasted space on your computer. If you don't like what you have written one day, leave it; there will be plenty of time for revising later.

Though you should spell check what you have written each day, save the major revising until the novel is complete. After you are satisfied that your novel is finished, take a break away from your writing for two or three weeks. Then come back to your novel and start reading from beginning to end. Correct and rewrite anything that sounds out of place.

After you have corrected your novel, consult some objective friends. Ask them to read your work and write down questions or comments about your novel and the page numbers where the problems appeared. This will be very helpful for the final revising stage.

Work with the suggestions from your friends, and make the needed changes. When you've finished, reread your entire novel. The more you edit now, the less you will have to edit when you submit your novel for publication.

Creating a novel can be a memorable experience. Like giving birth to a child, you will watch your novel grow, mature, and one day leave your nest to become published. I encourage you to use the easy steps that I have given to you or adopt some of the ideas to better suit your individual needs. Good luck with your novel and happy writing.

Lost & Found

Summer 1998

Mindy Hightower

I have not written with any purpose in over one year. I've done this thing called technical writing: reports, business letters, the blah-blah-blah of daily life. How boring format has become.

This year I saw daughter number one move into her own apartment and go broke within thirty days. I nurtured daughter number two through serious surgery and sent her away to college to complete a less-than-satisfactory first semester. I medicated a bad back, a bleeding ulcer, arthritis, and anemia. I have literally quit participating in everything I started or enjoyed in the past two years. For a while, I thought I was consumed by the dragons; my "self" was lost in constant battle.

At night, when too exhausted to think, the tears would simply well-up and run down my cheeks, the oozing sadness of my lost existence spilling on the pillow. Sometimes, I would feel dampness under my head in the morning and rationalize that I must have had another night sweat, a bad dream, or erratic hormones.

Where am I? The passions and flavors have turned to paste. My soul is a white nothingness, reflecting all light, all feelings; not letting anyone or anything in. My memories are buried under drifts of this whiteness.

So, tonight, I do not know why, I decided to write. The words come easily, like a cool glass of water. I have no worry that what I say may not make sense to the reader or even to me. I have quit caring for so long that criticism is just another blinding farce. What is important is that the words are giving me a vehicle to open my heart. The words might add color to my world, and, maybe, I will recognize something familiar about who I am.

My friend, an incredible woman, told me last week she has made a list of resolutions for this new year. She actually tabs them and journals everyday. When she records an achievement that happens to be on her list of resolutions, she celebrates! I did not make any resolutions this year. It seems a waste; I always break them, fail, forget, or get lost.

I feel the need to do something with my hands. I started sewing again. Nothing grand, but an exercise in taking flat fabric and placing raw ends together to create. Now, I sit typing on the keyboard again, feeling the need to see my hands and fingers move, creating a patchwork of words that are my own. They are not pretty, but it is me, trying to get back out.

I was an original member of the "Dragon Slayers" who started *The Quest for Fine Lines*, the predecessor of *Fine Lines*. I used writing as my defense. Since I stopped writing, I felt the dragons won, and I lost. Looking back at everything that has happened, I am wondering if what I have been doing is not really defeat, but a dance with the demons of life. I face the sadness, the disappointment, the heartaches, the frustrations, and wonder if I will make it out alive. I will not succumb to the depression, but I shield myself and convince the demons I am no longer interested in writing or creating or caring or loving.

In this way, I am a double agent of sorts, living one way to protect the inner sanctum where the real me lives. I am here. My heart still beats. I still read and write. I still care about people, and I still love. I have been found. My passion remains tucked inside the whiteness, bubbling out in nature. Now, I am chasing the dragons and catching their tails. I am on the hunt, looking for the next challenge. With my fingers moving over the keyboard on the coldest of nights this winter, I have been found.

A Scale of Journals

Winter 1993

Hanna Hinchman

Hail to all journal keepers. Over the years, I've watched my journal shift around from being an observational, informational record to a deeply personal, interior process and back again, always shifting. Below is an idea I call "a scale of journals" to help me understand which stage I'm in at the moment and what element I might want to introduce more of for balance.

The informational stage adds to the body of measurable data in the world: identification, distribution, populations, temperatures, etc. It is valuable and narrowly focused. I never considered it as an art form in itself, though it can include some meticulous drawings, diagrams, and maps.

My investigative stage always focuses on the outer world, but its emphasis is usually on the immeasurable, unnamed phenomena: effects of light, clouds, flowing water, and changing seasons. Opportunities for artistic interpretation increase dramatically with this stage.

The resonating stage is the ecotone section, where the inner world meets the outer world. This connection is between the point of awareness that is the writer and the surrounding universe. What is selected for the journal becomes far more personal and idiosyncratic. It is the highest possibility for artistry, and the whole becomes a work of art.

The deeply personal journal and explorations of the psyche are in the reflective stage. It becomes concerned with memories, dreams, interpersonal events, spiritual growth, and the problem solving of self examination. It usually is more devoted to human-centered events and exchanges. It can be an artistic vehicle, but like the informational journal, it is more concerned with content.

My favorite journals tend to fall into the two middle categories. Thoreau and Hopkins embody the best of the resonating journals, but they are not in any way visual. Keith Brockie, Janet Marsh, and Sara Midda reach a level of perception in the visual journal, but the content is disappointingly thin and dull.

If I were to send a message to a group of journal writers, it would be this: "Take Risks." We all talk about a reverence for creativity, but it can be scary when it gets a hold of us. It's a powerful force that has its own tidal influences. The journal is a perfect place to give free rein to the creative impulse, even if it results in maddened ravings or strange dark images from time to time. How I envy you out there, getting ready to open the doors! "The journal is a room of your own, a place of retreat, as well as a way of participating in the life around you."

Door :: Wipanan Chaichanta

Take Out a Piece of Paper

Spring 2001

Analisa Jacob

Of the four years in high school, I think my junior year was the worst of all. Deadlines, due dates, and curfews were all thrown at me in one big package. "This is the one year colleges look at, so make it count!" screamed the counselors, but every time a counselor, a peer, or teacher said that to me, I asked myself the question, "Make it count for whom?"

I wanted this year to count for me. This is why I took creative writing. Without creative writing, I would have missed out on some of the most impressionable experiences of my life. The people, the stories, the poems, and all the glory that came in and out of that class every day were impressive. We became a family, a family of writers. Not a day goes by that I don't thank my lucky stars for taking that class.

I can't say that it was fun and games that year; the junior year isn't supposed to be. At one point, I never wanted to come to school. I had no desire for it, but as time passed, so did that phase.

Without creative writing, I would never have taken the time to understand people. Creative writing taught me about myself, and I studied the people around me, more than I studied the eight parts of speech. I learned to accept, respect, and observe my fellow peers. I can't imagine my junior year without a creative writing class. I think I would have gone insane.

I am grateful for the opportunity to be in that class. I am grateful for the friendships I made. I am grateful for having a dedicated teacher who refused to see me as anything less than special. So much encouragement, so much love, and so much devotion came from that teacher. What did I learn? I learned respect for others and dedication to the writing craft, which I am still working on. This wonderful experience will always remain with me. "Write on."

The Boundaries of Freedom

Winter 1995

Yoshi Kardell

Jacob Fritz :: Killed in Iraq

A boundary is something that creates a limit. It is necessary to create perimeters to avoid chaos. Disorder creates change and creative improvements, sometimes, but uncontrolled variation will ruin the largest country. A limitation can be both physical and personal. In America, the boundaries of freedom are created by the United States' Constitution, the Declaration of Independence, and by citizens' responsibilities to their country.

The Declaration of Independence and the Constitution create the guidelines under which every American can live freely. The Declaration stated the right of the colonists to operate as a free and independent nation. Thomas Jefferson incorporated into The Declaration the three basic rights which are unalienable to every American citizen: Life, Liberty, and the Pursuit of Happiness. The Constitution guarantees our civil rights and establishes legal boundaries for our citizens. Both documents state that the government is run by the people. They claim that if the government becomes destructive of those rights written in these documents that it is in the hands of the people to change it.

To live in a free country does not mean that it comes free of accountability. The strength of freedom comes from citizens being liable for their actions and respect for the rights of others. People are free to do with their lives that which they choose to unless it is at the expense of another's freedom. Americans also carry with them a regard for their country. The forefathers of America upheld the cause of freedom with their lives. Today, Americans should recognize the commitment those ancestors had for freedom.

Americans tend to take their liberty for granted and lose their sense of trust in their country. This is when the rights of others are not respected and people discriminate against each other. I feel that Americans should continue to pledge our lives, our fortunes, and our sacred honor. We seem to forget all this country has to offer.

The responsibility of American citizens, the Constitution, and the Declaration of Independence create the boundaries of our freedoms. These boundaries are necessary for Americans to live freely. The physical boundaries are the written documents, which guarantee the rights of American citizens. The personal boundaries are created by the people's responsibilities and respect for their country. In Amercia, we serve each other.

"Knowledge is proud that it knows so much; wisdom is humble that it knows no more."

- William Cowper, English poet, 1731-1800

Dear Dragon Slayers

Autumn 1993

Jon Kathol

Writing to you now, I feel a bit like the prodigal son. Two years ago, I received the gift of journal writing from you, but like the prodigal son, I took the gift and blew it. Now, I have returned. I have a few pages filled with thoughts and emotions. I cannot give my journal a name, yet. However, through these years, the Dragon Slayers continued to share their wealth with me. For that, I thank you all.

I have been busy studying architecture. You see, I have transcended paper. I do not write on it. I build with it. My pen does not always write words. It spans a length. It supports a load. Words and phrases are ripped out and replaced with mortar and stone.

When I read *Fine Lines,* I often feel like I'm reading the instruction manual for some sort of role-playing game. The following words come to mind: sword (pen), battle-ax (typewriter), Winchester double-barrel shotgun (computer), shield (words), dragons (thoughts-language-overcoming obstacles), slayer (writer/feelings).

Enclosed in this envelope please find a check for one zillion dollars ($1,000,000,000,000,000) which should provide me with a lifetime subscription for *The Quest* for *Fine Lines.*

An Essay on Humor

Spring 1998

Kip Kippley

When assailed with the task of writing an essay on humor, one finds one's self hopeless, as if in a canoe. How can one assail in a canoe? Hence, it's the proverbial creek without a paddle. Since this is a family focused essay, I shall refrain from writing anything even remotely disturbing.

Intellectual humor is an oxymoron, but since I have never met any oxen with a fashion sense, then I can be assured that they never did want anything "more on." That would lend this essay more to a discussion of wild life, and I am determined to keep this rather tame, so as not to lose my audience. If you are reading this, at least I can be content with an audience of one.

When it comes time for the applause, please do not be too self-conscious, if you are the only one applauding in the room. I will still appreciate the gesture of good will. It may indicate your depth of decline into the realms of poor taste in humor, mind you, but good will none the less. Perhaps, in another article, we can discuss what actually less than none is, but I have decided not to be negative today.

I enjoy toying with the English language. It's my second language. My first language was unintelligible, I am told, so I switched to English at an early age on the intense prompting of my parents. Apparently, I succeeded. Other research may be necessary to replicate this hypothesis. Cloning is not an option, so I am told. It is illegal to put the world into a scenario of double jeopardy. The world has brought many humorists to trial, and this being the case, I will have to plead the fifth. So, indeed, I am only one by the grace of God, and this lifetime is my only shot at fame, though I am quite sure that many have taken aim at me from time to time. As far as I can tell, they have missed, so far.

Many have said that I have a magnetic personality, but I digress. Perhaps, that explains the bipolar personality struggles, but again I have concluded that negativity tends to repulse people of a more positive nature which, in and of itself, is against the laws of physics. I have never formally studied law. I have always worn casual clothes when reading legal briefs or while wearing them. I have found many such looms to be fruitful.

If you are having a difficult time following this essay, I have taken the liberty of making an outline of it. I hope that helps. I will try to stay within those bounds. Now that we have established some sense of order, I would like to be first. Secondly, with all due respect, is you. The rest is up to you as far as who you recruit to read over your shoulder. Have everyone else form a line behind them, please be courteous, and hold the applause until the end of the line. Pass it on.

In conclusion, I would like to point out but find myself constrained by the dotted line. I will point instead to the very fact that humor is a personal thing that is mystic in nature and is dependent upon the circumstances, education, breeding and personality of both the humorist and the one partaking in the vent of the humor in whole or part. With that in mind, it is a wonder we ever laugh at all. There are too many variables.

The equation is perhaps limited to $E=mc2$. "E" is equal to the elusiveness of humorous events and their short-lived duration. "M" is equal to the mode delivery which can be verbal, demonstrative, written or blasted over the airwaves in a continual assault of poor taste, sarcasm, and perversion which we call television. I prefer the written form, for any fool can be a television fool and have proven this ad nauseam, heavy on the nauseam. "C" is equal to content, and since it is squared, it is the humorist who is given the task to double, multiply, and compound the humorous content and attempt to tame it into a form of lasting duration and heightened potency.

In any event, the humor of the situation may be the product of mystical forces beyond the control of any and all parties involved, and I have been to many such parties that lacked that mystical quality. Do not take yourself too seriously, dear reader, and take a moment to relish the hot dog that has been given you. "Frankly, my dear, I don't give a lamb," because I certainly don't want to end this with a baaaaad joke.

Insert applause here. Pass it on.

1936

Spring 2008

Richard Koelling

 If you believe the history books, 1936 was a very bad year in the United States of America. The depression was raging unabated, war was thought to be on the horizon, and it was either too hot or too cold wherever you lived. Hindsight, though, is 20/20, especially when it erases bad memories – if there were any. For me, it was a wonderful year. It was the sixth year of my life, full of all sorts of wonders. In January, I was allowed to begin kindergarten. In those years, new classes began in September or January, depending on the birth date of a new student. If you were born no later than the end of September, you could begin school in September, otherwise January began your trip through academia. In January 1936, my long and undistinguished career as a student began in morning kindergarten.

We lived right across the street from the school but bundled up like Eskimos anyway, regardless of the humiliation level. Sheepskin coats, real sheepskin lining with leather on the outside; mittens large and heavy enough that nothing could be gripped; galoshes (overshoes), three-or-four-buckles were preferred; cap, earmuffs; and a wool, wraparound scarf that left only our eyes visible. The film, *A Christmas Story*, pretty well showed how we were dressed, except that we didn't have down-filled snowsuits then. The cold of those mid-1930s winters still penetrated the extremes of what we thought were warm clothes.

Unfortunately, kindergarten was a total bore. We were taught how to play "cat's cradle" with string, how to wind string around our hands to begin a ball of string, and how to count and tell time. Geez!! Who cared about the string anyway? All I did was get tangled up in the string and cut off circulation in my fingers, and I already knew how to count to 100 or so (they always made me quit before I got any farther.) We were told we would be allowed to begin learning to read in first grade. What a bummer! A whole year of fighting string and looking at the clock didn't seem promising.

Punishment was meted out by sending offenders to the "bench." It wasn't really a bench but more of a book cabinet away from the other kids. It was a fine place to draw pictures, though, and in my year of kindergarten I acquired some skill at drawing airplanes, trains, and cars of that era. Solitude was actually kind of fun, but once in a while, the teacher would examine my artwork and try to make me draw right-side up instead of upside down, which is how I drew best. That generated more solitude and more art practice.

School quickly lost its attraction as the center of my life, and all the other things that could happen became my focus. For example, the first fistfight: two little boys saying silly nyah-nyah stuff until one pushed the other and eventually one hit the other. Then a crowd of other little kids gathered around to cheer or heckle one or the other. Eventually, a teacher came out and stopped the fight or one of the boys quit – willing to be the loser. This was a fun fight – a fat little kid, me, against a fast little kid, him. I think I got a bloody nose, but he started crying – maybe at the sight of my blood – just as the teacher came out and threatened to take us to the principal's office. That was the surest way to stop a fight, but nobody quit, so apparently there was neither a winner or loser.

Pretty soon school was out. In Iowa, school finished in May, because some of the older kids had farm chores to do.

Summer of 1936 was hotter than blazes. It didn't seem like anybody cussed then, so we had quaint phrases to describe things like heat. Day after day, it was in the 90s and often reached 100. We sweated and got dirty, and the dirt stuck. It stuck behind our ears, under our fingernails, and in the lines of our necks. The dirtiest kid won the day, but at night the ogres of the households made us wash up – hands, necks, faces, everything! A whole day's work just plain got shot down, and victory was hollow, but dirty neck contests had a magic of their own.

There was no escaping the heat – day or night. Air conditioning might have been something my parents had read about, but I never heard it mentioned. Fans were located here and there around the house but were mostly effective at moving the warm air to somewhere else than where you sat. Basements offered some relief, but not until morning. An occasional thunderstorm cooled things off a bit and were exciting, especially when they knocked limbs off trees. They just made the night or next day more humid, but y'know, that's the way it was! What could we do about it?

September came, and school began again. Just like spring, some of the farm kids had work to do, so school started later than it does now.

Being an old hand at kindergarten, which was all day now, I went straight to the bench to claim my place. It was mine, and nobody else was going to get it. In fact, I'd already cheated and learned the alphabet which earned me the right to be isolated from those who obeyed the rules. My brother was really at fault, though, because he taught me the alphabet, a group of letters at a time. However, he still represented the establishment, refusing to teach me how to put the letters together to make words. I think he just wanted me to sit on the bench.

**

Early 1936 apparently hadn't been a banner year for my father, who sold canned fruits and vegetables for a major food processor (which no longer exists in the 21st century). He was paid straight commission and went three months without a check. We lived on savings. Fortunes changed somewhat in the spring, and the wholesale food distributors began buying again. Paychecks resumed, and we kept our car, a 1935 Dodge which had been bought in a moment of optimism. My father had many such moments. In that three month interim, we ate lots and lots of canned vegetables, fruit, pork, and beans as the company provided samples for their families' provisions. We never knew hunger, so we never knew we were poor.

The 1935 Dodge is relevant because it opened new vistas for me – about to become a world-wise six-year-old in the fall. Because I was already in trouble for knowing the alphabet, my parents decided we could miss school for a week or two or three by taking a long trip to visit my grandparents in New York state. What my brother's excuse was I never learned. Maybe, he just flunked that part of his life.

In October, we headed east to see the sights and my mother's family. We got to Iowa City at night after a 300 mile drive, and something escaped me about its beauty in the dark and only a few streetlights to illuminate it. We crossed mile after mile of flatland prairie, already harvested. Only signs and pictures of Alf Landon and Franklin D. Roosevelt broke the monotony. They meant nothing to me, being assured by my parents that Landon was a big time winner. The only other amusement was the occasional hurried stop at the side of the road and my father making a mad dash to get behind a billboard. Fortunately, the billboards were fairly close to the road and totally opaque from the ground up. He seemed to have some sort of a digestion problem. Parts of Illinois and Ohio were greener in 1937 for his efforts. By now, 1936 seemed to be a lot more fun.

We finally arrived at the farm in upstate New York – way, way upstate on the St. Lawrence river. In fact, the farm went right to the river just a football field's length away. The farm was wonderful. There were lots of dairy cows, a big barn, hay, and a tall silo which my brother said I could see the North Pole from, if I climbed to the top. The opportunities for adventure were endless. What might have happened in the barn or around the cows, besides getting squirted a few times direct from the udders, I never learned. My grandfather heard about my fight and decided to teach me a little bit. We put the boxing gloves on. Mine came halfway up my arms and were a lot heavier than they looked. He pretended a couple of jabs and told me not to hit over-handed like a baseball pitcher, but to hit straight or come around the side. So, I came around with a round-house right which he blocked but pretended had hit him, and he just flopped over on his back and made a few gargly sounds and then snored, as if snoring represented unconsciousness. At someone's count of ten, he got up and congratulated me.

Wow! Almost six years old, I was king of the hill, but there was more was to come.

The silo was yet to be conquered, the North Pole was yet to be seen. The silo was probably only 30 feet high with iron rung steps going up the side. That was a piece of cake, if there ever was one. I climbed to the top and could see Canada, the river, almost to Canton, N.Y., but no North Pole. I heard them calling for me from somewhere – somewhere way down below – with admonitions like, "Where have you been all afternoon?" "We've been looking all over for you!" and "Get your butt down here right now!"

There was the rub! I froze! "Down" was a long, long ways away, and I wasn't about to move an inch. I was petrified. My uncle had to climb up and guide me down one step at a time, but once down, my fear was gone, and I was king of the hill again, strutting around like a bandy rooster.

Shortly after we got home from New York we celebrated my sixth birthday, and 1936 was really a special year already, but the best was yet to come.

Winter was as severe as summer was hot. It was extremely cold with lots of snow. Christmas was sure to be good, because it was Santa's kind of winter. As Christmas approached, we got a nice big tree that we strung lights on and hung ornaments with great globs of tinsel. My job was the tinsel, so the lower half of the tree was pretty shiny. The stockings were properly hung with care, and they were real stockings. Since we wore "knickers" then, which was short for "knickerbockers" – knee length trousers which little kids, baseball players, and golfers wore – we also wore ugly, long brown or argyle stockings that went up to and under the cuffs of the knickers. The only possible good thing one could say about those stockings was that they were long and held lots of great stuff on Christmas morning.

My brother and I finished the decorating and the stockings and waited patiently for Santa. My brother was almost 12 then and infinitely wise. He told me Santa would be approaching from the back side of the house, so we parked ourselves at the back window, blew holes in the ice that formed on the inside of the window (That was common in those days. Houses were well air conditioned in the winter.), and waited. Suddenly, there he was! I saw a red light far away. My brother agreed – maybe it really was Santa!

I watched and watched, and as the holes in the ice would refreeze I'd make new ones and search again, but Santa never got closer and never seemed to move from one side to the other. Alas, it was just the light at the top of a radio tower. My faith in seeing Santa was obliterated, and I was only six.

The next morning his evidence was there. The stockings were full of oranges, apples, nuts, and some sugar candies. He brought lots of presents in 1936, too, and the best of all was my Buck Rogers ray gun. If you pointed it at something (not someone – that wasn't polite) and said "ZZZZZZZZZZ" loudly, you destroyed it. The ray was invisible, of course. I wanted more action; however, so I went down the street to show off the ray gun. Somehow, there was more action than allowed, and when I got home, the gun was taken from me and never seen again.

That was just a momentary disappointment. In a couple of days, the Christmas tree dried out considerably and was rapidly shedding. My father being a man of the moment decided we'd best burn it.

The fireplace was handy, and what the heck, that's what it was for. He started a small fire with the usual kindling wood and started to feed it twigs from the tree. They burned brightly, but too slowly. He fed it larger and larger pieces until we couldn't see the edges of the fireplace for the flames. It created its own firestorm with an upward draft, so we went outside to see what was happening. Flames and embers were shooting out of the top of the chimney dropping harmlessly – so far – around the neighborhood. This was really exciting!

We ran back in the house, and I watched him frantically working to quell the fire quickly. Most of the tree had burned by then, so the danger of spreading the fire had lost its immediacy, and the night soon ended. All was well, and in a few short days 1937 would arrive. Yes, 1936 was a very good year for a six-year-old boy.

The Sandbox

Autumn 1994

Penny Koenig

I don't understand why, but my father was a man who showed his love for his children in strange ways. He wouldn't say, "I love you." He showed his love for us by making things. I remember the hours he used to spend in the garage, making pine-wood derby cars, go-carts, and whatever else he thought would make us happy. Once, he spent two weeks making a covered wagon for my sister's dolls! He was so proud of his ability to make us happy.

Whether he realized it or not, his best creation was our sandbox. To my father, the sandbox was one of his simpler projects. It was four pieces of planking nailed at the corners into a square. The lower edges of the wood were sunk into the ground, so it wouldn't move. On one corner of the sandbox, he built into it another box with a lid in which we were supposed to put our toys away when we were done playing with them. The inside, of course, we filled with sand.

This was no ordinary sandbox. It was coveted by every kid on our block. Their sandboxes were the standard tractor tire sandboxes with no toy box built-in. Our sandbox was huge! It was 10' by 10', so we had more room in which to build things. Our sandbox design was emulated by all of the other good fathers on our block.

My brother, Jeff, (who is two years younger) and I grew up together in that sandbox. We spent countless hours building houses and roads that all connected, but led nowhere, for our Matchbox cars. Time was lost in that sandbox, as was my mother's silverware that we used (instead of shovels) to carve out the streets of our city. If someone were to go out to where the sandbox was today with a metal detector, they would strike it rich.

When Jeff and I were in our sandbox, the rest of the world disappeared. We never fought. For that matter, we hardly even talked. We simply lost ourselves in the world we were creating, enjoying the sunshine on our backs, the feel of the warm sand between our toes, and the quiet company of one another. We became the best of friends.

When I think back to my childhood, and especially the sandbox, my heart yearns to be a child again. I miss the quiet time spent with my best friend. Although my brother and I are still close, the hectic lives that we both lead do not allow us as much time to spend together as I would like. I often wonder if Jeff ever thinks about our sandbox and misses it too.

Last year, when my husband and I bought our first house, I sat on the deck in the back yard on closing day and pondered where to put the sandbox for our own children. Jim asked me what I was doing. He said I looked sad and that I should be happy, because we were buying our first house today. I never told him about the sandbox. He would have thought that I was silly. How could he understand?

I have since made up my mind where to put the sandbox. Maybe I am just being foolish, but I really do think that a sandbox is more than a place where roads and cities are built that only last as long as the weather permits. I believe that friendship and love are also created between siblings. However, unlike the cities of our past, this bond lasts forever.

> *"There is no luck except where there is discipline."*
>
> Irish proverb

Roller Coaster

Autumn 2004

Tina Labellarte

 Whenever my dad thumbs through the photo albums, he comments aloud to whoever happens to be nearby.

Today, he says, "It's sad you don't remember more about your grandfather."

Without looking up from my book, I replied, "It's not easy to remember someone you only met twice, especially, when he speaks Italian, and you speak English."

What I want to say, though, is that when I met Grandpa, I didn't have to speak much at all. Tony did the talking for both of us when we were little. Dad used to say Grandpa loved Tony the best, because Dad gave him Grandpa's name. Now Dad says nothing about Tony.

"I loved Tony the best, because he was my big brother." I imagine saying this aloud, but I don't do it.

Mom smiles and cries when she looks at the old black and white photos with white, scalloped edges that show Tony and me together. I am always looking up at him. Tony was a couple of inches taller than me, so I guess that's normal. In these pictures, the ones in the photo album, which I've studied over and over, Tony never looks back at me. Instead, he looks directly into whoever or whatever was in front of us.

"You must remember Grandpa. He brought us the cheese?" My father prompts me. He thinks he remembers everything better than I do. Dad loves very hard cheese, the kind that only comes in a special box direct from Italy. He grates and grates the small triangles of it for hours; until the pile becomes a mountain. Our mother, who is not Italian, puts the grated cheese into empty pickle jars. She boils them first, of course. The jars, I mean. She says it is a whole lot of work for something we could buy in the Kraft Food aisle of the grocery store.

"Yeah, Dad, I remember," I say, "that cheese smelled like dirty feet." My father frowns at me. He does not like me to be disrespectful, though I am eighteen now and no longer a child.

I was five when Grandpa visited the first time. I saw him go down into the basement carrying a package and the knife Mom always kept in the big drawer in the kitchen. Tony followed Grandpa, and I followed Tony. We pushed and shoved each other to get a closer look.

Grandpa heaved the huge round hunk of cheese wrapped in brown paper onto the old wooden table. He cut away the heavy string tied around it. He looked from the cheese to the knife and back again. Grandpa licked his calloused thumb and ran it along the edge of the long blade, then smiled in satisfaction.

All the muscles in his arms bulged up as he leaned his weight onto the knife handle and created the triangles. We clapped our hands. Grandpa laughed and raised the knife above his head, making little slicing moves in the air. Maybe, he was teasing us with an old, Italian custom we didn't understand, or maybe, he was just trying to wave us away. When Grandpa laid the knife down on the table, though, Tony thought Grandpa meant that it was his turn.

"I'm gonna help," Tony said and his hand landed on the knife.

"Noooo," I screamed. "Me, me, I wanna."

Tony held the big kitchen knife the right way, grasping it by the brown handle, the sharp blade pointed down. Tony was six, only eleven months older than I was, but that's a lot, really, old enough to know things I didn't. I liked that about him, but it made me mad, too. I grabbed for the knife. I had it, but so did Tony. My firm grip was as close to the handle in Tony's hand as I could manage. I clutched the blade between the thumb and index finger of my small soft fist.

"Let go, you're too little," Tony yelled in my face.

"No. Mine," I yelled back.

Tony yanked the knife back toward him, and that settled it. My cut was clean and deep. Luckily, I still have the thumb. Of course, I also still have the scar. My parents don't seem to remember how mad they got that time. Tony wasn't allowed to play outside for two weeks. Dad said Tony should have had sense enough to take care of his little sister. Mom said, "It's always the girls who have the most sense." I don't remember what Grandpa said. Maybe, that's because I was screaming and bleeding, or maybe, that's because whatever he said was in Italian. Anyway, I didn't see my grandfather again until I was eight. He came to this country for the last time after we had Angela's birthday party. She's my little sister.

Angela heard the doorbell chime, too, but she was so much smaller than us that she had no choice but to trail behind Tony and me, as we ran down the short, narrow hallway in our little red brick ranch house. Okay, so it was Angela's birthday, and it was her godmother at the door, as it turned out.

Red-haired and red-faced, Auntie Marlene stood on the front porch, already dripping with sweat in the July heat of the Chicago suburbs.

I was impressed with the height and color of Auntie Marlene's teased hairdo atop her short, fat body. I confided this to our Mother one night while I stood in the doorway of our parents' bedroom, watching her brush her long, dark wavy hair. Mom disagreed. She said Auntie Marlene's hair looked an awful lot like cotton candy at the circus. I didn't care. I thought Auntie Marlene's hair was wonderful, but I kept that to myself.

It wasn't fair that Tony and I got stuck with weird, old, Italian cousins for godparents and Angela was blessed with Auntie Marlene, whose husband died in a war before he could give her a baby. Mom explained that our godparents had kids of their own to waste money on at birthdays and Christmas. Tony was a nine-year-old, for heaven's sakes, and I was a second grader, Mom said, and the two of us were plenty big enough to forgive our aged relatives their limited gift-giving abilities. Mom never missed a chance to remind us that she had ten brothers and sisters and never had birthday parties or presents even. She said we ought to be grateful for what we had and not so damn selfish as to want someone who rightfully belonged to our sister. I couldn't argue with that.

By the time the three of us crashed into the living room, we saw pretty quickly that none of us had won the race. Mom beat us to it. She was already out of her straight-backed chair nearest the front door, blocking our path with her tall and slender frame. On days like this, we knew that we had the youngest mother and the prettiest. She wore a little mascara, some blush, and a bright red lipstick only when we had company, but she creamed her face every night before bed, using white stuff from a blue jar labeled Noxzema. Our mother was proud of her perfect skin. It was the only compliment I ever heard her give to herself.

Mom had prevented Tony, Angela, and me from plowing into our favorite guest, but at least, we could see Auntie Marlene through the screen door. Our three sets of dark brown eyes were riveted on the box covered in shiny, girlish, pink paper and gripped tightly by Auntie Marlene's pudgy bejeweled fingers. At four feet tall, the gift was as big as the birthday girl.

"Happy birthday, baby," Aunt Marlene wheezed as Mom guided her through a crowd of female relatives so she could settle into an empty spot on the sagging couch.

"What could there be in such a big box?" our mother asked. Mom's blue eyes flashed a warning in our direction, as she lifted the bulky treasure from Auntie Marlene to lean it against the wall. The reply Auntie Marlene formed on her orange lips was drowned out by the arrival of Uncle Vito,

Auntie Carol, and their children, who included my best friend Jane and
her brother Joe. Mom was momentarily distracted by her duties as hostess.
Angela, who really always was a sweet kid, climbed into Auntie Marlene's
lap and planted a juicy kiss in the folds of her perfumed neck.

"See. I told you she'd get it," Tony whispered to me, pointing at the
box.

"So what? I don't care," I replied, giving him a quick shove to prove it.

Four, pastel candles glowed on the cake from Cantoro's bakery. The
men had been cajoled inside from the driveway where they had been
sipping cold beer and admiring Dad's next-to-new 1962 Chevy Impala,
white with a red stripe. Mom tilted her head, giving Tony the signal. His
pure, clear voice led the loud rendition of "Happy Birthday." The heavily-
accented tones of our immigrant fathers mingled with the soft soprano
sounds of their American wives, but it was obvious that we children were
the only ones who really knew all the words.

"Make a wish, honey, but don't tell," Auntie Marlene yelled out. Angela
dutifully screwed up her face, closed her eyes tight, made the sign of the
cross, and pointed her hands to the heavens. Angela's short black curls
gleamed against her flushed cheeks as she filled them with air. Her gentle
breath blew out the candles in one sweet puff.

She needn't have bothered with the wish. After the cards with dollar
bills and the books and the Candyland game from Mom and Dad, Angela
was allowed to pull the huge package to the table. They had saved the best
for last. She tore through the pink wrap in a frenzy of delight. Through
the clear cellophane looking glass that made up the front of the box, I saw
a dream come true. It was her, all right. The life-size "Cathy" doll, just
as we'd seen it advertised every day after school on the black and white
console during "Bozo's Circus." Cathy was blonde, blue-eyed, and beautiful
in her blue cotton dress. Even the adults were awed by this spectacle.

"Thank you, Auntie Marlene!" Angela squealed, and everyone
applauded. Except me.

Angela would share. She always did. I was too big for a doll like that
anyway. Angela and "Cathy" sat at the table with the grown-ups. Tony and
I huddled with our cousins, Jane and Joe, in the kids' corner of the kitchen.
We grabbed for the paper plates the mothers passed our way, runny with
melting Neapolitan ice cream atop wedges of chocolate cake. We gobbled
the sticky treats with plastic forks and nimble fingers.

Jane was exactly my age, and I loved the family gatherings, because
we could play together for hours without too much interruption. We didn't
go to the same school or live in the same neighborhood, but we were close.

We understood what it was like to be scolded by foreign fathers, ignored by busy mothers, and tortured by our brothers. Jane's parents paid for her to have music lessons, so she taught me to play a song with her on the piano, a duet called "Heart and Soul." Tony surprised me with a big hug the first time we played it. The performance had been a gift from me at his birthday party the year before. I wasn't sure he'd like it, but he said it was a very nice present.

Tony became bored with all the attention Angela was getting at her birthday party, so he pulled on our bare arms, trying to drag Jane and me away from the kitchen and toward the coolness of the basement where a ping pong table had been set up for our distraction. Mom's eyes darted over to us, as we scrambled to our feet. "Don't disappear, you two. Both of you help your sister clean up all the wrapping and take the boxes to the garbage."

Jane escaped down the stairs with her brother. Tony and I knew better. We made no reply, but worked together in silence, gathering up what was left of the birthday festivities. Angela continued to sit in Auntie Marlene's lap, like a small princess, smiling and enjoying her subjects. We didn't mind.

"I've got an idea," Tony said to me on our second trip to the backyard garbage cans. I waited. He had that goofy look he often got when he was very excited about the mechanical possibilities of the world around us. Like the time he built the go-cart by taking apart milk crates he got from behind the grocery store and nailing them back together into a big contraption that he perched atop our rusty, old, red wagon. Tony wasn't good at school like I was, but he was smart in other ways. That go-cart would have worked, too, if Dad hadn't caught Tony when he pulled the car into the garage at the end of the workday. Tony was trying to take the engine out of the lawn mower. Dad was yelling so loudly that Mom came out of the house and told him to stop swearing, even though he was doing it in Italian so the neighbors wouldn't understand. Mom admired Tony's work. She even decided it would be great for the two of us to pull Angela around the block in the odd-looking wagon. The neighbor kids liked it, too. They sat on their porches, pointing and laughing at us.

"Look, Marie, this doll box is big enough to sit in." Tony attempted to continue our conversation. He placed his hands on my shoulders and shook me to make his point.

"So what?" I snapped at him and jerked away.

"It would make a great roller coaster," he said.

I stared. Idiot, I thought. I wanted the doll, not the box, or I would have wanted it if only I could have it. Anyway, what I wanted didn't much matter, and a box was not a roller coaster.

"What do you mean?" I asked him.

"Follow me."

We passed some of the adults on their way out, as we entered the house. Aunts and uncles drifted to the backyard where cold beer and wine flowed. Men set up tables on the cement patio, and red, white, and blue plastic poker chips appeared.

"Stop cleaning, and come out here, Karen," Dad yelled to the kitchen window where Mom was bent over the sink. "It's a party for Christ's sake," he added. She sighed.

"Keep an eye on the kids in the basement," she said to me, ignoring Tony. She didn't even notice the huge box he carried back inside. She passed him without a word and went out of the room and into the yard.

Now, Jane was calling up to me from the basement. "Come on, Marie, Angela is going to let us play with the Cathy doll."

"Just a minute," I yelled back and looked over at Tony. He closed the backdoor. He carefully positioned the box lengthwise, long and flat on the landing.

"What are you doing," I hissed. I was worried that Mom would return through the door the instant she noticed it had been closed without her command.

"Roller coaster," Tony said, looking down the stairs.

"It's twelve steps to the bottom," I said.

"We'll fly over them," he assured me.

I doubt it, I thought, but we had never been to an amusement park, and we had only heard about roller coasters from those neighbor kids who laughed and pointed and lived in bigger houses and whose families owned two cars.

"Forget it," I said. "It won't work."

Jane climbed up the stairs now to see what was taking me so long. She stopped two steps below us and looked up. With her hands on her hips, she said accusingly to Tony, "What are you doing with Cathy's box?"

"Roller coaster," he said.

Each time he repeated the two words, he grew larger and more confident.

"You're nuts," Jane said.

She'd never been impressed with Tony's ideas in the past, but I figured she might be jealous. Tony was definitely more fun than her brother, who was probably reading one of Angela's books in the basement, while we stood debating and sweating on the stairs.

"I want to go first," Tony said. "You guys can go after."

That seemed to motivate Jane, somehow. She advanced up to the landing.

"No, Tony, don't; it's too far down," I said and grabbed his arm. He shook free from me.

"Don't be a baby. It will be fun," Tony said. He climbed into the box and began to make a low "grrrr" sound, like an engine, I guessed.

"Energy. Electricity. Roller Coaster. Flying," Tony chanted to himself now.

Jane and I crouched behind him, flat up against the wall of the landing. I gazed at the back of Tony's crew-cut head, admiring that space inside where Tony kept ideas, and other people kept their brains. I was beginning to see the possibilities. I felt my heart soar in my chest.

"Push. Hard. Push up so I will fly," Tony commanded, eager and sure.

Jane and I were the same height, both skinny kids. Tony was bigger and had to be heavier. Jane and I looked at each other quickly. I calculated the necessary force and placed my hands low on the box, where Tony's back disappeared into the cardboard. Jane did the same.

"Now," Tony shouted. "Roller coaster!"

Jane and I moved in unison, throwing our combined frail weight against him. I saw Angela's small face peer around the bottom of the stairway just as Tony took flight. She jumped back, screaming.

He didn't fly far.

The front of the box slammed down on the third step, and he bounced up, higher than I had imagined. He catapulted forward without the box, the momentum of our push and his own weight carrying him through the air. I heard the fierce cracking sound as his neck snapped back when his head made a final bounce on the green and white, tiled, concrete floor.

I stumbled down the stairs, my legs tangling in the blind rush, reaching vainly to stop the moment. Tony lay still, his motionless body at an unspeakably wrong angle. I was close enough to touch him, but I could not. His face was very white. He did not breathe. He did not moan. He did not look up at me to laugh and say, "Your turn."

In every language, people screamed. The cries of the young and the old blurred together, rising and falling in confusion. I was shoved aside, as I watched my father's strong arms encircle his broken son and gather him from the floor.

"Don't move him," Auntie Marlene screeched.

"Hospital," Dad shouted.

Through the sea of legs and stairs, my eyes searched for a glimpse of my mother's face, but I did not see her. I could no longer see what was happening, though I was aware that the ocean of people receded up stairs and out the door. I was left sitting alone at the scene.

I felt the hard, cold tile beneath me. I locked my thin hands firmly together around my knees. I rocked myself slowly. The rubber soles of my shoes made a creaking sound with each movement. Forward and back. Forward and back.

I softly chanted, "Roller Coaster, Roller Coaster, Roller Coaster." The rhythm was steady and sure.

I could feel him near me. I gained speed, then altitude. I saw him above me. He reached for me, so I flew to him, higher and higher. I have never spoken of it, but I saw him. I did. I saw him as no one else ever had, and no one else ever will.

This picture exists. It is mine alone. In it, we are together, side by side, as always. He smiles at me, and we are released. We are not afraid. As the ground falls away, we throw our heads back and scream in a language only we understand.

Dear Mom

Autumn 1998

Lori Leuthje

We met one day in August. To be exact, it was August 19, 1980. I do not remember you. Newborns do not usually have much of a memory. Sometimes, I wish I could have seen your face, just once. I wish I could have burned it into my memory.

It seems so strange that you're my mother, the woman who gave birth to me, yet I know so little about you. I've thought about you a lot over the years. I gaze at myself in the mirror and wonder how much I look like you. It hurts when I see those families who look so much alike, when I can only sit and imagine.

I wonder if you ever think of me, if late at night, you wonder what's happened to me, where I've ended up, or how I've turned out. Did you hold me when I was born? I know that most times the mothers choose or are told not to hold the babies before they're given up for adoption, in case they become attached and change their minds. I always like to think that you held me in your arms, just once, before they took me away.

I can't help but wonder just how you ended up pregnant with me, anyway. I've always assumed that I was a mistake. Was it your decision to put me up for adoption? The only reason I ask is because, sometimes, young girls are forced or tricked into giving up their babies, but if you decided on your own, I understand.

You've got to be the bravest person I have never met, to carry and bear a child at the tender age of fifteen. I decided once that you must have loved me a little to choose life for me. Those nine months must have been hell! You gave up your life to give me mine. I can't even begin to tell you how special that makes me feel.

It's only been five years since I found out about my adoption, yet I think, somewhere deep down in my soul, I always knew. There is something missing in my family life, something I can't quite put my finger on, yet I know it's there. I love to watch other families together. I marvel at their closeness and how genuinely happy they are to be together. Then I look at myself and realize that I don't even know how to be close to someone. It terrifies me, the fact that I'll be turning 18 soon, and I don't even know how to hug!

I'm not saying that my family is bad. I had a comfortable childhood. They provided everything I needed, and I was happy, but somehow, underneath it all, I always felt like an outsider, an uninvited guest observing a family of strangers. I don't know what it was that made me feel that way. I'll never know.

Ever since that October day when I first learned of my adoption, I haven't stopped thinking about you. I wonder what your life is like now, if you have a family to love. I wonder if my creativity and my love of nature and adventure were inherited from you. I wonder if you're the one I got these crazy eyes from. My exotic, chameleon eyes that are too green to be blue, too blue to be green, and too gray to really be either.

I wonder about my father, too, though not as much as you. Was he a nice guy? A guy who would have stuck around had you decided to keep me? Or was he one of those guys who knocks a girl up and then splits instead of taking responsibility? I've seen lots of girls who look more like their fathers, so it occurs to me that maybe I inherited everything from him.

What if I've already met them? I sometimes wonder. What if you're one of those people I've bumped into on the street and never thought twice about? I love to watch people, partly because of my writing, and people watching helps me build characters, but I think the real, underlying reason is that somewhere, deep down, I think that if I ever saw you I would recognize you. I know it's just a crazy, childish dream, but I keep imagining that I run into you and look into your eyes, and at that moment, I just know, as if there was a bond that somehow spanned our 18 years of separation.

I do feel close to you, even though we've never really met, perhaps, because I talk to you so much. When I'm happy or sad, when my heart is breaking or bursting with joy, I find myself telling you about it, as if you were sitting right there beside me. I've started other letters to you over the years, wishing that I knew where to send them. Instead, I ended up crumpling them and shoving them into the bottom of my trash can, afraid that someone might find them and not understand.

People ask me all the time if I plan to find you, someday. I really don't know how to answer them. I would like to know your name and see you just once, and I really would love to talk to you. I'm just so scared. What if you don't want to see me? What if you're disappointed in me? I don't know if I could handle that.

We've missed out on so much of each other's lives! Little things like Christmas mornings, birthdays, the Tooth Fairy. You weren't there for my first steps, my first word, or my first love. You never got to tell me about Santa Claus or explain to me just how things work between girls and boys. We've never been on a family vacation. We've never even been shopping together.

I wonder, how different my life would be had you not decided to give me up. I wonder where we would be living, if we would be happy. I wonder if you and I would have the kind of mother-daughter relationship I've always wished for, yet never experienced. I wonder if I would have lots of brothers and sisters. I've always dreamed of having a big family. I wonder if you would understand me in a way my adopted family has never been able to.

My eighteenth birthday is coming soon; I wonder if you remember that. I can legally start searching for you when I am one year older. I could have found you earlier, but I would've had to have my parents' permission. I don't think they would have let me find you. A few months ago, I was supposed to have my family medical history for my college records. I asked my mom if we should find out in case I ever needed them. She refused. Since then I haven't mentioned anything about finding you. They just don't understand, but that's okay. This is something I need to do by myself anyway.

I've been dreaming of the day you and I would finally meet. The scene plays over and over in my head like a movie on rewind. I change little things every time, hoping to make it perfect. Do I call you by your first name, or would it be too presumptuous to call you Mom? Do I try to hug you, or would a handshake be sufficient? Do I try to stay in touch with you, or would you rather put the past behind you and forget about me, completely?

I'm probably digging up a lot of things that are best left buried, and I am sorry, but please try to understand that I wouldn't be doing it unless I had a good reason. Just once, I would like to see you and talk to you and have you actually sitting there listening and talking back to me. Just once, I would like to hear your story: how you met my father and how I came to be. Just once, I would like to know the truth about my heritage and be able to speak of my ancestors with knowledge and pride. I want to know my birthday story: what happened that day and what time I was born. Most of all, I would like to hear someone say, "Wow, she is just like her mother!" Just once, I wish I could hear someone say that and know they were talking about me.

I know this probably comes as a huge shock to you, because you've probably spent the last eighteen years trying to put all of this behind you, but please, please, understand that I wouldn't be doing this unless I had to. If you never want to see me again or don't want to be a part of my life, I promise I'll understand, just please give me this one chance. Give me one day, so I won't have to wonder anymore, so I can put all this behind me and get on with my life. I know it's asking a lot, but please, just think about it.

I sit here, writing an impossible letter, yet somehow, I find myself still clinging to the dream that it will all turn out perfectly. I can only pray that you'll understand what I'm trying to say and just how much of my heart I've poured out onto these pages. What I really hope is that I can somehow find the courage to drop this into a mailbox and start piecing together the parts of my life that have been missing for so long. I love you, Mom. I just wanted you to know that.

Chase :: Jimmy Reistad

Dream Schools

Autumn 1999

Chaia Lea Lloyd

My idea of a perfect school is comprised of many different factors. The most significant elements are ideal students, staff members, environments, and curriculums. The school's goal must be to allow the child to grow into a capable adult. There are many components that make up this simple method.

Students will become better scholars. The ideal student is one who is motivated and determined to learn and develop. Too many students simply slide through school without ever trying their hardest. I think this comes from bad teachers, along with poor parenting.

The ideal student is one who is optimistic, persistent, and serious about his studies. The student would keep social problems away from the classroom in order to concentrate solely on his work. The student would need to be optimistic and determined in order to achieve his goals. He needs to get right back on that horse and try again. Many students give up after one try because they feel they are failures. The student must be respectful and listen obediently to his teacher as well as be respectful to other students. That would drastically reduce the number of physical fights, verbal arguments, harassing, assaulting, and insulting. There would be fewer cliques, and everybody would be treated equally.

The worst aspect of high school is how cliquey people are. Many groups exclude people and make them feel unwelcome. It took me my entire freshman year and part of my sophomore year to find a niche. In a perfect school, the students would be polite and welcome each other instead of snobby and inclusive. The students would have to obey the rules of the school, provided they are fair ones. Instead of distracting elements such as cigarette smoking and skipping school, the students would focus on the matter at hand and put their effort into their schoolwork. I'm irritated when the students in my classes disrupt the class and are chastised. It takes away from my learning environment and makes me annoyed. Indeed, ideal students are needed to make the perfect school.

My dream school would not be perfect without the presence of great staff members. Some of the worst parts of my classes are the teachers who have no idea where they are going, how to get there, or where they have been. They do not know how to manage a class or teach anything. They may assign homework, but in truth, it is only busy work. Because they do not know how to handle the children, the kids become disruptive.

Instead of helping the kids to get back on track, these incompetent teachers just kick them out of the class. I can think of several examples of bad teaching from this school year alone. This situation angers me for two reasons. It is denying the students the opportunity to learn and develop their minds, and it is a pointless waste of time to pay a teacher to do nothing other than kick kids out of class. If that's all there is to it, I could be a teacher right now! Instead of letting these "wannabe" instructors get away with pretending to teach something they're not, we would need competent, capable teachers. Instead of telling the children what to do, they simply need to offer support and assistance to the children.

"Children are not minds to be molded but people to be unfolded" (Nicholas Jones.) Many teachers need to remember that. Certainly a perfect teacher is essential to a dream school.

A satisfactory environment plays a major role in making a perfect school. What I mean by this is that the school's setting, building, and surroundings are important to a person's education. First, the school's temperature needs to be regulated. As silly as that sounds, "It's pretty hard to concentrate on your schoolwork when you're sweating all over your papers" (Clinton Lloyd). I noticed that when I am unusually cold I can hardly focus on my work as well. The temperature affects one's thinking, especially the clarity of the mind, and needs to be kept the same at all times.

The school needs to be quiet. People should not be slamming lockers or yelling in the hallways when others are in class. I can remember countless times that a sports announcement has interrupted my class, as well. I think that those announcements should be handled in a more appropriate fashion as they have little to do with our academic day. The school must be accessible to all students so that they all have the same opportunities. So many times, I have been late to an important honors class simply because an overweight teacher was too lazy to walk up the stairs. These teachers fill up the elevator and think that they take priority over students, thereby leaving us to be late to class. I have been as much as 10 minutes late to a class this year. Plus, I cannot reach the classrooms on the fourth floor due to steps. A special situation was set up so that I could take physics, but I still am not able to take the art and pottery classes that I'd love to. Granted, the school is ADA accessible, but I still don't have the same opportunities that other students do. Finally, the ideal school would need more and better restrooms. They are too tight and crowded to use when needed. Most times, somebody has to wait in line and try to squeeze past another person. I have difficulty doing this due to my three wheeler. Therefore, the perfect school would have to be more handicapped accessible (with deaf and blind accessibility as well). Indeed, environment plays a key role in making a perfect school.

The school's curriculum is very significant to the school. A variety of classes need to be offered to everybody: some fun classes, some difficult, challenging ones, and some mediocre ones. Any class that I am required to take would make me hostile and annoyed enough the whole year for me to not try very hard. In addition, these classes need to be offered to everybody, not only select students. If students think they can master the class, who is a teacher or counselor to tell the children that their expectations are too high?

In some classes, I know I can ace the tests without doing any homework while in others, I have to review daily. If a school is truly preparing us for college, then they'll give us a list of assignments, and it will be up to us to decide whether or not to do them. It is up to each individual student what he or she wants to do at school. If the ideal students above were the ones doing this, then we would have no problems. Indeed, a perfect curriculum is important to a dream school.

Many components make up my dream school. Hard working students, capable teachers, a good working environment, and a flexible curriculum are all parts of it. The perfect school should only be interested in helping the child mature into a capable adult.

Every Child Counts

Winter 2002

Dr. John Mackiel

Much has taken place since we last celebrated Education Week. One of the simple lessons of the past year is that things can, and things do, collapse. Tall buildings and big companies, all have their hidden weaknesses, and under certain stresses, they can crumble. It is troubling to ponder, but entire societies have limits as well.

In 430 B.C., Pericles addressed the people of Athens. He observed that the blessings of freedom were being taken for granted; people were withdrawing unto themselves. He called upon the citizens of Athens to "preserve the good life, never forgetting the need to make sacrifices while investing in future generations." He challenged them to develop eros (to cherish, to love beyond themselves).

In 1716, as this great nation was emerging, John Adams (later to be the second president of the United States) sought to ensure the blessings of freedom. He called upon his counter-parts and declared, "It is the duty of government, not only to provide education but to cherish it," recognizing that education is the vital ingredient in preserving freedom and sustaining liberty.

The real inspiration in the Adams' family, Abigail Adams, later to be the second first lady of the United States, wrote to her spouse, John, that "unless the nation is universally educated, we will be unfit for freedom."

As we celebrate public school education this week, it is appropriate to consider our hidden weaknesses and our mounting stresses as a nation and as an institution.

We are the most powerful, the wealthiest and the freest nation on earth. Americans cannot fall under the illusion that each person holds his or her fate in their own hands-withdrawing into totally private concerns, private agendas, private communities, private clubs, private beaches, private schools, and private security. Self-interest and public education cannot become detached from one another.

As we attempt to preserve our good life, we can never forget the need to make sacrifices while investing in our future.

It is truly ironic that public education has witnessed the stresses of cynicism, sarcasm, and ridicule, and has suffered from weakened commitment and comprised support from the most highly educated and prosperous electorate in our history.

As we stand united during these unprecedented times, let us reaffirm our commitment to the blessings of freedom and the preservation of liberty.

On behalf of the Board of Education, let us celebrate public education and recognize that public schools are the only institutions that are positioned to preserve our good life, our great freedom, and our blessed liberty.

Summer Camp Thinker :: David Martin

What Baseball Is...

Autumn 1995

David Mainelli

When I was young, my father took me to the College World Series every year and to at least one game in Kansas City when the Yankees were in town. What I did not realize was the very special thing that happened between my father and me. Baseball helped me get closer to my father.

The baseball strike left millions of people distant and disenchanted from the game. The players want more money, and the owners do not want to lose more money. It sure sounds like the regular business world where employers and employees struggle with each other, but baseball is supposed to be different. The players and owners already make too much money. This may be true, but what has happened is that the fans have lost track of what the game is really about. Is baseball only about bats and gloves, players and owners, and charging the mound? Are we that shallow to only look this far?

Baseball is about a father telling his son he loves him as they leave the ball park, and that he loves him so much that he can mow the yard when they get home. Baseball is about little league players who can't keep their pants up without wearing one of mom's belts or the kid who could never get a hit but finally did. Baseball is apple pie, beer, and hot dogs with extra relish on top. It is about sticky bleacher seats, big pretzels, and people dressed funny walking up and down the bleachers looking for their lost dogs, Pepsi, and Budweiser.

Baseball is about getting ready to watch the big game on television and falling asleep by the second inning, but waking up in time to see the ninth inning excitement. Baseball is about running home from school to tell your sometimes-uninterested mother who your new favorite player is and then crying for that same player when he retires. Baseball is about digging through the baseball card package only to find the most inedible, rock-hard piece of cement gum, and enjoying it. It is about Hary Caray yelling, "Holy cow," Bob Costas poetically tracing the game through its past using historical markers, and the president of the United States throwing the first pitch out to start a new season.

Baseball might be the only sport where the fans get excited to hear the national anthem. Baseball is about girls in bikinis and half naked guys with painted letters on their beer bellies that spell out "GO TEAM!" Baseball is about sharing with friends, whether it is the beer or the stories told, like how you skipped class to be at the game. It is about first dates and how you wonder if she came to the park because she really likes you or has a thing for the first baseman. Baseball is about bringing your new mitt to the game and not even coming close to a foul ball but still bringing it to every other game you go to just in case. It is about rain delays, double headers, and chewing tobacco. Baseball is about Babe Ruth, Mickey Mantle, and Reggie Jackson, not the persons, but the legends they leave behind. Baseball is folk-lore and little league. Baseball is America.

Children believe in Santa Claus, the Tooth Fairy, and baseball, necessarily in that order. Without baseball, we are left with less to believe in. Very few things in society are able to bring together millions of people from all races and creeds like baseball. What better teacher on how to live in harmony than the players on a baseball team. As family, they strive for the same goals. All races act as one unit by sticking together during the hard times and celebrating together during the good times.

Do not let baseball die. Save baseball, not for the players, but for ourselves and our children. Let us not forget that baseball is a way of living. Let us not let it die, because grandfathers will lose so much to talk about that still relates to their grandchildren. Let us rise up and be bigger than the game itself, appreciating it for what it is, rather than what it is not. Let the players and owners do the fighting over pay and what does not pertain to us. Let's use this experience with strikes to teach our children how not to quit, and if we love to do something, then we do it. Put love first before money, and for heaven's sake, "PLAY BALL!"

Humane Borders: Offering Water in the Desert

Autumn 2003

Dr. Stan Maliszewski

Since the summer of 2001, Tucson based Humane Borders' volunteers have distributed thousands of gallons of water throughout the southern Arizona desert, the deadliest crossing point for illegal immigrations into the United States. For migrants, Humane Borders' water tanks, designated by blue flags flapping 30 feet in the air, can signal the difference between life and death. The Border Patrol count for border crossing deaths in Arizona, since the start of the year, has now reached 268, with three more months of sweltering heat in the desert remaining.

The Border Patrol initially voiced concern that the water stations gave migrants a false sense of security, but it since has developed a working relationship with this organization. The Border Patrol does not stake out water stations. They support the sole objective of Humane Borders, saving lives. Volunteers only offer assistance with providing water, food, and in some cases emergency medical attention.

Robin Hoover, a no-nonsense articulate and compassionate pastor of Tucson's First Christian Church, is the founder of Humane Borders. Weekly, Wednesday evening meetings are attended by volunteers who discuss successes and challenges of filling water tanks strategically placed at thirty-eight sites throughout the Sonora Desert.

During the meeting, stories of filling water stations and encountering migrants in the desert are shared. One volunteer told us how a mother and father approached the volunteers, pleading for water for their two-year-old daughter. The parents appeared to be disoriented, and their feet were covered in blood. Another volunteer reported that often water station hoses are cut, and the water is poured out in opposition to those crossing. A vigilante organization is increasingly voicing opposition to the mission of Humane Borders.

Volunteers come from a variety of backgrounds, work closely with an educational organization called Border Links, and for the most part receive training by assisting a seasoned volunteer. On a recent early Saturday morning, eight volunteers and a news correspondent from Germany met at a parking lot and traveled to Altar, Mexico, about five hours south of Tucson. Migrants meet in Altar to prepare for the four to six day walk across the desert. The town plaza is a gathering site for the migrants. There they connect with an hombre called a "coyote" who guides them across the desert and often provides transportation in overcrowded vehicles with little ventilation for $200 - $600 dollars. The bumpy road from Altar is used and would not compare to the worst Midwestern potholes in the winter.

The purpose of the day-long visit to Altar is to meet with migrants, listen to their stories, and grasp the idea of what limited resources the migrants have available to them for their journey across the desert. Jason, a soft spoken and humble Border Links guide, greeted the volunteers and presented an itinerary for the day. Chris, another guide, was to join the group in Nogales, Mexico. In addition to the guides, half of the volunteers spoke fluent Spanish. As the van departed, all of us were quietly wrapped up in our own images of what to expect from this journey. The common bond of wanting to save lives quickly ignited a conversation about the plight of the migrants.

In the crowded border town of Nogales, Kris, hair wrapped in dark blue cloth protecting her from inevitable perspiration, suddenly appeared at a shopping plaza parking lot waiting for Jason. She immediately introduced herself, speaking Spanish and English to those in the van. We were only three hours away from Tucson, and friendly relationships were forming, food was shared, and the group sensed a closeness formed from the common mission of wanting to gain additional insight into the people served by Humane Borders.

After driving through arid terrain and several small villages, we came to Altar. The volunteers divided into two groups, each with a guide, and started to talk to migrants who were preparing to cross the desert, some for the third or fourth time. It didn't take long for the migrants to gather around the volunteers. Initially, some expressed anger, then desperation and despair. It took a while for the migrants in the plaza to "trust" the intentions of the volunteers. Out of respect for the dignity and confidentiality of the migrants, photos were not taken.

Several men, shared how the Border Patrol found them three hours north of the border, near Marana, and immediately drove them back to Mexico without offering water and food. One man was still angry; he hadn't eaten in twenty-four hours. This was his third attempt to cross the border and find work in the fields, so he could provide for his family. Once he understood that the volunteers were there to learn and not judge, he invited them to walk with him across the desert, then understanding would take place. Work to provide for their families was the only reason mentioned for taking the risk of passing across the desert.

Only about a fourth of the few dozen migrants were aware of Humane Borders and the water stations. They eagerly listened, wanting to know where the water containers were located. An intense expression, "hope," was apparent on their faces. Many of the men prepared for the journey with only food, water, clothing, and sandals provided by a shelter located about a half mile from the town plaza.

After leaving the plaza area, the volunteers had lunch at the shelter, supported by the Catholic Church. Although there was no air conditioning, the shelter was clean and had an ample supply of water and food. Although many men chose to sleep outside in the coolness of the night air, housing was available. Welcoming staff treated the migrants as "guests" and honored them with dignity and respect.

Throughout the shelter were constant reminders of the perils of crossing the desert and the names of those who died holding onto the dream of meeting the responsibilities to their families. Dehydration is a horrible way to die, irrespective of a person's citizenship and nationality. The names posted throughout the shelter represent only a partial list of those who experienced the most undignified death anyone could anticipate. Seeing these names, remembering the faces of those in the plaza, and learning the needs of migrants and their families, left the volunteers to their own thoughts. The lively discussions, even laughter, during the last few hours before arriving in Altar, gave way to silence during the drive back to Tucson and an increased desire to offer a drink of water to those in need.

Soon, these volunteers will join others, meeting just before dawn, to deliver water to migrants whose faces will now be as familiar as neighbors' faces. Church groups and good Samaritans from across the United States have come to Tucson for a few days or weeks for the sole purpose of doing what they can to save the lives of migrants. Anyone interested in learning more and joining Humane Borders' volunteers for even a brief period of time can check the website <www.humaneborders.org> and email Robin Hoover at <humaneborders@gci-net.com>.

I arrived back in Tucson exhausted after the trip. The highlight was an opportunity to talk with migrants in the town plaza. We also talked with some "betas," folks who offer emergency first aid near the border on the Mexico side. I was able to take some black and white photos at the migrant shelter; however, I just couldn't bring myself to take any photos of these migrants. Their looks of desperation, fear, and disappointment were symbols of living a hard life. They were too hard on me, emotionally. Even with permission, I just couldn't take their pictures. When I have a reason that will contribute to promoting their cause or saving their lives, then I will feel better about taking their pictures and sharing their souls.

Windmere :: David Martin

Random Acts of Kindness

Winter 1996

Kathleen Maloney

In the past, people told each other to "stop and smell the roses," advice which was intended to make humans more aware of life and the goodness found in many small things. This book which takes this advice a step farther and suggests ways to actually "stop and smell the roses," wherever they might bloom. Numerous people, who share their own experiences both as receivers and givers of such acts, are the ones who made this book possible.

Lock your cynicism up for an hour and read the book. Throughout are anecdotes of "gifts" (random acts of kindness) which people have given others such as the man in San Francisco who would leave his store and drive frightened tourists up over the top of a steep hill. Or, the plumber who installed a water filtration system at no charge for a customer with cancer. The customer later found out the plumber's father had died of cancer.

In addition, are suggestions for committing random acts of kindness: give a bouquet of flowers to someone anonymously, or send a greeting card to a name you select from the phone book. Also, on nearly every page are comments culled from a variety of individuals such as Marcus Aurekius' "Do every act of your life as if it were your last."

A word of warning is necessary. Don't give this book to someone who is self-absorbed or to one who finds happiness spending hours in the local mall; they just won't get it. Also, be careful if you read it yourself. It can become a habit which starts out small and, gradually, as the days pass, becomes addictive, until you find yourself thinking of more and more ways to commit more and more acts of kindness.

Random Acts of Kindness, introduction by Dawna Markova; 1993 Conari Press; ISBN
0-943233-43-7; pb. $8.95.

Long's Peak at -60F

May 1994

Bradley Martin

Mountaineering and rock climbing activities are often associated with individuals who seem to be thrill-seekers and dare-devils. Initially, this judgment may seem accurate, considering the risks involved. There is no such thing as a "safe" climber, only one who practices risk management. However, nothing we ever do is 100% "safe." If we are never willing to take risks, we will never fulfill our potential.

Lately, I have been asking myself a question regarding one of my favorite activities, rock climbing. What makes one person foam at the mouth with anticipation at the sight of an exposed traverse and another throw up his hands dismissing the activity as ludicrous? Sometimes, I think I should listen to the warnings of my mother and stay home. Nevertheless, it is my internal battle, this desire for adventure versus the security of a safe life.

The answer to the question, "Why do I climb?" lies in the experience itself. This winter, I embarked on one of my most difficult and rewarding climbs. Three others and I left the week before Christmas on a weeklong expedition to climb Long's Peak, one of the highest mountains in Colorado. This mountain is climbed successfully every year; however, in the winter conditions of December, it can be very technical.

Our first two days consisted of snow-shoeing with full packs and pulling sleds loaded with equipment and food to our base camp at 11,000 feet. We tested our avalanche transceivers, one of the items I hoped I wouldn't have to use. Our base camp became the "Taj Mahal" of snow caves. The project took hours of burrowing, but it cozily slept four people. A handy cooking area was located at the mouth of the cave, and an insulated candle put a roomy finish to our new temporary home. As I dug through the hard-packed snow, I thought of all the people who were in a warm living room awaiting Christmas, while I tried to light a small stove before I lost feeling in my fingers from the howling, below zero wind. After being rehydrated from dinner, my partners and I discussed plans for the next few days, and then, we snuggled into our down cocoons and dreamed of beaches and bikinis.

Our route up the windswept, southeast side of Long's Peak was relatively free of avalanche danger due to the high winds the night before. I climbed with one crampon boot on the rocky face and the other in snowy waterfall ice. Each time my ax sunk into the ice, I reflected on comments I often hear from non-climbers about this activity: "Surely, the motivation for this must be the thrill of danger and the consequent rush of adrenaline." The reasons for climbing are seldom stated in terms of risk or danger. Instead, the question becomes, "Why did I climb that mountain?" All I can say is, "Because it was fun."

As I completed the last pitch of mixed climbing (ice and rock), we all agreed to pick up the pace because it was already noon. If we were to summit and get off the mountain by dark, we would have to hustle. I spent many hours kicking steps into the packed snow, placing my ax for balance, shifting my weight to the other foot, and repeating the motion over and over and over. The tedium of this never ending dance was complimented by the concentration I couldn't allow to slip away. At 14,000 feet, there is only a fraction of the air that I am used to as a Nebraska "flatlander."

"Crazy Climbers! They must not value life very much," was one local person's voice I remembered, as I watched the rope from me to my partner stretch up into the snowy void.

"On the contrary," I thought. "The whole reason I'm here is to get the most out of life that I can, including as many experiences as possible. I want to do more than simply exist in the hum-drum of everyday living." The higher I climbed, the colder and windier it got.

The last 100 yards slowly came into sight. I removed the "chocks," which protected our team in case of a fall and followed the kern mantle line to my destination. On my left, I placed my ax, and on my right, snow pushed from my steps slid and fell into oblivion. The wind was so fierce now that any uncovered skin became frost bitten in minutes. My goggles kept fogging up so that I had to protect my face with my glove from the blowing snow that felt like tiny pinpricks. I could only see a few feet in front of me. The feeling of pushing myself to the limits of endurance and to keep going through these difficult situations propelled me from the "groan zone" to the "growth zone."

Finally, we reached the summit. The feeling of accomplishment was exhilarating, not to mention the view. Knowing that I did not see another person for six days and that there was not another person around for miles left me with a feeling of calmness and serenity. However spectacular it is, the final goal is not the most impressive sensation. The memories we keep from intense experiences like this winter climb show that value of the journey is greater than the destination. The biggest value that I receive from climbing is to learn more about myself: how I deal with extreme conditions, and how I react to various stimuli from exposures, both human and natural.

Standing on the peak at 14,225 feet with a wind chill of -60F, I looked at the snowy ranges in front of me and felt very humble. The view made me realize how small I am in the universe, but I am significant, nonetheless. Just as a small flower may be aesthetically valuable to a passing hiker in a wide field, a lone climber has value even though he stands on top of a mountain range infinitely larger than himself. Seeing the beauty of climbing and everything else that gives us and our environment value is my driving force.

Snowing Road :: Shari Morehead

How *Fine Lines* Began

Summer 2006

David Martin

Jungle Out There :: Yolie Martin

In 1990, one of my English classes was filled with downtown, street-wise, tough high school teenagers who were one step from expulsion. All of them failed English class before, at least once, some of them several times. They did not want to be in school, and they couldn't wait to leave those classroom walls. They did not do homework for other teachers, when it was assigned, and they stared at me like they dared me to teach them anything. Half of the class was black. The rest were Caucasian, Latino, Vietnamese, and Native American, but the meanest looking and most physical was a white boy named Jack.

Every day, this group of "at-risk" juvenile delinquents fluttered around our school, like little birds with broken wings. Lacking direction, scared of their futures, possessing few marketable skills, trying as hard as they could, they were unable to get off the ground and take flight. When they became bored, which was often, they created drama by starting fights and inciting

121

riots. Often, it was a bad thing, when they were quiet, like the silence before a storm. However, if they misbehaved in this "class from hell," they knew their days as students in that urban high school were over, and the street was the only thing they had waiting for them. Most of them knew what that meant: gangs, hard work, bills, more drugs, prison, welfare, trips to the hospital emergency room, and an early death. They all had friends and family members in one of those places.

Jack never talked to anyone in class, including me. For all I knew, he was mute. From the first day of class in August to the week before Thanksgiving, he did not talk to anyone. He turned in enough work to maintain a passing grade, but when I asked him a question, he shrugged his shoulders and refused to reply.

He never took his eyes away from mine. Whenever I turned around, after helping another student or when I looked up from my desk, his eyes were on me. After a few days, I was leery to turn my back on him. When I did things in class, I always faced him. He sat in the next to last seat in the second row from the door, and I planned all my classroom activity so I had one or two rows between us. Jack only let one student sit behind him, George, who was everyone's friend and always seemed happy. George was slow and worked with behavioral development issues, but he tried to read and write, even though he had fourth grade abilities.

Some of the girls in class had children. Carlotta was nineteen-years-old and had three. It was forbidden in school to flash gang signs, but when she wasn't paying attention to me, I could see her give a sign to another girl across the room. She was pretty and smart, and all the boys spoke to her every day, except Jack. When she spoke to him, he glared at her. After a while, she ignored him.

Some of the boys were scarred by fights, and they never relaxed, even in class. They were always looking over their shoulders, like the worst thing that could ever happen to them was to be caught off-guard or surprised, and where they came from, they were probably right.

The first day of class, I walked through the door and looked at this collection of races and attitudes, of dark sunglasses and darker souls, of defensive body language and silent despair, of low motivation and lack of hope. I said to myself, "Oh, Lord, why me?"

The next day, when I saw the principal, I asked him, "Why me?"

His answer was, "No one else would take the class, and we thought you could make them work. You've coached seven sports. You get along with any student who tries. Give them a chance. They all know that if they don't do what you tell them, they will fail the class and won't be allowed back in school."

I agonized about how to teach this unusual collection of young adults who did not fit into any group in the school. How would I get them to write essays, learn poetry, and read the standard curriculum? They didn't do those things before, so I knew I had to try something different. I threw the school's traditional way of doing things out the window, metaphorically. I decided we would write every day and keep a journal of our own work. Our writing notebooks became our textbooks, and I graded their work by the pound. In this class, the sweat that appeared from pushing a pen across the lines on the paper would earn credit. Three days a week, I would bring ideas for us to write about, and two days a week, different students would bring ideas from their personal lives for the class to write about. In effect, they would share in teaching the class. We sat in a circle, and everyone was equal.

Chemistry started to build between us. Slowly, trust crept into the room, silently and unseen. I would not let students enter class, if they didn't bring their journals every day. I brought photocopies of chapters from many classics, and we read those, often out loud. Text books scared these students, but they would read, discuss, and study anything that was photocopied. One reading I handed out that created the biggest stir from these young, angry rebels was "The Song of Hugh Glass" in *A Cycle of the West* by John Neihardt.

I introduced Neihardt's epic poem and talked about defeat and victory, rejection and acceptance, revenge, and forgiveness. I thought I saw Jack's lips move in response to something I said, but when I called on him, he shook his long hair that touched his shoulders and refused to speak. I knew he wanted to ask a question, but he would not verbalize it. He sat there in his long, black, leather coat, years before Columbine, and I thought, "Will I ever reach this one?" When I read his journal entry about Hugh Glass's true story, I felt a strong passion come out of his pen that started to show a different aspect of his character.

Over the next few weeks, everyone helped read Neihardt's long poem in class, except Jack. We slowly read every word, and I took my time, like I was walking beside Glass and giving a "play by play account" of this unusual, adventure experience. Outwardly, Jack gave the impression that he was too good to participate or too cool; however, his journal relayed another story. After each verse, after each page, we stopped and talked about what we read. I helped interpret many words and put the lines in a context everyone could grasp. Each time I looked up, Jack's eyes met mine.

When he turned in his notebook to me, as the others did, every Friday,

I made sure to write something about his thoughts on every page. All my comments were positive. I believe in the power of positive reinforcement, and he had so much rejection in his life that I did not want to add to that long, negative list of "downers." I was surprised to find out that he was a deep thinker. No one could see what he wrote but me. I was amazed. His words were philosophical and intellectual. The sentences and paragraphs were not filled with the anger he generated with his body language and glacial stares in class. There was a good mind leaking out between the lines of his writing. Was there a heart in there, too?

I read to the class from "The Song of Hugh Glass":

"Alas for those who fondly place above
The act of loving, what they chance to love;
Who prize the goal more dearly than the way!
For time shall plunder them, and change betray,
And life shall find them vulnerable still.

A bitter-sweet narcotic to the will,
Hugh's love increased the peril of his plight;
But anger broke the slumber of his might,
Quickened the heart and warmed the blood that ran
Defiance for the treachery of Man,
Defiance for the meaning of his pain,
Defiance for the distance of the plain
That seemed to gloat, 'You can not master me.'

And for one burning moment he felt free
To rise and conquer in a wind of rage.
But as a tiger, conscious of the cage,
A-smolder with a purpose, broods and waits,
So with the sullen patience that is hate's
Hugh taught his wrath to bide expedience."

Jack shifted in his seat and rocked back and forth. He leaned forward and squeezed his pen so hard that I thought it would snap in half. While I asked other students how they interpreted those words, Jack stood up, slowly, left the group, and went to the windows and looked outside, quietly. He stood there for twenty minutes and only left when the bell rang to end the period.

The next day he wrote about rage and anger for ten pages. There were no paragraphs, just a stream-of-consciousness writing, like Holden Caulfield on steroids. He told of the injustices he witnessed, a death in the family, depression, fear, no strong male presence at home, loneliness, all the "phonies" he met in his short life, unable to control his anger, and why his court probation was connected to fighting.

The next day, I asked the students for permission to print some of their work in a four-page pamphlet that I would bring to class and share with them. Each person would get a copy, and they could take extra ones home for their family and friends. I got a verbal acceptance from everyone in class, except Jack. When I looked at him, he simply nodded. That was the first, positive gesture he made since school began months ago.

In 1990, our school had ten, old Apple computers, and they were always in use with a waiting line of teachers hoping to use them, so I bought my own and planned to do the layout of the student writing at home for our first, little publication. I didn't mention my ideas to the class again, because I was preoccupied with learning how to turn on my new computer so it would not explode in my face, teaching myself how to run a desktop publishing program, not swearing loudly while my own children were at my desk, grading papers from school, doing lesson plans for all of my classes, getting enough sleep to stay awake in class, and staying sane.

Many weeks later, I walked into class, and without saying a word, I started passing out our first class newsletter. All the writing came from students in Jack's class, and I could hear a few gasps and "Wow's" as they started reading their own copies. By the time I got to the next to the last row passing out the copies, I heard Jack yell out loud, "What is this?"

All the students and I jerked around like we had been shot. Jack talked, and he was on his feet and walking toward the front of the room. He was 6' 4" and weighed 225 pounds. He should have been on the football field daily after school, because he was such a good athlete, but he had such a poor, grade point average, the head coach would not let him come out for the team.

As he strode down the aisle, I thought he was coming for me, but when he got to the front of the class, he turned and walked directly through the open door, out of the room, and into the hall. He stopped out of sight of the other students, turned around, and motioned for me to come into the hall with him. I told a student in the front seat, "If I am not back in five minutes, go to the office for help."

I walked into the hall and said, "Hang on, Jack, you can't leave our class."

Jack surprised me. His eyes got wet, and he began to cry. Tears came down his cheeks. With much anger, he asked, "Why did you put my writing on the front page?"

I didn't know if he was going to hit me or what. I said, "Jack, your writing is consistently the best writing in the class. It deserves to be on the front page. You have talent. I hope you write a lot more, and I am proud of you."

Then, the tears flowed heavily. "No one ever said I had talent in school before. What do I do, now?" He hung his head and stared at the floor, as water splattered on his shoes.

I felt him change in front of me. I placed my hand on his shoulder. "Go down the hall, and get a drink of water. Take ten deep breaths. Then, come back into class, because this is where you belong. From Monday to Friday, from 2:00 to 2:50 p.m., this is your home. Hold onto that notebook, and tonight, write into it like you are writing to your best friend. Tell it what you are thinking. Hold onto your pen, like it was your life-line. Don't let go of it, until you are so tired of writing that you have no energy left. Whatever you do, tell the truth with your words. Make every word ring with honesty. It doesn't have to be pretty. It doesn't have to be fancy. Just write. Tell the truth. When you are done, let your "new friend" talk back to you, and all you have to do is listen. Write everything down. You don't have to show it to anyone, unless you choose to do so. Now, go get that drink of water."

As he turned to leave, he stopped and moved toward me. I froze. He looked at me. I will never forget those black eyes looking down into mine: part animal, part divine, part confusion, part determination, part anger, and part pride. Those eyes haunt me still. Then he hugged me and said, "Did Hugh Glass ever survive?"

Tears came to my eyes, and I had to look at the floor. I said, "Come on, I will go with you. I need a drink of water, too."

As we walked down the hall and back to the classroom, several students looked out the door, trying to find where we went. When Jack and I entered the room, the other students wanted to know where we went. Jack smiled. It was now the week before Thanksgiving, and none of us had ever seen him smile in class.

As he sat down in his seat, he said to the other students, "Come on you guys, relax. I want to see what happened to that mountain man. Can you imagine crawling 100 miles after being half-eaten by a grizzly? That is some kind of courage. I don't think I could do what he did."

After that day, there were many more class newsletters. Jack's writing was in most of them, and he was the primary inspiration who sparked that anemic, classroom pamphlet to grow into *Fine Lines*, now a quarterly magazine for new writers of all ages. What started as a classroom motivator to encourage marginal students to write more after they saw their work in print and read by other students, teachers, and administrators became a publication which is used today in all grade levels: elementary, middle, high school, college, and graduate school.

Jack's grades slowly began to rise. He came in to see me after school and asked for help with his homework in other classes when he needed it. He still had to check in weekly with his probation officer, but he did graduate from high school. I found out, years later, that he stayed out of jail, worked his way through a two-year community college, graduated from a small, four-year college in another state, majored in journalism, and got a job with a small newspaper in South Carolina. He moved on from there, and I do not know where he is today.

I remember the last entry of Neihardt's *All Is But a Beginning: Youth Remembered, 1881-1901*. An old man tells of his youthful vision quest and how he felt like a failure after experiencing the three-days and nights of fasting on a lonely hill praying and hoping Wakon Tonka would appear and provide a spiritual message as he entered manhood. The old man admitted he had no great dream to tell when he returned to the tribe.

"If I have no vision to give me power and guide me, how can I ever be a man? Maybe, I shall have to go far off into a strange land and seek an enemy to free me from this shame."

Then, just as he had this bitter thought, a great cry came from overhead like a fearless warrior hailing his wavering comrade in the heart of battle. "Hoka-hey, brother – Hold fast, hold fast; there is more!" Looking up, he saw an eagle soaring yonder on a spread of mighty wings, and it was the eagle's voice he heard.

"As I listened," the old man said, "a power ran through me that never left me, old as I am. Often, when it seemed the end had come, I have heard the eagle's cry, 'Hold fast, hold fast; there is more.' "

When in Turkey

Autumn 2004

Erin Martin

Some of the hardest lessons people learn are the ones experienced when we are nowhere near a school classroom. Life lessons come in different locations. For athletes, their classrooms are fields, rinks, and courts, but for me my classroom was a country called Turkey.

My dad and I went on a two-week excursion through Italy, Greece, and Turkey, before my freshman year of high school. We had a blast. We saw the sights and took hundreds of pictures. We ate exotic food, but I mostly stuck with oranges and water. We experienced a huge culture shock, and I learned a lot about myself and how fortunate I am to be an American.

After we toured Italy and Greece, my dad and I went to Ephesus, Turkey. This ancient city had been under water for hundreds of years, and as the sea receded archeologists began their excavations. In the city, there had been an enormous library. The people held town meetings and government social events there. The shelves were filled with thousands of written works. We listened to our guide talk about every detail of the library. She also said that men used to say they were going to the library as an excuse to visit the brothel across the street.

I got tired of looking at the old inscriptions and ruins, so I wandered ahead. I was in my own little world, taking in all the sounds and smells. On the way to the bus, we had to walk through a small market place just outside Ephesus. I entered alone. I looked at jewelry, rugs, and clothes. It was a little, unique, Turkish strip mall filled with kiosks and vendors. I was enjoying myself when it hit me that there was something missing.

I continued walking, but then I realized that all of the sales people were men. There was not one Turkish woman anywhere. I began to feel uncomfortable, as the vendors started yelling things at me. In Turkey, the women are suppose to have their skin covered when in public, and I was wearing a spaghetti-strapped shirt with Bermuda shorts. It was very unsettling, but I put my head down and walked quickly to the tour bus. I sat on the bus for fifteen minutes, wanting to leave, and waiting for my dad, but he never came.

I got off the bus to look for him when an older, American woman who was also on our tour said she would walk with me through the vendors to find my dad. She heard the men before and did not want me to go alone. I thanked her.

We walked through the cat calls, and I found my dad. He was just entering the "strip mall." I linked arms with him, and the thoughtful woman followed. Even with my dad, they called to me. This was the first time he had been through the crowd, and he was trying to listen to what they were saying. I knew what they were saying, and I pulled my dad through quickly. He and I were within thirty yards of the bus when a group of men stopped us. The leader, the most outspoken man of the group, stepped forward. He walked right up to my dad, looked him square in the eyes, and said in a strong, Turkish accent, "How many camels would you take for her?"

"WHAT?!?!?!" I screamed silently in my head, as my mouth dropped open. I looked at Dad who was equally as shocked as I was. We stood there for what seemed like hours.

"Uhmm... no, no thank you," Dad said politely over his shoulder, as we walked away.

We boarded the bus, and I thanked the woman again for walking with me to find my dad. He and I did not talk until we were almost to the boat that would take us back to Greece.

I do not remember what we talked about then, because I kept playing that moment over and over in my head. Was that man serious?

What if my dad jokingly would have said, "Sure, twenty camels sounds like a good deal to me?"

Do dads really trade their daughters for livestock? Then I wondered, "Where's the airport? I want to go home!"

Cultural differences are important to understand. "When in Rome, do as the Romans do," or should I say when in Turkey do as the Turks do. I should have learned about the Turkish culture, before my short visit there. A little information could have saved me from a culture shock moment that I never want to relive.

My High School Prom Dress
Winter 2003
Deborah McGinn

Dress Up Week :: Deborah McGinn

My mother has started moving some of her vast collections to storage rentals in Lincoln and O'Neill, Nebraska. I predicted that her full house would begin to show signs of space, but where there are old things in storage, new things have appeared. This is the way my mother likes it, to have her home engulfed in things that make her happy.

She asked me to come and look through my college textbooks, and it took me five minutes to toss all of them in a recycling box. She's thinking about a retirement community, someday, for active older women, and she's mentioned having a large auction.

I don't think that auction will ever take place, but it would be a full day affair. My mother will dance until she's past ninety and have enough tambourines saved for everybody. She has too many things, but it's none of my business.

I was thinking about my junior prom dress from 1976 that she made for me. It was floor length cotton, white, with print blue and yellow flowers. It tied in the back, and she made a ribbon for my hair out of the same material. She used lace for the collar and sleeves, and it was once one of the prettiest dresses she'd ever fashioned. There is so much of my mother's artistic strength in that dress. I think she loved me years and years in that dress. I'd hear the purr of the sewing machine at night, while I was in bed, careful not to fall completely asleep or she'd have to wake me for a fitting.

There were so many pins that poked across my skinny sides, and I'd giggle when she moved her fingers to pin and fasten. She'd tell me to stop wiggling.

"I'll take a little in here, let a little out here," she'd say. Then she'd sit back on her heels and compliment herself. "Your mother is going to make you look stunning!"

I'd go back to sleep, and in the morning, it hung for my approval in a place so I could see her progress. My friends had dresses from Miller and Paine, Ben Simons, and Hovland Swanson, but mine came from a personal designer. I was privileged. It never occurred to me that my dress wouldn't meet criteria; I knew it would be just right for me.

I loved wearing my mother's fabric around me on prom night. My date's name was Sweeney, and my corsage had more blue ribbon than rose, and his own big bow tie and brown tux didn't go with my dress, but the seventies were more about clash than perfection.

My shoes were all wrong under my beautiful dress, and I knew it. I had a pair of light beige sandals that weren't exactly delicate, with gold buckles that stood out whenever I gathered up my gown to climb steps or excused myself from a linen tablecloth to dance.

I must have forgotten to save for pumps or ballerina slippers. I thought I had covered everything from my homemade dress to homemade facial to homemade hair curls, but I forgot the importance of shoes.

I was sixteen when self is all I thought about and had convinced myself that everybody would notice my feet in bulk and point. I have come to understand that everyone was having their own thoughts, and not one of them had anything to do with me. At some point, someone suggested we drop our shoes anyway, and that's when the fun really started.

I have that old prom dress today, still dancing shoeless, still showing love.

Ars Poetica

Spring 1998

Dr. John J. McKenna

It was, as I recall, Ezra Pound who said, "Poetry should be at least as well written as prose." I, too, believe that poetry must be DAMN good writing. By this I mean it should have DENSITY. All the words should count --at least as many as possible, as much as possible. You should not be able to pick up a poem and shake a lot of unnecessary words out of it. Also, the poem should have AESTHETIC impact. It should use language patterns beautifully -- both gracefully and harmoniously. The sounds of words, syllables, phonemes are the notes out of which the poet constructs his or her melody to make the language sing.

The poem must have METER, at least it should have periodicity. Units of expression, whether they are patterns of stressed and unstressed syllables or longer syntactic units like Whitman's and Ginsberg's, should give order and rhythm to poetic expression. In some ways, rhythm is the most important component of a poem , and most disappointing poetry, especially free verse, fails because the poet has established no sense of rhythm in the poem, and so, it lacks drama and coherency.

The poem should use METAPHOR. I mean this term in a very general sense. Metaphor shows the connection or correlation between two things ordinarily thought unlike. This metaphoric connection shows that there exists a potentially ubiquitous and universal web of connections between what Lao Tsu in the *Tao Te Ching* calls the "ten thousand things" and

132

"tao." Thus, metaphor shows the underlying coherency of the world, which to the casual, unpoetic eye at least, looks chaotic and unknowable. The poet illuminates these connections with poetic expression, especially with metaphor, and shows that understanding is possible.

As for myself and my method of working, I write about half the time in pretty conventional forms: sonnets and quatrains, using a fairly regular meter and rhyme scheme. I try to mute the effects of the traditional forms by modifying them. I might write a sonnet in couplets with no stanza breaks for example, use a lot of half-rhyme, or loosen the meter, so it's as subtle as the violas in the adagio section of Mozart's Piano Concerto #21. I think Phil Larkin and W. D. Snodgrass are about the best at making well-crafted poems and achieving this artistry with such subtlety that you won't notice it, unless you look carefully. About half of the time, I struggle with free verse and other forms which, contrary to the belief of beginners, are actually much harder than working in pre-established forms.

I write about my daily life, my family, my love of the natural world, and the change of the seasons here on the Great Plains. As Vonnegut admitted, "What the hell else do I know?" I think it's a great privilege to be able to write, to live in a society where people who work in offices and businesses and on farms will help support my writing through the University of Nebraska and other public institutions. "If I have only a little sense," Lao Tsu writes, "I will stick to the main path." I have to confess I often do not stick to the main path, which for me is surely making poems. I get sidetracked with other tasks and duties. I know those other things are mostly detours, because when I return to the main path and get a poem to be the best I can, then I feel a special inner satisfaction, a peace that passes understanding.

The American Way

Spring 1998

Jane Meehan

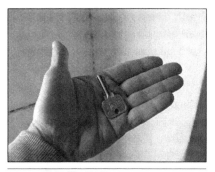

Key to Life :: Stan Maliszewski

"It's the great American way!" they say. "It's in the American tradition."

What I see is clutter, display, disarray, clothing hanging from fences, tables laden with miscellaneous, lamps without shades, great bowls with cracked lids, drawers without pulls, coats without hoods, and rubber boots in all sizes with many holes in them.

Decades ago, a gypsy or a migrant worker might have stopped at the edge of town to clean his wagon. The tacky contents might have appeared much as the driveway I share with my neighbor looks today. If the gypsy didn't move through his task slyly and nimbly or do it in the dead of night by kerosene and moonlight, then the sheriff would soon be upon him, leaving his possessions awry and driving him from the scene with threats of jail and vagrancy. My neighbor puts signs on all the trees (large, magnificent, old oak trees), in the parks, on the lamp posts, and in the newspapers for all the world to come and view his eviction-like junk. He puts prices (rather high) on each and every one of the thousand garage items; he invites his friends to bring their junk and do likewise, and his brother from the farm brings manure-corroded antiques upon which he places home-made price tags with high numbers.

Then, the vehicles come and fill our beautiful street: little, tiny, red and yellow toy-like sports cars; open, square jeeps; big, rambling station wagons with lots of windows and children; small Datsun pickups; medium-sized trucks with home-made racks; and large, white, windowless vans. The people emerge from the vehicles: old people with white hair and canes; young couples with hot, crying babies; lovers holding hands; school-age children chasing my dog; toddlers pulling my cat's tail; black people;

white people; sun-burned people in tennis togs; and church-going people in summer dress-up fashions. They all flow up our joint-easement driveway (for everyone wants a bargain. That, too, they say is the American Way!) I run to my porch for protection and shelter and whatever privacy it will afford.

I didn't always run to the porch. The first time it was fun, and I was in the garage, too, with the rest of the neighbors, buying and selling. The second time, it wasn't as much fun, and the novelty began to wear off. The third time, I resumed my habit of taking my surplus items to the Goodwill Store and the Salvation Army. The fourth and fifth sale times – a way of life it became.

This summer, when my folks' 50th wedding anniversary rolled around and we decided on a backyard pig roast celebration, I invited my neighbor. The invitations were sent three weeks in advance, and one day I stopped to chat with him about the upcoming event and the farmyard setting I was trying to create. He smiled and told me he purchased another apartment house, and then he showed me his garage sale sign. I cried, I begged, I implored, but he smiled again with his dollar sign eyes and shook his head.

Today, with the sun on hot and high, the guests and the buyers together flow up the mutual driveway in its "gypsy" farm-yard setting. My carefully procured and precisely laid hay bales mingle with the clothing flopping in the breeze from every fence post, adding to the mayhem, instead of to the party's theme. I mentally shriek; I visually grimace; I orally curse, and I wonder if my neighbor's monetary profit tallies more than the good will it cost him. Is this the American Way?

Muskets, Missiles, and Meaning

Winter 1996

Mary Binder Misfeldt

On New Year's Eve, Molly thought of the times when Little Molly was growing up in Wyoming and how she tried to stay awake until midnight. If she fell asleep earlier, she expected her father to waken her. The reason? She would be allowed to go to the door in her night clothes and bang a large metal spoon against the dishpan and call to the dark world outside, "Happy New Year."

Vaguely, she remembers hearing that New England settlers announced the beginning of a year by firing a musket into the air at the stroke of midnight. Today's youngsters may sometime equate parades and football games with the New Year.

While checking the musket story in a reference book, Molly's attention was directed to a portion of *Little Boy Blue* by Eugene Field (1850-1895):

"The little toy dog is covered with dust,
But sturdy and staunch he stands;
And the little toy soldier is red with rust,
And his musket molds in his hands ... ."

She re-read this rhyme and glanced at a colorful wooden soldier standing under the Christmas Tree. The gift was fashioned from a spindle of an old kitchen chair. Attached to it was a note quoting II Timothy 2:3, " ... *endure as a good soldier of Jesus Christ.*"

She thought of service people, around the world, who presently are engaged in what their leaders refer to as "peace keeping." She thought of those she and her husband met in November, at Norfolk, Virginia, while escorted on a tour of the *U.S. Ramage*, America's newest guided missile destroyer commissioned July 22, 1995, fifty years after the end of World War II.

Visitors saw the pads from which missiles, fired at the push of a button, hit targets 1,000 miles away. The young sailor who explained the basics of modern warfare technology, said solemnly, "Once a missile is fired, it cannot be retrieved."

Other service people on missions demanding hand-to-hand, face-to-face encounters know, too, the awesome responsibility of striving for the vision of true world-wide peace. Touring the destroyer left Molly with a deeper meaning of Christmas peace proclaimed by the angels "to all" people.

The vision of personal peace is attainable to people wherever they are, because the true peace of Christmas is in individual hearts – not on signed documents. It is a peace which passes understanding, comforts those who grieve, and provides emotional, spiritual, and mental stability when the world seems to be crumbling. Mark 14:7 explains, " ... *When ye shall hear of wars and rumors of wars, be ye not troubled."*

Instead of making a list of resolutions, Molly decided to strive for this reassuring type of peace. Whether her husband's favorite football team wins, whether nations are engaged in military action, or whether discouraging problems or illness come, the one important meaning to her, personally, is how she plays her own game of life.

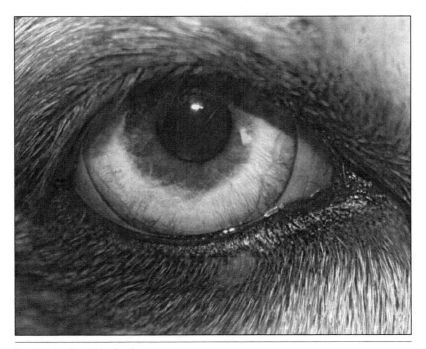

Dog's Eye :: Shari Morehead

My Imaginary Writing Toolbox

Summer 2002

Jacquelyn Morgan

When I was young, my mother was heavily into crafts. Every ornament that graced our Christmas tree, as the years passed, was homemade. As Christmas approached, my mother and I would search out new and different designs to try to create on our own. My favorite ornaments were the Oscar the Grouch ornaments we created using film canisters and green cotton balls.

After getting an idea about which projects we would be attempting and the materials needed to formulate them, we would make a pilgrimage to Mangelsens' Craft Store. After arriving home, burdened with dozens of bags stuffed full of goodies varying from pipe cleaners and beads to paints and brushes, Mom would take out her craft box into which she would organize everything.

As a child, I was taught not to covet anything that belonged to anyone else, but a secret desire to own her craft box with all of its amazing contents burned through me every time I saw it. The box itself was not my object of affection. Actually, I've always believed it to be quite ugly. It was approximately twelve inches long by twelve inches wide with about a six-inch depth. It was a lovely yellow, the color that reminds one of bile or some equally disgusting bodily fluid. Speckled here and there across the surface were silver, gold, and brown diamonds. The handle was clear plastic, held on with bronze fasteners. I didn't want the box because of its beauty. I wanted it because of all of the happy hours it symbolized. Her graceful hands guided my awkward ones.

About two years before my mother died, I received a very bulky birthday present. As I pulled the bright colorful paper away, I was delighted at the drab yellow, silver, gold, and brown sight that I beheld. Smiling, my mother looked on as I joyfully ripped the paper from the box and excitedly opened it.

Inside, awaiting my eager eyes was a treasure trove of craft materials: felt, beads, markers, string, glue, squiggly eyes, puffy paints and other baubles to spark my creative genius. I was nine when I received this, and if I had as many hormones then as I do now, I would have burst into tears at the thoughtfulness of the gift. Instead, I jumped up, hastily planted a thankful kiss on my mother's cheek and sat down to open some other presents.

As the years changed, so did the appearance of the box and its contents. In anger, one day, I picked up the closest object in my reach and threw it forcefully against the wall. Regretfully, it was my precious, ugly box. When I came across the wreckage after I calmed down, I was broken-hearted at my own impetuousness and immediately set out to mend the broken box with a roll of duct tape, covering the hideous yellow with shiny silver.

Whenever I write, I picture that box in my mind. Upon opening it, I visualize my intense love of the written word in the form of a magic pen with which I am able to compose great works of art, even if I am the only one who believes in their gloriousness. Under the pen are the folded up pieces of paper that symbolize my above average vocabulary. I have always been gifted with the ability to find the proper words to say for any occasion without being too redundant. There is also a ruler buried inside, a constant reminder of the grammatical rules I should keep in mind as I write. The most prominent of all objects in my box are the beads that are my memories. Because of my memories, I am able to write from the heart, and I am always able to relate anything to something I have already experienced.

The ugly box, its bottom covered with duct tape, came with me when I moved out of my parents' house. Ten years passed since the box came into my possession, and though a smack against the wall dislodged the bottom, I couldn't throw it away. It doesn't hold crafts anymore. It makes a very convenient place to store all the articles necessary to womanhood. Though the box changed over the years, the image of it remains the same in the cavernous wasteland of my imagination. It contains everything I need. Daily, I open it to store new memories for future influence on my writing,

India

Winter 1998

Hilary Moshman

The smell of burning incense pervaded the dry, dusty evening air of the traveling train. It was an ever so familiar scent associated with India and its ubiquitous religious ceremonies. The practice had become quite popular with the country's foreigners. Several more sticks of Nog Chompa (an incense) were pulled out of a package and lighted by the dirty hand of a foreigner from Switzerland. (I learned his nationality through a later conversation). He had long, blond, dirty dreadlocks and wore a soiled maroon loongie (a long piece of cloth wrapped into a skirt, the traditional wear of working-class men in Southern India). He was in his late twenties, but assessing his appearance, I came to a quick conclusion that he had not lived a normal and structured life in the past, nor would he, if ever, in the future. My friend and I struck up a conversation with this man and two other men he had just met on the train. One was a similar looking hippy from England, and the other was an Australian military cook on holiday.

The particular part of the train the men, my friend Yael, and I were occupying was covered in filth. It was the small entrance area at the end of the car with a side door open to the air and a metal sink on each side. This space divided the berth area from the bathrooms. It was also a place where, through the wide open doors, one could escape the stale air of the over-crowded berths of second class Indian passengers.

Yael and I discovered this place at a most opportune moment: the beginning of a gorgeous sunset on the horizon of the flat plains of northern India. We crouched on the floor of the open doorway. The glowing golden sphere of the sun was descending, gradually silhouetting the passing landscape of the world's largest alluvial plain. Yael and I were sharing her earphones, listening to the music of India's most famous classical instruments: the sitar and the tabla. The melody of Ravi Shankar set the perfect mood I was aiming for, as I beheld the beauty before my eyes.

We were leaving Varanasi, the Hindu's holy city on the Ganges River, where all who die there are guaranteed moksha, liberation from the ongoing cycle of rebirth and death. Varanasi, the city of the ghats where bodies are burned and their ashes strewn into the sacred waters of the river, is one of India's seven sacred Hindu pilgrimages. Every year, tens of thousands of devout Hindus visit one of the two thousand temples along the banks of the Ganga (Hindi for Ganges). Mendicant monks meditate in solitude, living the ascetic life of non-possession of material things and money. It is a sacred city where the locals daily bathe, wash their clothes, and collect water to boil for their early morning chai (Indian tea made with sugar and milk) with utmost faith in the ancient belief of the river's purifying qualities and healing miracles.

Yes, I visited Varanasi for four days and loved it, from the spirituality in the air to the constant hustling and stratagems of money-hungry Indians.

Yael and I met many interesting foreigners from around the world: Canada, England, Italy, Germany, France, Australia, and Israel. I conversed with these people like the three men sitting near me on the train. I learned of their experiences in India, why they decided to come here, how long they were staying, and how they were traveling.

At sunrise, we had taken a boat on the Ganges and watched hundreds of Hindus wash themselves in the bitter-cold water, repeating their ritual prayers and dipping themselves.

I struck up a conversation with five sadhus on the ghats with my limited Hindi and ate lunch (rice, yellow lentils and curried okra and potato) on banana leaves on the stone ground with them. We exchanged questions and answers about our contrasting lives, sometimes laughing at each other's peculiarities.

I specifically remember spending two hours of savored solitude at a mini-restaurant on the ghats. I sat, overlooking the Ganges River, writing my thoughts in my journal. I ate toast and drank several cups of hot chai, relaxing among India's laid-back "OK. No problem" atmosphere and experiencing its slow-paced lifestyle.

I recall vainly looking for a hotel room upon arrival, one to fit our pocketbooks. We found a simple room and registered our names in the hotel's record book, only to find that the room had already been reserved for a couple we previously talked to. My friend and I told the desk clerk and the couple they could have the room. The fat, old desk manager then told us we must pay for the room anyway, because we wrote in a "government book," and by law, we had to pay. Being wary of possible ploys to get our money, we easily sensed the intention of his request, laughed in his bewildered face at our refusal to pay, and walked out. That, to me, was hilarious, so ridiculous it was funny. It was the mock innocence on the man's face and insistence in his voice, like a child trying to convince his mother that he never ate out of the cookie jar when the truth was so obvious, that made us crack up, as we descended the steps from the hotel.

Varanasi was an experience I'll never forget. From this trip, I gained a whole new outlook on the country I had been living in for the past six months, a whole new appreciation for my temporary home. It would be no exaggeration if I said I had fallen in love with India, as one person falls in love with another. I had met India, and she swept me off my feet. We "clicked" from the start; my open frame of mind and high level of tolerance mixed well with her Eastern culture and various religions, disorder, and chaos. Her customs and beliefs became mine. Living in the country was like living in a trance, in a dream, where reality was no longer a part of my life.

Central India seemed like another planet when compared to the United States, and the myriad differences between them. I had become attached to the country and most everything it entailed: the culture, religion, and especially, the Indian people. It's hard to explain the feeling I got from walking through the crowded market or experiencing India's warm hospitality, or making offerings and praying at her many Hindu temples. The Indians' devoutness to Hinduism was never more apparent than in Varanasi. To the secular Westerner like myself, the vital role religion played in the people's lives induced admiration and awe.

Besides Indian life, I had fallen in love with India's craziness. For example, you walk down the road and people say the most ridiculous and random things to a foreigner.

"Hello, Madam. You like to smoke? You like hash? Heroin?"

"Hello, Madam, Sir. You like sheep fight? Yes. Sheep fight right here. You like?" (What?)

If you need directions and ask an Indian who doesn't know, he will give you wrong directions (hoping he is correct), rather than disappoint you and tell you he doesn't know. Some foreigners might find this irritating, but I found it quite comical.

After learning how to deal with the country's chaos, I became ready for the Indian experience of adventure. It is traveling with backpack, a torn, two-inch thick Lonely Planet guidebook, an open-ended plane ticket, and a small budget. The Indian experience is not really having any definite plans, meetings, traveling with other interesting foreigners, and staying in cheap hotels or youth hostels for $1.50 a night. The fun in India is the adventure, experiencing the ridicule and disorganization of Indian life. It is testing your patience and tolerance, experiencing Indians trying to deceive you to get your money, technology breaking down, dealing with Indian bureaucracy, getting a room reserved for somebody else, being dirty, and sitting on a toilet with cockroaches swimming below. The fun is getting food poisoning from street vendors, going to government opium emporiums, getting pushed by Indian women into a jam-packed city train during rush hour in Bombay, having your belongings stolen, seeing Indian men relieve themselves on the side of the road, and having Indians stare at you non-stop on a two hour bus ride. Now, that's the adventure. That's the fun. That's why I love India. It's the craziness of everything. I've learned to relax and view everything crazy as a comical situation, rather than become annoyed as a typical Westerner. I've learned to sit back and relax.

Relax I did, as I leaned against the wall of the train car, with my legs bent close in front of me, gazing out the door. The burning sun was quickly dropping below the horizon, creating a background with shades of orange and grapefruit pink. It was like the sun had some special power, the way it could transform the sky into a beautiful mural of nature. The sun touches all material things on Earth, like Brahman (Hinduism's ultimate God), the infinite, omnipresent and all-pervading God.

There were black silhouettes of dispersed pipel trees with their wide spreading branches, the distant hills and other activity. I noticed several old village women in the distance, crouching in the wheat fields, relieving themselves after a hot day's work. A small man walked slowly beside his two meandering oxen pulling a cart full of hay. They were heading towards a cluster of small houses made of straw and dried cow dung.

The air was mixed with Nog Chompa and the burning of hash emanating from the activity of the three men beside me. I closed my tired eyes and listened to Ravi Shankar over the quiet rumbling of the rolling train.

Why Write?

Autumn 1997

G. Lynn Nelson

"What we really are searching for is a language that heals ... that takes the side of the amazing and fragile life on our life-giving earth ... ." (Linda Hogan, *Dwellings*).

Why do we write in our journals? What about this work so compels us? Sure, some may write to become famous, to be on *Oprah*, to become rich, but we who lug ragged journals with us and sit in quiet corners of coffee shops and under trees in parks writing, we who steal scribbling moments from our work, like shoplifters at Circle K – we are not they. We are after more. Though we may not know just what it is we are after, we are following a need as deep and ancient as that of the Paleolithic artists who drew on the walls of the Caves of Lascaux some 20,000 years ago – the need to tell our stories and find meaning in our lives – a need more denied now than ever before.

"We write to escape the trap of our training, to take back our eyes, to recover our hearts and spirits. We write to save ourselves from our primary training in America: to be consumers."

I would suggest (without exaggeration) that, at the end of the twentieth century, we write for no less than to save ourselves. We write to escape the trap of our training, to take back our eyes, to recover our hearts and spirits. We write to save ourselves from our primary training in America: to be consumers. We write to escape the trap of having watched 20,000 hours of television by the time we graduate from high school, to escape the approximately 3,000 advertisements we are exposed to per day. We write to find a deeper vision of life than the deadly mechanistic, I-It vision that we have been given. Aware of it or not, we write for no less than this.

Now, if all that sounds ideal and grandiose – don't be intimidated. Just do as you have done. Open your journal daily, religiously, and say what you see, inside and out. Tell your stories. Scream your anger so you can let go of it, so you will no longer be trapped in it. Tell of your wounds, your hurts, so they will heal. Tell of your losses, cry your grief, so you can go on. Look closely at everything, and write what you see. After doing this, you will see more – have more to write – and writing more, you will see more. This work is never done – on and on, learning and growing into greater visions, better being.

"We reach out with our words and touch the world – the world touches us back, and we are never the same."

Writing thus, dare I say it, you will come to care, to love. Everything. It is inevitable. Because, writing thus, all those "Its" we have been trained to see and start to come alive, no longer mere "objects." They start to become "Thou's," as in "I and Thou," as in "Thou art that." Our words break them out of their cages, and they ravish us. We reach out with our words and touch the world – the world touches us back, and we are never the same. Those people, those trees, those amazing creatures, this grass beneath our feet, those clouds, and that sky. On and on, the world comes alive for us. We stagger through it, taking notes, properly amazed.

Writer, do not sell yourself short. Do not think small of your quiet scratching, your word-work in this world. For if you are writing with a good heart, if you are writing with soft eyes and a beginner's mind, then there is no better work for you to be doing. You are doing more than any millionaire CEO in this world. Write on. Write on toward peace, and know that you are not alone, that others are on this journal-journey with you.

"Lick a finger: feel the now." (Annie Dillard, *Pilgrim at Tinker Creek).*

Life Is Good

Winter 1999

Jill Parker

I've been in Guatemala for 3 ½ weeks. The first 2 weeks were spent studying the Guatemalan health care system and other social/public health services with 25 Tulane University students. It was a great class with lots of speakers and field trips including the 3-day stay in El Retiro. I learned a lot. I've spent the last two weeks traveling around and seeing what I could. I have not been writing in my journal as much as I wanted, but I have been writing and hope to do some more this afternoon, before my second round of salsa lessons!

Five friends and I are catching a bus in an hour to head to the Caribbean coast. I'm "planning" to be back in Antigua on Tuesday. Then, I'm heading west to see the sights in that direction.

Last weekend at Tikal (the northern part of Guatemala) was great. The Mayan ruins were so beautiful. We got lots of exercise hiking through the jungle and climbing to the top of the ruins. I took tons of pictures. Then it was off to El Retiro. We left the hotel Monday at 7 a.m. and drove about 2 ½ hours and then walked another ½ hour into the village. It was like a completely different world. We first took a little walking tour around the village and then met in our small groups to discuss our projects we would be working on there. The official theme was "biodiversity and public health." The unofficial theme was "can the gringos survive the hard life in a Guatemalan village!"

We all got placed with families to live with. I met this little 9-year-old-girl, Elva, during the tour. She chased me with a big bug, and then we started chatting, as well as two people who don't speak the same language can, and I ended up being her gringa for the week. I totally fell in love with her and cried when I left.

Their house was made of mud bricks and bamboo rods with big leaves for the roof. There was one room for cooking and one for everybody to sleep in. Every morning we were up by 5 a.m. and walked a long ways to get water. Elva could carry more water on her head than I could. Then, we'd walk some more to get corn ground into masa, which was used to make the tortillas for that day. They tried to teach me how to make tortillas, but mine were always too thick and definitely not round. In any case, I'm sick of eating tortillas.

We also ate these giant winged ants that were "fried." Sick. I tasted one, but that's all I could get down. Some people said they tasted like corn nuts. I think they tasted like burnt bugs. During the day, we'd work on our class project, and at the end of our stay, we presented what we learned to the community through skits. This is where we tried to repay our family's hospitality with some cheap entertainment! I'm still not sure if everybody was laughing with us or at us!

Art :: Eddith Buis

Save the Planet with Music
Autumn 2010

Karl Paulnack

"One of my parents' deepest fears, I suspect, was that society would not properly value me as a musician, that I wouldn't be appreciated. I had very good grades in high school. I was good in science and math, and they imagined that as a doctor or a research chemist or an engineer, I might be more appreciated than I would be as a musician. I still remember my mother's remark when I announced my decision to apply to music school.

She said, "You're wasting your SAT scores!" On some level, I think, my parents were not sure themselves what the value of music was, what its purpose was. They loved music; they listened to classical music all the time. They just weren't really clear about its function. So, let me talk about that a little bit, because we live in a society that puts music in the "arts and entertainment" section of the newspaper, and serious music, the kind your kids are about to engage in, has absolutely nothing whatsoever to do with entertainment. In fact, it's the opposite of entertainment. Let me talk a little bit about music and how it works.

One of the first cultures to articulate how music really works was the ancient Greeks. This is going to fascinate you; the Greeks said that music and astronomy were two sides of the same coin. Astronomy was seen as the study of relationships between observable, permanent, external objects, and music was seen as the study of relationships between invisible, internal, hidden objects. Music has a way of finding the big, invisible moving pieces inside our hearts and souls and helping us figure out the position of things inside us. Let me give you some examples of how this works.

One of the most profound musical compositions of all time is the *Quartet for the End of Time* written by French composer Olivier Messiaen in 1940. Messiaen was thirty-one years old when France entered the war against Nazi Germany. He was captured by the Germans in June of 1940 and imprisoned in a prisoner-of-war camp.

He was fortunate to find a sympathetic prison guard who gave him paper and a place to compose and fortunate to have musician colleagues in the camp: a cellist, a violinist, and a clarinetist. Messiaen wrote his quartet with these specific players in mind. It was performed in January 1941 for four thousand prisoners and guards in the prison camp. Today, it is one of the most famous masterworks in the repertoire.

Given what we have since learned about life in the Nazi camps, why would anyone in his right mind waste time and energy writing or playing music? There was barely enough energy on a good day to find food and water, to avoid a beating, to stay warm, and to escape torture. Why would anyone bother with music? Even from the concentration camps, we have poetry, we have music, we have visual art; it wasn't just this one fanatic Messiaen; many, many people created art. Why? Well, in a place where people are only focused on survival, on the bare necessities, the obvious conclusion is that art must be, somehow, essential for life. The camps were without money, without hope, without commerce, without recreation, without basic respect, but they were not without art. Art is part of survival; art is part of the human spirit, an unquenchable expression of who we are. Art is one of the ways in which we say, "I am alive, and my life has meaning."

In September of 2001, I was a resident of Manhattan. On the morning of September 12, 2001, I reached a new understanding of my art and its relationship to the world. I sat down at the piano that morning at 10 a. m. to practice as was my daily routine; I did it by force of habit, without thinking about it. I lifted the cover on the keyboard, opened my music, put my hands on the keys, and took my hands off the keys. I sat there and thought, does this even matter? Isn't this completely irrelevant? Playing the piano right now, given what happened in this city, yesterday, seems silly, absurd, irreverent, and pointless. Why am I here? What place has a musician in this moment in time? Who needs a piano player right now? I was completely lost.

I, along with the rest of New York, went through the journey of getting through that week. I did not play the piano that day, and in fact, I contemplated briefly whether I would ever want to play the piano again. Then, I observed how we got through the day.

In my neighborhood, we didn't shoot hoops or play Scrabble. We didn't play cards to pass the time; we didn't watch TV; we didn't shop; we most certainly did not go to the mall. The first organized activity that I saw in New York, on the very evening of September 11, was singing. People sang. People sang around firehouses; people sang "We Shall Overcome." Lots of people sang "America the Beautiful." The first organized public event that

I remember was the "Brahms Requiem," later that week, at Lincoln Center, with the New York Philharmonic. The first organized public expression of grief, our first communal response to that historic event, was a concert. That was the beginning of a sense that life might go on. The US Military secured the airspace, but recovery was led by the arts, and by music in particular, that very night.

From these two experiences, I have come to understand that music is not part of "arts and entertainment," as the newspaper section would have us believe. It's not a luxury, a lavish thing that we fund from leftovers of our budgets, not a plaything or an amusement or a pastime. Music is a basic need of human survival. Music is one of the ways we make sense of our lives, one of the ways in which we express feelings when we have no words, a way for us to understand things with our hearts when we can't with our minds.

Some of you may know Samuel Barber's heart-wrenchingly beautiful piece "Adagio for Strings." If you don't know it by that name, then some of you may know it as the background music which accompanied the Oliver Stone movie *Platoon*, a film about the Vietnam War. If you know that piece of music, either way, you know it has the ability to crack your heart open like a walnut; it can make you cry over sadness you didn't know you had. Music can slip beneath our conscious reality to get at what's really going on inside us, the way a good therapist does.

Very few of you have ever been to a wedding where there was absolutely no music. There might have been only a little music, there might have been some really bad music, but with few exceptions there is some music. Something very predictable happens at weddings; people get all pent up with all kinds of emotions, and then there's some musical moment where the action of the wedding stops, and someone sings or plays the flute or something. Even if the music is lame, even if the quality isn't good, predictably 30 or 40 percent of the people who are going to cry at a wedding cry a couple of moments after the music starts.

Why? The Greeks. Music allows us to move around those big invisible pieces of ourselves and rearrange our insides, so that we can express what we feel, even when we can't talk about it. Can you imagine watching *Indiana Jones* or *Superman* or *Star Wars* with the dialogue but no music? What is it about the music swelling up at just the right moment in *ET* so that all the softies in the audience start crying at exactly the same moment? I guarantee you if you showed the movie with the music stripped out, it wouldn't happen that way. The Greeks. Music is the understanding of the relationship between invisible internal objects.

I'll give you one more example, the story of the most important concert of my life. I must tell you I have played a little less than a thousand concerts in my life so far. I have played in places that I thought were important. I like playing in Carnegie Hall; I enjoyed playing in Paris; it made me very happy to please the critics in St. Petersburg. I have played for people I thought were important; music critics of major newspapers and foreign heads of state. The most important concert of my entire life took place in a nursing home in a small, Midwestern town a few years ago.

I was playing with a very dear friend of mine who is a violinist. We began, as we often do, with Aaron Copland's "Sonata," which was written during World War II and dedicated to a young friend of Copland's, a young pilot who was shot down during the war. Now, we often talk to our audiences about the pieces we are going to play rather than providing them with written program notes. In this case, because we began the concert with this piece, we decided to talk about the piece later in the program and to just come out and play the music without explanation.

Midway through the piece, an elderly man seated in a wheelchair near the front of the concert hall began to weep. This man, whom I later met, was clearly a soldier. Even in his 70s, it was clear from his buzz-cut hair, square jaw, and general demeanor that he had spent a good deal of his life in the military. I thought it a little bit odd that someone would be moved to tears by that particular movement of that particular piece, but it wasn't the first time I've heard crying in concerts before; we went on with the concert and finished the piece.

When we came out to play the next piece on the program, we decided to talk about both the first and second pieces, and we described the circumstances in which the Copland piece was written and mentioned its dedication to a downed pilot. The man in the front of the audience became so disturbed that he had to leave the auditorium. I honestly figured that we would not see him again, but he did come backstage afterwards, tears and all, to explain himself.

What he told us was this: "During World War II, I was a pilot, and I was in an aerial combat situation where one of my team's planes was hit. I watched my friend bail out and watched his parachute open, but the Japanese planes which had engaged us returned and machine gunned across the parachute chords so as to separate the parachute from the pilot, and I watched my friend drop away into the ocean, realizing that he was lost. I have not thought about this for many years, but during that first piece of music you played, this memory returned to me so vividly that it was as though I was reliving it. I didn't understand why this was happening. Why now? Then, when you came out to explain that this piece of music was written to commemorate a lost pilot, it was a little more than I could handle. How does the music do that? How did it find those feelings and those memories in me?"

Remember the Greeks? Music is the study of invisible relationships between internal objects. The concert in the nursing home was the most important work I have ever done. For me to play for this old soldier and help him connect, somehow, with Aaron Copland, and to connect their memories of their lost friends, to help him remember and mourn his friend, this is my work. This is why music matters.

What follows is part of the talk I will give to this year's freshman class when I welcome them a few days from now. The responsibility I will charge your sons and daughters with is this:

"If we were a medical school and you were here as a med student practicing appendectomies, you'd take your work very seriously because you would imagine that some night at 2 a.m. someone is going to waltz into your emergency room, and you're going to have to save their life. Well, my friends, someday at 8 p.m. someone is going to walk into your concert hall and bring you a mind that is confused, a heart that is overwhelmed, a soul that is weary. Whether they go out whole again will depend partly on how well you do your craft.

You're not here to become an entertainer, and you don't have to sell yourself. The truth is you don't have anything to sell; being a musician isn't about dispensing a product, like selling used cars. I'm not an entertainer; I'm a lot closer to a paramedic, a firefighter, a rescue worker. You're here to become a sort of therapist for the human soul, a spiritual version of a chiropractor, physical therapist, someone who works with our insides to see if they get things to line up, to see if we can come into harmony with ourselves and be healthy and happy and well.

Frankly, ladies and gentlemen, I expect you not only to master music; I expect you to save the planet. If there is a future wave of wellness on this planet, of harmony, of peace, of an end to war, of mutual understanding, of equality, of fairness, I don't expect it will come from a government, a military force, or a corporation. I no longer even expect it to come from the religions of the world, which together seem to have brought us as much war as they have peace. If there is a future of peace for humankind, if there is to be an understanding of how these invisible, internal things should fit together, I expect it will come from the artists, because that's what we do. As in the concentration camp and the evening of 9/11, the artists are the ones who might be able to help us with our internal, invisible lives."

Journaling at 2:30 A.M.

Winter 1993

Irv Peckham

This is the time when I generally get up to write in my diary and then move into whatever novel or story I am working on. This is the part of the day before the rest of the world gets up, which has always seemed to me the appropriate time to write stuff no one else reads. At any rate, while having my first cup of coffee, I read David Martin's last contribution in the NAG Journal (*Nebraska Association for the Gifted*) and wanted to make some remarks and subscribe to the *Fine Lines* newsletter for 1993.

I find myself so often (and very much so this morning) in the space you describe. I certainly find myself harried, which is why I got up this morning at 2:30 a.m. rather than 4:30 a.m., my normal rising time. There I am, at my age, lying in bed at 2:30 a.m. and thinking of all these things I have left undone. Finally, I have to shrug my shoulders and say, well, let's see what happens, but still I can't get back to sleep. I, of course, know I have constructed (or allowed others to construct) all these mental debts, but this knowledge doesn't make them any the less real. So, relating my harried condition to yours and to a lot of other people I know, this seems the general condition. I know I vow not to accept responsibilities for certain things, but then there they are; they sneak in under the door, somehow. I guess we are left with the challenge of how to maintain a kind of Emersonian perspective on, as Thoreau would say, the baggage we carry on our backs.

You and I both write. You write your way into existence by journals. I do something of the same and also write stories, when I know damn well I should be writing more articles, because I am in the publication grind. There is that part of us that says, *what the hell, I am going to write what I like to write*, and maybe that is why we both continue to write. If I were writing to demand all the time, I know I wouldn't have the same easy feeling about writing that I do.

Okay, you haven't fulfilled your potential, part of the subject of your gifted journal. I remember I was in the same quandary before I went back to grad school to get my PhD. I was of two minds: just keep teaching and writing these stories in the morning (the ones I never get published) or go

153

back to school. Well, I went back to school, mostly a consequence of a new principal I wasn't too fond of and who, by the way, was later prosecuted for falsifying his academic credentials. I earned my doctorate and continue to write these stories in the morning. For me, the PhD was worth it, but one shouldn't dismiss all the things one has to go through to get it. I was 40 when I started, and it worked out so I could handle the disruption financially, but boy did I take an economic loss – which continues to this day. On the other hand, and this is no secret, it is ten times easier to teach at the college level than in high school. College teachers are very privileged, period, although they wouldn't say so.

If our focus is on this writing that no one sees, which is to say on personal growth, dedication to finding a richness in each morning, knowing how to bless the mere fact of being alive, saying *thank God I have words that let me know who I am and what I'm about and how I relate to the world*, then what we do on the outside, or shall we say, on the periphery, doesn't make a whole hell of a lot of difference. Another side of me keeps working toward erasing the boundary between the periphery and myself. I wish I could be what I do. I wish I could just sing self like Whitman, but the world is out there, and I have to function in it, and so I have to shift (or what is song to me) into prose.

Well, gotta get to some self-writing this morning before everybody wakes up.

Little Henry

Summer 2005

Marty Pierson

Little Henry was a sophomore in an inner-city, Midwestern high school. He stood about 5'2". His diminutive body was proportional to his height and weight. Henry's daily dress was laundry clean: an unpressed, over-sized khaki shirt with long sleeves and worn work jeans. The leg bottoms were rolled into two, three-inch cuffs. He was clean, though a comb had not met his hair.

Henry was my student during the 1970s. He sat directly in front of my desk. His class attendance was nearly perfect. He read what I wrote on the chalkboard and then copied school announcements. He made few attempts at academic assignments. I offered verbal encouragement, pencil, and paper.

"You know I don't do this stuff," he said repeatedly.

He slept or feigned sleep through most of our classes. One eye often opened and looked directly at me, but then he switched his arm to pillow his head on the desk.

There was a strange experience for the students and me, one early morning. A harried administrator entered our room and stated in a loud, authoritarian voice, "All black students to the auditorium in five minutes. You escort your students there, Mrs. P, and then return to this classroom."

Silence prevailed in the classroom. I looked at my eighteen students; they looked at me. They were black. I am white.

Henry suddenly jumped from his desk. He scurried to the aluminum cabinet. All the students' eyes and mine followed him. He opened the

155

cabinet and looked up. He needed a chair to reach to the top shelf. Henry took something from the shelf, leaped to the floor, and returned to the front of my desk. The silence continued.

"Gimme your hand," Henry instructed. I stretched out my hand. He slapped a generous amount of black shoe polish on my hand and wrist. "There, now you can go with us."

The silence was broken with murmurs and some smiles. I took a huge breath and slowly released it.

"Thanks, Henry. Come on! We're going to the auditorium together. Let's go!"

Henry sat next to me in the auditorium. He propped his legs on the back of the seat in front of him and slept through the presentation.

In the midst of change, some things will always remain the same.

A Piece of My Mind

Summer 1994

Donald F. Prince

I must share with you one of the highlights of my practice of medicine. I practiced medicine for 33 years and am almost 67 years old. That covers a rather short time when compared to the age of my patient and friend, Veva, who was 106 years old on January 15, 1991.

Veva is a retired school teacher who lives in our small hospital at her own choosing. She just retired when I arrived in this community to be in general practice. She is of a slight, fragile build, so I told her I did not mind making house calls on her on my way to or from the hospital.

Most of my calls on her were to reassure her that her heart and blood pressure were OK, but at 83 she developed abdominal pain that localized. Her workup revealed a RLQ tumor, and our surgeon removed it with the nodes that were visible and palpable. Two or three days post-op, I presented to her the option of seeing an oncologist for therapy of her cancerous bowel tumor. Her response was, "I've lived a good life and a fulfilling life, and let's just let nature take its course."

At 90 and still living at home, she had a neighborhood arrangement in which she would raise her shades each morning, and the neighbors would know that she was all right.

One Saturday, the signal was mixed up, and the unraised shades were not noted until late in the evening. The neighbor called me, and on arriving I told Veva, "You have broken your femur."

The response was, "I know that, but what is important is, I haven't had a radio on all day. Did Nebraska beat Kansas?"

I told her, "Yes," and she said, "Good, let's go and get the leg fixed." With an intramedullary pin, she still walks with a walker and gets about with help.

I still see her each morning before going to my office. She asks about the weather, Nebraska football, school activities, and church work.

I'm not sure if I am seeing her for therapy or if she is my therapist. She is one of the reasons general practice (family practice) is such a delight. With all of the alphabet soup we have to deal with, interesting people and friends are what make the practice of medicine so appealing.

A Mean Mom

Autumn 2004

Kathleen Pugel

Student Wrapped ::
Deborah McGinn

I'm a mean mom. Just ask my son. I won't buy him a game system or let him have a television, computer, or phone in his room, ever.

He wants to know why he can't have all the things that most of his friends have already. He's almost eight. He thinks I'm unreasonable. He's analytical by nature. According to him my explanations have to be logical.

What a headache! I am constantly having to think on my feet. At times, I get so flustered by his questioning my rules, my authority, and my explanations that the overused, "Because I said so," comes out. That explanation doesn't mean much to him, but I don't care. It's my job to form him into a decent human being, one who can be comfortable in social situations and who can function at all levels in our society.

I didn't have any of those things in my room until I was in college! I encourage him to read, write, and play outdoors, as much as he can. I'm such a mean mom.

I'm not saying, "No," to those things because he's a bad kid. I simply want to retain as much control of him, as I possibly can before he becomes a teenager. I don't think I'm being unreasonable, no matter how loudly he yells. I want him to remain the bright, energetic, and thoughtful boy he is thus far. I've seen what repetitive game playing can do to kids, and that's not a road I want my son to travel down.

It's certainly not easy being one of the only parental units from his circle of friends who has not bought her child a Game Boy, Game Cube, Play Station, or whatever else there is out there that does about the same thing. My husband was our son's basketball coach last year. After Christmas break, as an icebreaker before practice started, he asked the boys what their favorite gift for Christmas was. Six out of eight boys mentioned the game system they received. The dark look my son shot at my husband spoke a thousand words. I don't fault the other parents for their choices, but I've made mine, and I'm sticking to them, no matter how badly I'm hounded.

My point in limiting what my son has or doesn't have in his room or elsewhere is that I want to be able to see what he's doing, know with whom he's talking, and see what he's watching. I want to protect him and educate him so he's equipped to deal with things that will be thrown at him much sooner than he'll probably be ready for. There are too many scary people and scary things in the world. If he's in his room with the door shut with so many things at his fingertips, how can I be an influence in his life?

When we watch television or movies, we do it together. There are teachable moments, and we have to utilize them. When he uses the computer, it's with approved sites and educational CD-ROMS. Reading is something I want to encourage him to do more. I love to read, and I've tried to instill this in him as well. It's fun to share books with my son that I read when I was a child; it's another connection, an important one.

It's not fun being the bad guy. It would be great to be the cool mom, the one who is adored, but that is not my lot in life right now. Maybe later on. At least my little guy doesn't have a clue as to what is in store for him, yet, so I still have a little peace (and a little adoration) here.

Will my older son grow up to resent me for the limitations placed on him? Probably, until he's a parent and his child tells him that he's a mean dad! Then, I'll know I did my job.

Life in the United States

Autumn 1997

Armando Salgado

Once we were in the state of Washington, everything was much harder. We didn't have transportation, and the nearest town was about ten miles away. The manager of the ranch lent us a small house. It wasn't even a house; it was like a small garage with no heat or ventilation. I remember when we got there, a lot of people tried to help us, people who had gone through the same thing, people who knew how it felt not to have anything, and we didn't have anything. We didn't have anything to eat, and I was starving and crying all of the time.

I could tell my dad was really worried about not having anything to feed me. He asked some of his friends to lend him some money and to give him a ride to town, so he could buy some food. By this time, there wasn't much work to do at that ranch, so my parents set off with some other people to look for work at other ranches.

Since we didn't have transportation, we always had to pay for the rides that other people gave us. Sometimes, when we didn't have any food, my dad had to walk ten miles to the nearest store to buy supplies for us. Life, at that time, was really hard. Sometimes, when we used to get sick and we needed to go to the doctor, we couldn't because we didn't have a car. I remember one day, my dad had a really bad toothache. It hurt him so much that he couldn't take the pain anymore. He walked all the way to town and when he got there, the doctor wouldn't see him right away, so he walked all the way to the next town which was another ten miles away. They did see him there. Lucky him! When he returned, he got a ride from another Mexican man who knew my dad. Dad was so mad! It's still funny to him, because he tells us that he thought the doctors took out the wrong tooth since his mouth still kept hurting.

Because of a money shortage and the lack of English as their language, many Hispanic people are forced to live like this. Some people are afraid to leave their homes; the only reason they leave is to buy food, and they usually buy enough for the whole week.

The ranch manager picked them up to take them to the field they had to clean out. The jobs they had to do were not a day at the office. I would see them work like slaves. That's how my parents had to work.

I got enrolled in school and started to learn the language my parents so much wanted me to learn. In first grade, I caught on quickly. In one way, I had to because I was the one who was going to do all the talking. When I started to learn English at first, it was so cool because I could talk to people and start knowing what everybody was like here in the United States. Then came the great obligation. You wouldn't believe me, but at the age of eight, I had to send the payments for the electricity and the phone bills. We didn't pay the heating bill because we didn't have any.

I remember all of this very well, and I hated it! Since we didn't have any money to buy a heater, my dad built a fireplace. He built it out of this big heavy barrel with a hole in the middle. He added some tubes to it, and he made a hole in the window and slipped the pipes through there to let the smoke out. That darned thing worked! My dad made a fireplace without even knowing how to start one. That small house was so cozy after that, we never got cold.

The hardest thing was to go outside and chop the wood. I hated that so much. Sometimes, I would sit down and cry and ask God why we had to suffer, but I would later see the starving people in Africa, and compared to them, I was living like a king. They would probably wish they were in my position, and I was trying to get out.

I got on the bus every morning, and my parents set off to work. Sometimes, I would go to their work with them, and I just wanted to cry. I would see a big group of people bent over cleaning the hops trying to take out the weeds while the hot raging sun would burn its hottest. Instead of watching them, I would help them, not much, but I saw their faces light up, and that made me happy for a while.

When I used to come home from school, I would be embarrassed over the house that I lived in. I was embarrassed that the other kids would see where I lived, so I would start walking to another house close to mine pretending it was mine, and when the bus was gone, I would go home. That's how embarrassed I was, and there was nothing that I could do other than accept who I was and where I was going.

My parents got the hang of the way the Americans lived here. We lived like this for a long time with no car, no phone, nothing. We bought things one by one until we had a TV and some heaters. My dad took a test for a driver's license, and he passed it. Now, he could drive. By this time, my parents applied for residency. They had to fill out a ton of papers and pay a lot of money, but that's what they were saving for. To be legal in this country is hard on people who mean no harm.

Writing with Music

Spring 2002

Patricia Schicker

Sitting here at the end of my day, and listening to Jim Brickman play "Part of My Heart" on his piano is sweet. Music is part of my spirit and imbedded deep within my soul. It can smooth even a most frustrating day when I select the genre and artist I need.

I have over 150 CDs in my collection. I play some of them everyday, as I challenge myself and continue to grapple with my roles. My five portable Loge Cases are not large enough to hold my precious works of art.

I have been a member of the *BBC Magazine*/CD Club for over eleven years. Each month a new collector's gem arrives at my front door. The *BBC Magazine*, my *Opera News*, and *Fine Lines* adorn my bookshelves. I am in need of a cabinet to protect and store my CDs. I do not know where a new piece of furniture would fit in wall-to-wall bookshelves.

I am writing from my free spirit not my editing hand, as Natalie Goldberg would say in her book, or in the Collector's Edition of audiotapes, *Writing from the Bones*, given to me by my son, Benjamin. It is difficult for me to let the controls go. I do not wish to lose my grammar and syntax for content, but, hey, if that's what the experts say, I should give it a go. Yes, everyday is "writing practice" day, and I can use all that time and energy to devote to promoting the long lost art called "composition." Good music frees me up to do this nightly, whether in my journal, as an exercise or J-ON THE NET, journaling electronically.

On the Internet, I have all my sites categorized by topics. Music has the most websites saved for easy access. The George Maurer Group, www. gmjazzz.com, is based out of St. Cloud, MN, but plays big time at the Jazz Mine, downtown Minneapolis, the Dakota Bar in St. Paul, and all over MN and WI.

George has played piano solos with ensemble or sans his group for over a decade nation-wide in very impressive places. I enjoyed with delight the live performances of both piano solos at St. John's University and elsewhere with his talented jazz group plus vocals and special guest performers. My son, Nicholas, who plays violin is a recent graduate of Saint John's

University, so he shares the unique status of being alumni with George Maurer. George took the initiative to cut a CD of Nicholas' performances with the 7-piece Collegeville String Quartet. "The sly and irreverent George" is the proprietor and producer of Pine Curtains Records in St. Cloud, MN. It is reported in his web site that George started producing from his sophomore dorm while studying music at SJU.

The next love in my music sites is The Bocelli Network at www.bocelli. net. Andrea Bocelli is touted as The Fourth Tenor. Born in Tuscany, Italy, he has been climbing both the pop charts with *Romanza* in 1996 and *Toscana* in 2001 to the soundtrack of his first live debut of a well-renown opera, *La Boehme*. Playing the lead role as Rodolfo is one acclaimed aspiration for him. He has been singing worldwide in solos, duets with famous artists, et al, during the '90s to the present. Bocelli has been "sightless" since age twelve due to a soccer accident. He and his works are a huge inspiration to me. His courage and tenacity to "ride horses that throw him and neigh as if laughing at him" is another role he took on as a champion to overcome obstacles in his life. His brilliance as a lone star in the night is enough to illuminate my existence.

I write with many musical genres. The classical Russian musicians give me an extraordinary boost with their long and sweeping, romantic melodies. I will name a few from the first and second generation composers, which I revere. First generation songwriters like Peter Ilyich Tchaikovsky, Glasanov, Milay Balakirev, Alexander Borodin, Nicolay Rimsky-Korsakov, and Mikhail Glinka (known as the "Father of Russian Music") makes my flesh stand up in an ovation of bravos.

The second generation masters, who also fill my soul with their music, include Sergei Rachmaninoff, Sergei Prokofiev, Alexander Scriabin, and Igor Stravinsky (known widely from the dazzling video *Fantasia I*). A Sergei Rachmaninoff repertoire can actually cause me to stop writing, when tears well up as my eyes reflect his genius like a prism. I believe strongly in "The Mozart Effect."

Dmitri Shostakovich demands such concentration from me that I cannot do both, write and listen to his musical works. Much like the Austrian conductor and composer Gustav Mahler in his later symphonies, these pieces exact a distraction in my spirit and hinder my flow of ideas. Those works are deep, and my writing is still on the surface of the crown jewels. Their works, which push some of my expressions to delve into their profound minds, are better left for mature writings. I have more classical CDs from many nations, which serenade me with surround sound.

My own choice of music allows me to freely follow where "part of my heart" wants to venture and leaves my journaling open-minded. In the future, I hope to plunge into deeper musical landscapes, but currently, I want to enjoy and skim the surface of my dreams and my life.

Charcoal :: Jasmine Kitchen

In Case of Fire

Spring 2003

Jayne Schlosser

Every person has one big fear in life: what to do if the house catches on fire. You're supposed to get out of the house quickly, and adults make sure the children are safe. Most people also worry about saving their most prized possessions.

Growing up, I remember having a specific item to save, if I could do it on the way out of the house. One time, it was the baby's favorite blanket. When I was older, it was my musical instrument. Fortunately, the only fires at our house were in the fireplace, which Dad watched with an eagle eye until the last ember was stone cold.

When I became an adult, I set up fire escape routes and thought about things to save. The first years of my marriage, I told my husband to save my camera because I was saving the wedding pictures. Later, I changed the plan to save the two dogs and my camera. Once we had children, there was no question. We save the children, the dogs, and, in the mad flight from the house, my camera. We never had to put the plan into action.

We've now reached the point where the children are grown, and worrying about escape routes is no longer a concern, but the other evening the news got me to thinking about updating the old escape drills. Not needing to worry about children, I am free to focus on saving the most important items in my house.

If I can save only one thing, what would it be? I should save the wedding pictures, but I'm not sure where the album is. I could save the baby albums, but each of them has two boxes of mementos, and I can't remember which boxes have the actual albums. We should save the guitars, but the fire department would be packing up and leaving before I found the cases for all eight instruments. Forget the amplifiers; they require two people to lift them. Which one of my quilts is most valuable? As I thought through the accumulation of thirty-plus years of marriage, I realized the choices were simpler when the children were small.

I spent the evening and the next day pondering what to save and decided. That evening as my husband walked in from work, I made my announcement, "In case of a fire, you grab the dog. I'll save the bread machine."

Barn Jackets :: Raleigh Wilkerson

Beautiful

Autumn 2001

Bill Schock

I recently resumed a somewhat torrid love affair that ended rather disastrously 56 years ago, although the memories have lingered on.

To dispel any rumors, which might quickly surface, it was strictly platonic. It was with a B-17 (Flying Fortress), the workhorse of the mighty 8th Air Force in World War II. My affection for the four-engine bomber wasn't singular. I would guess that everyone who ever flew one was similarly infatuated.

My emotional fire was rekindled at the Lincoln, NE, airport recently where the EAA Aviation Foundation of Oshkosh, WI, brought the restored B-17, "Aluminum Overcast," to give rides and to open it for walkthroughs by aviation and history buffs, as well as old WWII types in search of nostalgic boosts.

Bruce Morehead of San Jose, CA, son of John and Amy Morehead, who does his flying as a serious hobby, was eager for a ride in the historic bomber, and he flew us up to Lincoln.

Getting back to my love affair, it began as a blind date. Some of us had just graduated from advanced flying school in New Mexico and considered ourselves very hot pilots. We were ordered to Boise, ID, where we thought we were going in to B-25s, the twin-engine plane in which Jimmy Doolittle and his airmen made the surprise attack on Tokyo early in the war. The Army Air Corps needed B-17 crews to fill the ranks in England, which were depleted by heavy losses in bombing missions over Europe. We were a perfect fit for the co-pilots so badly needed.

So, hello, B-17! She and I became an item, as they say today. I thought about that first meeting as I walked and crawled my way through the restored and well-traveled "Aluminum Overcast" that Friday morning some days ago. It seemed like a big airplane, both then and now.

I sat down in the jump seat they gave me behind the two pilots, stowed for takeoff. Right off the bat, they "buzzed" the Seward airport. I smiled to myself. It brought back the most, and maybe only, fun I ever had in the four-engine bomber. It was in August 1943, and we just picked up a new

B-17 in Grand Island to fly overseas to England to become a replacement crew in the 8th Air Force.

The day before we left, we took our new plane up to calibrate the instruments. What better place to calibrate instruments than over Falls City? We "buzzed" Falls City for about 45 minutes, going east and west, then north and south, then west to east and south to north. What a blast! Even after 56 years it was fun to recall. I figured it was one heck of a goodbye to my hometown.

The B-17 and our crew went through some tough times together over Germany, but the rugged bomber always (well, nearly always) brought us back to our base in England. On a mission to Anklam, Germany, she kept us airborne through nearly three hours of continuous fighter attacks at 20,000 feet. However, it was her last hurrah. The battle damage to her was so extensive that she never flew again. She did bring us home, badly wounded as she was.

On another day and another circumstance, a different B-17 gave up her life for us. Between missions over Europe, we had been on patrol over the North Sea in search of Royal Air Force crews, which were forced to ditch in the sea after night raids over Germany. The Air Force left us out too long, and when we were recalled, the east coast of England was "socked in" by murky weather, as darkness had begun to set in. We were awfully low on fuel, and while going through the murk, we spotted a landing strip of a fighter base under construction, so we tried to land. After two unsuccessful passes, the landing strip became barely visible. When we were over the middle of it, we knew we had to set down. We were all but out of gas. We missed most of the runway and went bounding along on grass. Suddenly, a small creek appeared out of the gloom. The plane had just enough speed to bounce across the creek. When it came down, the wheels sank and stuck into a very soft Brussels sprouts field, and our hectic ride ended. It gave us a terrible jolt! The B-17 became perpendicular, the four props also sinking into the muddy field. Everyone scrambled out through the cockpit windows and escape hatches before the bomber settled back down on the ground.

While the ten of us were standing there shaking in our boots and thanking our lucky stars, a terribly upset British farmer came running up and began berating us for ruining part of his Brussels sprouts field. Sympathy was nowhere to be found. The B-17 again had been good to us, and all of us were still in one piece, but for that plane, the war was over.

Then there was our last goodbye to another faithful airplane. We were on the way home from bombing a German fighter aircraft factory at Marienburg, East Prussia, on Easter Sunday, when our plane was hit by flak over the Schleswig Peninsula (where Germany meets Denmark). She was burning badly, and we all knew it was time to desert her. On our 25 missions, we had seen too many bombers explode in mid-air after flak or fighter hits. On automatic pilot, the B-17 flew a level course long enough to give us time to parachute out. She had been faithful to the last. Then, she exploded.

One of her favorites was killed in his parachute when the Germans kept firing at us. Another lost an arm from the flak, when he was hit in the ball turret. Two more were wounded so badly they spent most of the rest of the war in German hospitals. The "lucky ones" of us, those without serious injuries, finished out the war in prisoner of war camps.

My intimate "affair" with the B-17 ended that Easter Sunday in 1944, but I knew I would never forget her. She had been too good to me. Then, presto! Fifty-six years later I was privileged to sit in the pilot's seat once again at the Lincoln airport. The adrenalin reached flood stage. Corny? Absolutely!

I'm sure she acquired a new suitor in Bruce, my young compatriot, who looked admirably at her when our 30-minute flight was over. A very experienced old head at matters of the heart, I could tell right off he was smitten.

I'm not jealous. How could a guy who knew her in better days keep from loving her, when she had been so faithful in times long ago, and when she sat so majestically on the runway, her four big props taking man-sized bites out of the hot and humid Lincoln air in anticipation of another quick trip into the wild blue yonder? Exactly as I remembered her. Beautiful. Simply beautiful!

Have a Nice Day, or Not!

Autumn 2004

Madelon Shaw

According to the dictionary, a cliché (or platitude) is defined as a "trite phrase or expression; a hackneyed theme or situation; something that has become overly familiar or commonplace." I think the use of clichés is increasing, or maybe I'm just noticing it more. Regardless, I'm annoyed, and if one more person suggests that I "have a nice day," I'm going to scream. People who tell me to "have a nice day" are invariably total strangers who don't care what kind of a day I have or don't have.

Does the check-out person at the grocery store honestly care about what kind of a day I have? I doubt it. I can do without "a helpful smile in every aisle." I dislike shopping for groceries, and taking time to respond to, "Hello, how are you?" interrupts my concentration and renders me incapable of continuing my search for the perfect silver polish (which is never located with the rest of the cleaning supplies, where it should be). I've considered responding, "Actually, I've been better. I've been undergoing a series of radiation treatments for breast cancer, so I'm tired and crabby." I'd be willing to wager $100 that the store employee to whom I responded would say, "That's good," and continue reorganizing the low-carb products on the shelf. Please! If you don't genuinely care how I am, then don't ask!

I don't understand the meaning of many of the clichés I hear. For example, "crazy like a fox." Is a fox notoriously clever? I don't know, and I'm too lazy to investigate. It's "water under the bridge." Does this mean that when whatever it is terminates, it's finished, and is this the same as "what goes around, comes around?" Or is it "what comes around, goes around?" I'm never sure. Are the above similar to "crying over spilt milk?" I doubt that we need several clichés for the same semi-meaningless thought.

"You can't teach an old dog new tricks." What makes a dog owner think an old dog might be even remotely interested in learning new tricks? Or any tricks? Have you ever tried to teach a young dog or a middle-aged dog a trick? The process takes months, and when you think the dog has finally mastered the stunt, it'll be forgotten as soon as you want to show it off to your friends. Maybe the dog hasn't forgotten; he just might not be in the mood to perform. I know dogs can be taught to sit up, shake hands, roll over, locate drugs in luggage, jump through hoops, and tear your throat out, but who really cares? Dogs are supposed to bark and wag their tails when they see you, go to the bathroom outdoors in a designated space, and spend the rest of their time gazing at you, adoringly. Personally, I prefer cats, because they already know everything and prefer not to waste valuable nap time learning tricks.

"A bird in the hand is worth two in the bush." My guess is this means that if you already have something, it's better than expending any effort toward obtaining something else. This seems the same as "the grass is always greener on the other side." Aren't both of these clichés promoting laziness and sloth? I'm certainly not suggesting that it's up to me to change them to "a bird in the hand is NOT worth ..." or "the grass is NOT greener ... ," but perhaps a slight modification is in order. "Life is just a bowl of cherries." This strikes me as beyond inane. I don't know anyone (and I know a lot of people) who hasn't experienced at least one major disappointment as she/he navigates through life. Why cherries in a bowl? Why not strawberries, blueberries, Jell-O, or chocolate-chip cookies?

"Too many cooks spoil the broth." I don't like to cook, because I'm not very good at it. When I have a dinner party, I make sure my guests feel involved by giving them a non-challenging food preparation assignment. By doing this, I don't louse anything up, and everyone has something fun to do, while consuming adult beverages before we dine. If whatever the guests help prepare doesn't emerge in edible condition, it's not my fault. "You can lead a horse to water, but you can't make him drink." Does this mean you can convince people to do something, but when the time comes to actually do it, they might not? Or does it suggest that you can make sure the horse will arrive at the designated watering hole, but if he isn't thirsty, you've wasted your time? You tell me.

"Do as I say and not as I do." I understand this. My father used to say it to me all the time, only he omitted the second part. "A stitch in time saves nine." About this, I am clueless. Maybe because I don't sew. Perhaps, it suggests that if you take your time, whatever it is you're taking your time with will be done better than if you hurried. Nine what? Stitches? The person who said this in the first place probably used the word "nine," because it rhymes with "time."

"It's a small world." This is good. It's what you say when you're in Tibet and encounter someone from Chicago who used to know your next door neighbor's cousin. "There's no fool like an old fool." Wrong! We all know lots of fools, many who are in their 20s, 30s and 40s and not old. Perhaps, I've misinterpreted this cliché, and it's actually a compliment to old fools. I hope so.

In spite of all of the above, or maybe because of it, the next time a stranger asks you to "have a nice day," feel free to respond, "Sorry, I've made other plans."

Called Up from the Minors

Spring 1992

Tim Shestak

I've been taught that actions are the foundation to all my growth, mental and spiritual. All I ever learned from ignoring what I needed or wanted to get done is that it doesn't work. Nothing gets done when I sleep for fourteen hours. No knowledge can be absorbed when I am in a coma.

Time has been a patient teacher. Time has allowed me to have a kitchen where my experiences can go, where they can cook until they can be used to save me from making the same mistakes again. Time has taught me that I didn't have to have it all figured out yesterday, that I won't get kicked off the planet for using the phrase, "I don't know." It has, thankfully, robbed me of the stately intellect I had at seventeen, that great thinking that led me to quit high school to go surfing.

My education has been one of experience. Watching friends die, being trapped thousands of miles from home: broke, fighting through nights where I felt my only option was suicide, and having my father tell me one sunny afternoon that the only way our relationship could continue is if he never saw me again. These have all taught me deep lessons. Being educated is a frame of mind for me, where I can approach new ideas with my pride and ego displaced, so that with an open mind, I might see the world in a richer way.

A proper education would be one where I would grow each day in my dealings with others, where I would grow spiritually; my faith and wisdom giving me the ability to attach each problem with strength and hunger. To deal with life on its terms and come out smiling, knowing I did the best I could. I have only recently become interested in what I can learn at school. I have been called up from the minors. Every day I do my best to swing for the fences.

Elvis has left the building.

Watching His Woods

Spring 1995

Jan Shoemaker

A fine mist was falling, as we pulled up to the spotless, L-shaped, white house. Square corners and fresh paint concealed its age. It seemed newly constructed by neat little carpenters wearing white work clothes. We pulled around back and walked up to the side of the barn part of the L. I imagined Robert Frost's children playing on piles of hay in the loft.

After watching a video of Frost reading his own poetry, we moved on through the L into the potato storehouse, the bathroom, and finally, the kitchen. Even the places where the animals stayed were "New England neat." The animals were kept, and the crops were stored for winter in the L, so the Frosts could reach them during bitter blizzards of December and January. Rows of canned vegetables lined the storehouse wall, just as if Mrs. Frost had carefully arranged them. After apple picking, Frost must have piled baskets with sweet-smelling apples in this room.

As we passed through the New England neat kitchen, I imagined Mrs. Frost paring apples at her gray zinc sink and setting plates at the round table, as golden sunlight slanted through her white curtains. The next room was my favorite. In the center of a large parlor sat a big, old, lumpy, green chair with wide wooden arms. It was in this very chair where Robert Frost had written his poems. I could just see his white shock of hair sticking out over his forehead as he began, "Two roads diverged in a yellow wood ... ."

Seeing the excitement in my eyes, my friend urged me to crawl under the rope to sit in the chair – right where my hero wrote his poems. It didn't take much urging for me to yield to the temptation. My friend made it easier by distracting the guide. As I gingerly sank into the chair, careful not to disturb the ghost that seemed to hover over the chair, I felt strangely inspired by the simplicity of the room. Great work, after all, often comes from simple surroundings. Greatness must be all around us, and we don't even know it.

Later, we strolled beside the mending wall that had inspired Frost's famous poem. I imagined Frost's ancient, simian neighbor trudging on the other side as they rebuilt the wall each spring. Instead of adding a

175

rock, I succumbed to temptation again and "borrowed" a small, flat stone. There were plenty to replace it, and I knew that Frost never liked the wall anyway. That rock sits on my mantle now, and sometimes, when I touch its flat, smooth coldness, I can smell the wet mist again and hear Frost's New England twang.

We followed the wall to the wood in back and then followed a little road through the trees. Lush, green ferns, red-berried vines, and thick undergrowth carpeted the ground under tall bone-white birches. Deep in the woods, a small stream slipped quietly over dark rocks. Then, the little road diverged into two paths. My friend wandered down one; I took the other, and that has made all the difference. I think Frost would not mind our stopping there for a while to watch his woods fill up with moisture. I don't think he'd begrudge the flat stone either or even my sitting in his chair. He would know we needed that pause in life and time, before we moved on to the promises we had to keep and the miles we had to go.

Boats :: Jay Worden

Sowing Seeds for a Spring Harvest

Spring 1997

Roxanne Slattery

Henry David Thoreau was born on July 12, 1817, in Concord, Massachusetts. He considered writing as his primary vocation and began to write journal recordings at the age of twenty; by the time of his death on May 6, 1862, Thoreau's journal writings consisted of over forty manuscript volumes. In an 1850 journal entry, Thoreau wrote that "our thoughts are epochs of our life; all else is but a journal of the winds that blew while we were here."

Thoreau's literary and spiritual mentor was Ralph Waldo Emerson, who nurtured Thoreau's literary and philosophical development with "Self-Reliance" and other writings about existentialism. Developing theories and followings of his own, Thoreau eventually surpassed his master's teachings; although Emerson served as the teacher, it was Thoreau, the student, who left the greater impact upon society.

Thoreau's teachings of transcendentalism greatly influenced intellectual and literary movements. His book, *Civil Disobedience*, inspired Mahatma Gandhi's passive-resistance movement. Thoreau taught that securing the basic human necessities would facilitate personal fulfillment. Consequently, Thoreau also asserted that when an individual exceeds the most basic requirements of sustenance and material goods, the likelihood of reaching personal contentment is greatly impaired.

On Independence Day, July 4, 1845, Thoreau moved into a self-made hut that was located on Emerson's property. Thoreau inhabited an area known as Walden's Pond; the uncivilized location of the pond provided the setting for the experiences that are chronicled in Thoreau's most famous work, *Walden*, originally entitled *Life in the Woods*. It illustrates the Naturalists' ideal mode of life and provides a prototype for obtaining personal contentment.

Thoreau uses *Walden* as the vehicle to deliver a challenge to the reader – a meaningful life is promised as the reward for an individual who is non-conforming enough to endure a Spartan-like lifestyle. Thoreau argues that physical isolation from commercialized society is necessary in order to gain such enlightenment. The author asserts that humanity may only repair the societal errors of materialism and egocentrism as a result of transcendental ideologies and pursuits. The recurrent images and metaphors of nature symbolize Thoreau's self-proclaimed state of utopian contentment when stating: "There are probably words addressed to our condition exactly, which, if we could really hear and understand, would be more salutary than the morning or the spring to our lives ... morning is when I am awake and there is dawn in me." Henry David Thoreau identifies the state of self-fulfillment as the earning of and spending of life's "morning."

According to Stanley Cavell in *The Senses of Walden*, Thoreau found great inspiration from other literary works when constructing *Walden's* first chapter, "The Economy." Cavell notes the specific parallels between this chapter and the writings of Xenophon 6, especially, concerning Oeconomicus and Memorabilia. In "The Economy," Thoreau states, "a man's rich in proportion to the number of things which he can afford to let alone." In Memorabilia, the character of Socrates orates, "my belief is that to have no wants is divine; to have as few as possible comes next to divine." Both authors refute the popular theory that a man's wealth and success depend upon the amount of property or material goods owned; furthermore, Thoreau's writings define an object's worth as the quantity and quality of effort spent in securing the property.

In *The Roots of Walden* and the *Tree of Life*, Gordon Boudreau compares "The Economy" to Benjamin Franklin's *Autobiography* and to the verses of "Poor Richard." The teachings common to both Thoreau and Franklin include: the construction of an economic and efficient dwelling; the building of a conveniently-structured house; the virtues of diligence, early rising, and industry; and also, the pitfalls of society's economy and industry. The works of both Franklin and Thoreau caution others against financial and material dependency. Thoreau taught that this self-sufficiency should extend to an individual's manner of living. Regarding deliberate isolation, Thoreau wrote that "individuals, like nations, must have suitably broad and natural boundaries, even a considerable neutral ground, between them."

Henry D. Thoreau devotes the first chapter of *Walden* to the dispelling of common misconceptions regarding labor, property, and spending habits. The items which are "necessary of life," according to the author, consist of: "Food, Shelter, Clothing and Fuel." Thoreau asserts that most of humanity attempts to secure gains beyond the bare essentials. According to Thoreau's calculations, only six weeks of manual labor (other than self-employment) are needed in order to afford an entire year's worth of life's basic necessities; furthermore, those who exceed such a regimen merely manage to clutter their lives and houses with worthless materials. The person who labors for others, his entire life-long, is left without the time to create a meaningful life.

In Edwin Way Teale's book *The Thoughts of Thoreau*, Teale illustrates Thoreau's dedication to self-education and philosophical pursuits; in a letter to Harrison Blake, Thoreau expressed his feelings of "guilt" over burning trees for fuel – explaining that the concerns of humanity should not be over keeping warm, but instead, over what an individual accomplishes while he is kept warm.

Walden's chapter entitled "Reading" defines Thoreau's views on proper self-education. Thoreau explains that all of humanity should be scholarly in the ancient classics and in the ancient scriptures; a true reading of such ancient classics must be accomplished in the works' original language. In "Reading," Thoreau states that "books are the treasured wealth of the world and the fit inheritance of generations and nations." Being quite well-versed in classic literature and in classical languages is only the first step to literary scholarship; the transcendentalist also advocates that "we need to be provoked" by literature and by life. In defining the concept of "good readers," Thoreau states: "I think that having learned our letters we should read the best that is in literature, and not be forever repeating our a-b-c's, and words of one syllable, in the fourth or fifth classes, sitting on the lowest and foremost form all our lives. Most men are satisfied if they read or hear read, and perchance have been convicted by the wisdom of one good book, the Bible, and for the rest of their lives vegetate and dissipate their faculties in what is called easy reading."

In "Reading," Thoreau acknowledges the importance of learning from humanity's founders and from humanity's past in order to shape an enlightened future. Regarding the literary historians such as Homer, Shakespeare, and Confucius, Thoreau reveals that "there are the stars, and they who can, may read them." A reader must "laboriously seek the meaning of each word and line"; in other words, all works and lessons of life must be actively deciphered if one is to ever bask in the glory of dawn. By accepting the challenge of a provoking life, an individual learns how to identify and develop the "I." To discover how to commune with the "I" during life's most wakeful hours is the purpose of *Walden*.

Thoreau's day of departure into the woods was no accident; the author chose the Fourth of July because of what the day symbolized – in gathering the material for *Walden*, Thoreau embarked upon his own Declaration of Spiritual Independence. Thoreau's quest was to discover and define the

"I"; the author of "Reading," Thoreau creatively displays his mastery of linguistics by selecting words which have a duality of meaning. According to Cavell, the word "radical" is used to symbolize a deepening spiritual journey." Central to the art and meaning of *Walden*, the principles of organic growth and vertical travel are combined with the principle of isolated and untamed location. As the radical is part of the plant embryo that develops the primary root, because it serves both as support and a means of nourishment, the radical also serves as the metaphor which proclaims Thoreau's affirmation of independent life.

Thoreau uses the word "seeds" in a dualistic manner; Boudreau explains that the reference is both of a place of residence and, of a plant seed – through metaphors of "making his head a radical burrowing instrument," it is the rooting seed of hope. According to Boudreau, Thoreau's statement, "I think that I shall not buy greedily, but go round … it as long as I live, and be buried in it first," suggests that the seed about to be sown is himself, the "I."

Thoreau insists that "these beans not harvested for economy's sake, went for the sake of the troupes and expression, to a parable-maker"; *Walden*, the parable, reaches a climactic moment in the chapter entitled, "The Bean Field." Man's capacity to survive is put to the test in agricultural terms. The beans are harvested and later, Thoreau remarks that man's "generative energy" might produce such fruits as "Genius, Heroism, (and) Holiness" – that is, if he has within himself the "seeds of a better life."

In the first summer, Thoreau did not read books. Through raising beans, the radical spirit was also cultivated. Thoreau describes the process of being revitalized as "an early twilight ushered in a long evening in which many thoughts had time to take root and unfold themselves." The seeds of intellectual inquiry were beginning to germinate when the author asked of himself, "Am I not partly leaves and vegetable mold myself?"

In "Winter," the seed has been planted below the frost-line, and the pond is a solid sheet of ice. As the pond is imperishable, so too, is the metaphorical land that it reflects. Spring, however, is perennial and everlasting. The melting pond becomes a pure "sea-green," and the renewal of man is described by the earth's melting. Thoreau asks: "What is many but a mass of thawing clay?" Thoreau depicts both the thawing of man and the thawing of nature in the following: "The symbol of perpetual youth, the grass-blade, like a long green ribbon, streams from the sod into the summer, checked indeed by the frost, but anon, pushing on again, lifting its spear of last year's hay with the fresh life below." The seed and root have grown into clay itself; Thoreau praises nature's germination in the pond and asserts that any pond, no matter how deeply frozen, may also become revitalized by nature. Nature demands that humanity abandon its conceit, and in doing so, mankind may flourish as a result of new growth.

According to Boudreau, "Spring" is a time of expressions of truth that combines the outer and inner selves. Thoreau describes Spring as an expression of holiness and divinity. Walden Pond also contained a reflection of tiered, or deepening, realms of reality. In *The Roots of Walden* and the *Tree of Life*, Boudreau illustrates how the pond represented the different degrees of self-knowledge and the knowledge of nature: "Gazing into the 'bottomless' pond was like looking to the backing of a magic mirror wherein one could not only see a reflection of the animal (or animated) self, but also catch a glimpse of an image or shadow divine, a similitude of the 'ungraspable phantom of life' Melville's Ishmael sought in his watery reflections."

Walden's purpose and definition of the word "divine" is difficult to identify. It dramatizes the search to identify the role of God and the nature of divinity. Thoreau wrote: "By the divining rod and thin rising vapors I judge; and here I will begin to mine." Thoreau suggests that God used a divining rod to create Walden Pond. In "Self-Reliance," Emerson argues that a divine god dwells within every man; however, Thoreau appears to acknowledge the existence of a separate divine being. I believe that *Walden* contains an entity which is referred to as God and Nature, synonymously; God and Man exist independently, yet neither may exist exclusively. Francis Bacon, in *Advancement of Learning*, says "the glory of God is to conceal a thing, and the glory of a king is to find it out." Thoreau sought to find out those things – yet, argued that God assisted in an individual's search. Regarding God's role in *Walden*, Thoreau wrote: "Heaven is under our feet as well as over our heads... and he concluded to dig a well here ... who is reported to have dug Walden Pond; a perennial source of our life ... God's Drop (and) a spring of springs."

Thoreau is quite clear about one issue, how individuals must cultivate an understanding and communion with the self. A person should not fear solitude, for if one does, the fear is of knowing one's self. Thoreau's most adamant teaching is that of seeking contentment – a state which may only be reached in the absence of self-deception.

In Walden's "Conclusion," the naturalist returns to civilization; however, the author has not abandoned his convictions. Much like Dante's *Divine Comedy* and Plato's *The Allegory of the Cave*, the enlightened Thoreau returns to the masses to spread his insight among those who remain civilization's captive. According to Boudreau, Dante's writings inspired

Thoreau to depart. In illustrating the parallel between *Walden* and *The Divine Comedy*, Boudreau explains: "Dante Alighieri ... (was) about to pass beneath an arch that proclaimed the loss of hope to all who entered, but instead gave entry to a passage ultimately leading to a heavenly vision of redemption. Thoreau left the woods ... caught glimpses of his inner self ... and (in a land far less forbidding than Dante's) proclaimed the discovery of hope, not its abandonment." In Thoreau's third volume of journal writings, the author wrote: "I see distinctly the Spring Arc thus far." Thoreau has sent out to help humanity mediate the battle between the loss of hope and the regeneration of Spring.

Thoreau did not intend for *Walden* to proclaim the meaning of life; however, it is my belief that he proclaims to know the prescription which will enable a meaningful life to take place. Cavell suggests that the hut is dismantled to symbolize the nation is also being dismantled. I believe that a metaphor to the radical is more accurate; in order to ensure a vital blossoming the following season, a plant will be stronger if pruned – perhaps, the nation must also die back to the root in order to become stronger.

Thoreau identifies the state of self-fulfillment as the earning of and the spending of life's "morning" in order to accomplish the dawn's awakening, the seed must be sowed, and "the root is faith." Thoreau wrote, "So we saunter toward the Holy Land, till one day the sun shall shine more brightly than ever he has done before ..." although both the sun and humanity fall in the West, *Walden* provides the inspiration to seek the Light. Through self-discovery, faith, and the scholarly pursuits, an individual has the power to shape and guide the self to contentment.

"The light which puts out our eyes is darkness to us. Only that day dawns to which we are awake. There is more day to dawn. The sun is but a morning star."

Sandhills Memories

Winter 1996

Mary K. Stillwell

Every summer, except for the year the polio epidemic hit Omaha and we headed west to the relative safety of Seattle, my grandmother and I set off to visit Aunt Helen and Uncle Leo in the Sandhills. Each summer, I was taken by surprise.

Suitcases appeared without warning by the front door, and Grandma called, "It's time to go." We caught the street car at the corner down to Union Station where the announcer listed the towns we'd pass through – West Point, Wisner, Norfolk, Meadow Grove, Tilden, Neligh, O'Neill, Atkinson, Bassett, Long Pine, Ainsworth, Wood Lake – as though they were the ties of the track along which we would travel into the heart of Cherry County.

We boarded the train quickly and quietly, eager to hear the "All Aboard" and feel the first lurch forward. I remember the acrid smell of coal dust in the air, the bite of the dense wool seat covers, the crinkling and the crackling of waxed paper that accompanied the bouquet of bologna and Velveeta that bloomed through the car as soon as the train cars curved north, then picked up speed.

I have no recollection of ever arriving or being met at the station in Valentine. As far as I know, I just suddenly woke to sunlight in my cousins' bedroom where great pink roses and peonies bloomed from their own deep mossy green bed on the floor.

Aunt Helen and Uncle Leo, along with my grandparents and their other brothers and sisters who still lived in Cherry County, represented the prairie and homesteading to me, and they seemed to carry in their actions and features the treasures of my heritage. To wake in the Sandhills was to feel an immediate connection to a determined, courageous, smart, funny, and sometimes cantankerous tribe of pioneers.

Summers were busy. By the time I was out of bed and dressed, ready to start my day, Aunt Helen was frying more bacon and another platter of eggs in the kitchen. Try as I might, I never made it up for early breakfast, even in order to catch sight of Edgar Fisher, a dark and mysterious man who fascinated me one whole summer for reasons now lost. Instead, I ate during the second breakfast shift, long after the men were gone. I dawdled, listening to Aunt Helen and Grandma talking in the kitchen.

There was always talk. As far as I know Aunt Helen and Grandma never ran out of things to say to one another. Uncle Leo joined them in the evenings while my cousin, Bob, played the piano, and I crunched the Indian corn that Marlys, my cousin closest in age, roasted in the cast iron skillet.

Outside there was always plenty of excitement. Aunt Helen and Uncle Leo's house was perched at the edge of a canyon – with its quick, quiet creek where minnows shot back and forth under the glint of the sun and through the small dark rifts of shade and where all sorts of wild and mysterious things lived and grew. I have a dim memory of my older cousin, Ella, taking me for my first horseback ride, a walk around the corral astride Buttons. And Strip, certainly I remember Strip. He was the first – but not the last – horse to toss me from his back.

I remember getting into plenty of trouble for climbing up the windmill and for giving the neighbor boy a black eye after a 4-H meeting. There nearly always seemed to be chokecherries, wild cherries, wild grapes, and sandburs, too, plenty of mud to go wading in, plenty of envy the summer when Marlys got her first bra.

Like two sides of the same coin, Aunt Helen always made me glad to be just who I was, and Uncle Leo reminded me I could be a little bit better. They called each other Mother and Father, and while I was there, I was a child of near paradise.

"It's time to go," I call to my own family now, and when we arrive in the Sandhills, Aunt Helen and Uncle Leo welcome us with the same warmth and hospitality as they welcomed my grandmother and me years ago. My husband and I take our children back, time after time, so they, too, will remember the murmur of adults talking late at night, of grasshoppers flying across the grasses. I want them to recall how we followed the twin crescents of deer tracks deep into the heart of the canyon, walked along the quick, quiet creek where minnows still shoot back and forth under the glint of the sun and through the small dark rifts of shade, where all sorts of wild and mysterious things live and grow.

I Believe in Music

Spring 1996

Michael Strauss

When I ran the "Outreach Program" for the Omaha Symphony, I brought classical music into high school rooms creating "Classic Classes." I related music to the subject studied, usually English or the Humanities. I played music on my viola to enhance the ideas I taught. At the end of a class, I'd say, "If you enjoyed this experience, you can recreate it by attending an Omaha Symphony concert. I can get you great seats for only $6. I am not interested in warehousing bored teen-agers into the Orpheum, so you really have to want to go." In the third year of the program, I addressed more than 1,000 students at 12 different high schools and colleges and sold more than 500 tickets.

I developed different approaches in my classroom visits. The first was culture. Many feel intimidated by the idea of "culture." They equate it with high-brow boredom, but when we look up the word in a dictionary, we find that it arises from the Latin root, "colis," to till the soil. Your "culture" is the ground on which you grow.

What would you like to grow in your own personal culture? Agar is the culture of choice for nurturing bacteria. Nazi Germany cultured genocidal hatred. Some consider Nebraska to be the Number One culture in America for growing football players. In what direction do you see you and your friends moving? What are the cultural influences that nudge you in that direction? Do you ever feel bombarded by messages of violence, rage, sex, narcissism, noise, and cruelty all hiding behind the façade of "cool?" Is there any way for you to take control of your own personal culture?

I believe listening to beautiful, flowing, thoughtful, classical music creates a culture of reflection, gentleness, integrity, and passion. If you experiment and admit to your own personal culture, such music and listening to it with your whole being, affects your thinking, feelings, and activities.

Let's pretend that this article is a classroom visit. We sit together listening to a recording of "Prelude to the Afternoon of a Fawn," an orchestral composition by Claude Debussy. This music makes a world unlike our everyday world, but it is only the first step in our journey. This beauty is an invitation to explore a strange land, yourself.

Listen to this exquisite flow of colors and shapes. Sensuous. Transparent. Moist and alive. It has no words. Nothing to tell you what to think or feel, except for the constantly shifting chords and melodies, which are gone before you can blink. If you relax into the flow, the music creates a world of its own. If you find yourself hearing a story, it is your individual and private dreams.

If you can't imagine classical music, tune your radio to Public Broadcasting. Now that you can hear it, what does it mean? A psychology researcher with a difficult name, Mihaly Csikszentmihalyi (Me-cha-ye-Chick-sent-me-hi!) developed an idea that he calls "flow," the second idea I brought with me into classrooms.

Three elements create a flow situation. There must be a goal, rules, and feedback. This explains why games are fun. In basketball, the goal is to put the ball in the basket. One rule is you're not allowed to push a defender out of the way, and one element of feedback is the score.

If your opponents are too good for you, you may get discouraged and not have fun, unless you change the goal from winning the game to learning more about how to play. If your opponents are too easy, you may get complacent, lose interest, and possibly get shocked and lose! There are limitless combinations possible, but the ideal situation is one in which both teams challenge themselves to the max. When that occurs, everyone is in the flow.

Reading can be a flow experience. The goal may be to gather information with the hope of creating new choices for yourself. The rules are to read accurately and critically, following along with words, phrases, sentences, and paragraphs, thinking at every step about what the writer is trying to communicate. Feedback comes when you ask, "Can these ideas be useful to me? Does Michael Strauss have anything to share about culture, music, and thinking which I might apply to my own life?"

Bored? I hope not, but if you are, say so out loud. It's okay. My feelings won't be hurt, but it's too late for me to do anything about it. These "fine lines" have already been published. If you are bored, take it as feedback that these lines may be either too complex or too simple.

What to do about it? You could stop reading, or you could get a dictionary to help you with the words you don't know, or you can put some effort into reading between the lines. Reading between the lines raises the challenge. The dictionary raises your level of understanding.

Still reading? Good! How do these ideas relate to music? When I play viola for classes, I explain that a Back Prelude is harmonically far more complex than pop, folk, or rock tunes. Becoming absorbed in the flow of the complexity provides a challenge that promotes intellectual and spiritual growth. It's like weight training and running; if you don't extend yourself, you don't get stronger and faster. Once you get into the habit of challenging yourself, that process becomes satisfying, and anything less becomes boring!

The flow of music is like the flow of thought. Students discover when they immerse themselves in the flow of complex music; it deepens and enriches the flow of thinking and writing. I've heard students say, "I looked up from my writing while you were playing and looked around the room and everyone was writing and thinking, and it was totally quiet except for the music and the sound of pens on the page."

My third major idea, borrowed from the ancient Greeks, is we all live in two worlds. We live in a world of our own. We also live in a world with others.

Listening to music together brings people into a shared world. Many people lead lives in which the two worlds have grown out-of-balance. They lack the energy to notice the world we share together. Listen. Debussy. "Prelude to the Afternoon of a Fawn." In my private world, the music is happening. Borrow a recording from the library and listen. When we listen to music together, we share a public world while also enhancing the experience of our own private worlds.

That's the paradox: the more we focus on respecting and sharing common goals with others, the more we express and experience our private goals. This paradox is the message great music brings to us, to sensitize ourselves both to others and self. The paradox works in reverse: the better we take care of ourselves, the better we care for others.

That's the end of today's class. If you enjoyed it, continue the experiences by getting tickets for the Omaha Symphony. Call the box office: 342-0635. Tell them Michael Strauss sent you.

Dr. Seuss: Oh, the Stories He Could Tell

Winter 1996

William Tarbox

Have you ever seen a Sneetch, a Snarf, a Lorax, or a cat in a hat? Have you ever met a Zook or a Yook or a man named Sam who likes to eat green eggs and ham? If you've ever picked up a book by Dr. Seuss, you've met these and other strange and unusual looking people and animals, with equally strange and unusual names. Dr. Seuss entertained us with his drawings and writings for fifty-two years.

Ted Geisel, better known as Dr. Seuss, had a passion for putting his incredible imagination and talents onto paper in the form of cartoons and books. His books always seemed to have a greater purpose than just teaching kids to read. Some of his books displayed his anger and sadness over the terrible things that he noticed happening in the world around him. Others were comments on the lighter side of life.

From an early age, Ted Geisel was fascinated with writing stories and drawing his unusual characters. His father was the zookeeper at the city zoo in his hometown of Springfield, Massachusetts. Ted would often accompany his father to work. While his father worked, Ted would draw the animals that he saw at the zoo. Of course, his illustrations of the animals were often quite different than how they really looked. One of his animals had ears three feet long. Some were brightly colored, while others would adopt human characteristics and would often sport shoes, hats or clothing. He drew upon these childhood memories when he wrote one of his best-selling books, *If I Ran the Zoo*.

After high school, Ted went to Dartmouth College, and with the encouragement of an English teacher, he began to write. Ted could write about almost any subject and make it sound interesting. By the end of his junior year, he was the editor of the school's humor magazine called *The Jack O'Lantern*. Geisel wrote news for the college newspaper, *The Daily Dartmouth*. He was far from the "perfect" student, and after getting into trouble during his senior year, he was asked to resign as editor. To get around this ban, he submitted his cartoons and stories using his mother's maiden name of Seuss.

After graduation, Ted went to England and attended Oxford University. While a student there, he met his future wife, Helen. Ted dropped out of school and came back to the United States. He felt he had to get a job in order to marry Helen, so he held several jobs drawing cartoons for local papers and magazines. He was doing a regular cartoon feature called *Boids and Beasties*. He signed his cartoons with the name Dr. Theophrastus Seuss to make them sound more professional. Later, he would shorten it to Dr. Seuss. One of Ted's editors read a report in *Life* magazine that stated children were having trouble learning to read. He gave Ted a list of 250 words that every first grader should know. He challenged Ted to write a book using only these words. Ted was unsure that anyone could write a book using so few words. Ted took up the challenge, and after nine months, he wrote his most famous book, *The Cat in the Hat*. Ted wrote the book using only 220 words. Because of the success of *The Cat in the Hat*, the firm that published the book, Random House, developed a new children's book division. They put Ted in charge. He became very interested in helping kids learn to read, and this inspired him to write many books.

Ted loved a challenge. His publisher, Bennett Cerf, bet Ted that he couldn't write an entire book using only fifty words. The book he wrote was another classic called *Green Eggs and Ham*. Ted was inspired in many ways to write other books. His book, *Horton Hatches the Egg*, was inspired when a breeze blew a sketch of an elephant onto another sketch of a tree. Ted wondered what would make that elephant be up in a tree. The answer, as it turns out, is that Horton had volunteered to baby-sit an egg, while the mother took a vacation. Through this book, Ted teaches a lesson about faithfulness to promises.

Ted visited the city of Hiroshima after it was bombed in World War II. This sorrowful visit was the inspiration for the second book that featured the elephant Horton. It was called *Horton Hears a Hoo*. The book was about the importance of every life and that each person deserves to be safe no matter what his size. As Horton would say, "A person's a person, no matter how small."

In the *Butter Battle Book*, Ted depicted two opposing armies, the Zooks and the Yooks. They disagreed over how to butter their bread. The disagreement quickly escalates, and the two groups are poised in their bunkers with weapons aimed at each other waiting for the other to attack. In this book, Ted was voicing his disgust with the nuclear arms race and tried to show how silly it was for people to fight. The last page of the book is left blank inviting the reader to visualize an ending.

Not all of Ted's books were well liked. *The Lorax*, was about greedy creatures called the Once-lers who were cutting down all the trees in the forest. The Lorax was another creature that lived in the forest. He tried to persuade the Once-lers to stop cutting down trees before it was too late. Those in the logging community felt threatened by this book and tried to ban it. The message that Ted was trying to teach children and adults was the importance of preserving the environment and standing up for what they believe in. Ted left the last two pages of this book blank also. As with the *Butter Battle Book*, he left the ending up to the imagination of the reader.

Although most of Ted's books were written for children, he did write two books for adults. One was called *You're Only Old Once*. It was based on the many people he had seen in the waiting room at the office of his doctor. The second book, *Oh the Places You'll Go*, was written for adults and children alike. It encouraged his readers to take chances and try new things.

Ted Geisel won many awards for his unique cartoons and writing style. He received a Pulitzer Citation, an Emmy for *How the Grinch Stole Christmas*, an Academy award for a film he made during World War II, and several Peabody Awards.

On September 24, 1991, at the age of eighty-seven, Ted Geisel died. It is fortunate for us that he was able to mirror that imagination onto paper and share it with the world. He was always ready to accept a challenge. When that challenge was to help children learn to read, he met it with a passion. Ted Geisel is not really gone; he will always live on in the character of Dr. Seuss. Ted Geisel and his array of unique characters are as close as the nearest library.

Lessons on Leavenworth

Summer 2002

Ted Theisen

My basketball leaves small round craters in the soft snow where I
dribble it on the frozen sidewalk. My breath tags close behind me, a small
cloud following me home as I walk back from the downtown YMCA.
The snowdrifts muffle the sounds of the sleeping city slowly awakening
to Saturday morning. The police siren is barely audible until the officer's
snow-frosted car passes me; the sound of the snow crunching beneath its
tires is as loud as the slow wailing of its siren. My bitterness towards my
parents "encouraging" me to move out after high school is almost as cold as
the weather. I yearn for the comfort of their home in suburbia. I feel out of
place. I feel too young to be living on my own.

My run-down apartment looms closer, as my toes go numb. The
moisture from the snow creeps through my basketball shoes. A mass of
people loiter in front of the door, trying to warm themselves from the fire in
a trash can. The smell of burning trash and body odor rapes my senses. They
try to warm themselves more with their bottle of breakfast vodka, which is
wrapped in its own brown-bag parka.

While I descend to my basement apartment, I forget about the broken
corner of the last step and knock it to the ground with a thud. I swear under
my breath. That step has been broken, since I moved into the apartment
last summer. My blood boils, as I wonder when my lackadaisical landlord
will fix it. When I crouch down to replace the worn step, I notice an elderly
woman doubled over an orange snow shovel, which appears to have
impaled her body. She attempts to clear the snow from her sidewalk. I
shrug, turn away, and creep into my apartment to hide from society, hoping
to sit down and pout about how rough I have it. I ponder what brought me
to this low point in my life. I have my own problems. I am about to realize
that I don't have a clue what it meant to be thankful for what I have. I am
about to find that I am incredibly fortunate to have what I do.

The art-deco turquoise refrigerator I lean against stands in sharp
contrast to the white snowdrift against the kitchen window. I can barely
see over the snow as I peer out at the woman who is attempting to shovel

her walkway. She grasps the end of the shovel and tries to push with every ounce of energy that she can muster. A sharp wind rips through her clothing, swirling snow around her ankles, nearly blowing her over. When the wind passes, she continues scooping her teaspoon-like scoops of snow, making little progress. While kneeling over the archaic cast-iron radiator watching her, I char my hand; leaving pulsating red grate marks on my palm. I curse at the landlord for leaving me to rot in such God-forsaken living conditions. I feel sorry for the old woman. I am confused as to why the vodka-drinking vagrants out front around the blazing trashcan won't help her. Hypocritically, I think to myself that they are truly worthless. I feel the urge to pray to God to help her out, so I pray that God will provide some help for her.

As I pray, my stomach twists in my gut, and I realize how heartless I am. I cannot believe the hypocritical thoughts in my mind. I am in disbelief that I walked right past this woman, while I was dribbling a basketball, and she could barely hold up a shovel. I know that God wants me to help her out. God is probably disappointed in me that I didn't offer her help when I walked past her the first time.

I put my coat back on and jaunt back up the cement steps, careful not to knock the corner off the bottom step this time. I step around the people huddled by the trashcan and make a beeline toward her small home. I wave and introduce myself in one motion.

She seems very grateful and relieved when I offer to finish for her. She hands me her tiny shovel, and I proceed to finish what she started. It is a very easy job. As I work, I glance at her house. Her home is camouflaged nicely within the urban jungle. Its exterior matches every other aspect of the buildings around. There are cracked windows with tinfoil accents to cover up holes. A screen door screeches, begging to fall from the frame of the house, as it hangs from one hinge. The house doesn't appear to have more than three rooms.

Upon completion, I open the front screen door, careful to not break the remaining hinge, and quietly knock. When the old woman answers, she invites me in. I set the shovel outside the door and enter. The slamming of the interior door disturbs several cockroaches and sends them scuttling to find other hiding places. The old woman scrambles away as well, leaving me and the roaches to wait in front of the breezy door. The woman returns, fumbling through a beige purse that is so overstuffed she is unable to close it. Old handkerchiefs and abandoned papers escape from her purse and float to the floor, as she continues her rummaging for some loose change. I interrupt her quest and inform her that it isn't necessary to pay me. She pauses, shrugs, and smiles.

She says, "At least come meet my husband."

I agree and follow her to the interior of her house, stepping over stacks of old newspapers that are adorning the green shag carpet of the hallway.

The living room looks more like a hospital room. The coffee table is littered with numerous, brown prescription bottles and a green, oxygen tank. A hospital bed takes the place of the sofa and engulfs the majority of the room. The old man occupying the bed shakes off his quilt and extends his hand toward me. When I grasp his hand, his firm grip crushes my knuckles. A smile shapes his mouth. After he settles down, they both talk without pausing. I learn of the history of their home, their family, the neighborhood that we live in, their medical history, and what they believe is the cure for the common cold. The both talk to me, but they rarely look at me. With each story they tell, they harvest numerous smiles from one another. They are truly in love with each other and are incredibly happy even amidst their poverty and their sickness. I stay and listen to their stories.

Webster defines one of the definitions of wealth as "characterized by abundance." This couple definitely doesn't have an abundance of material possessions or money, but they are wealthy. Their wealth was accumulated through the investment in their relationship with one another. This is something that no amount of money can purchase.

There is a pause in the conversation, so I stand and thank them profusely for their hospitality. As I step outside, I realize that the jaunt to my apartment looks much more inviting than it did earlier in the day. I kneel down, pick up an empty vodka bottle, and toss it into the now abandoned trash can. There is black smoke slowly billowing up from the can, but it doesn't bother me so much.

I grasp the cast-iron railing as I start down the cement steps and descend slowly into my apartment. The broken corner of the step is protruding from the snow like a miniature tombstone again. I don't bother to pick it up and fix it this time. I let the broken step stay in its resting place and accept the fact that getting the step fixed is out of my control.

"Hopefully, the landlord will take care of it soon," I think to myself. I know now that He is in control.

I am instantly warmed as I enter my kitchen once again. I don't feel like I did a good deed for society. I feel like society did a good deed for me. I am thankful for what I have. Even though I don't have much money, I am able to play basketball, I am healthy, and I have good friends. I pray to God that He will someday give me a life with a fraction of the happiness that the old couple has.

I realize that the least of the reasons God wanted me to help out the old couple was because they needed a clear path in front of their house. The main reason He wanted me to help them was so they could help me. They showed me many things that are more important than money and comfort. They gave me a new outlook on life, and I also made new friends in the process.

> *"I never had a policy; I have just tried to do my very best each and every day."*
>
> - Abraham Lincoln

They Knew It All!

The word "skyscraper," used first in 1840, referred to a four-story building.

"This 'telephone' has too many shortcomings to be seriously considered as a means of communication. The device is inherently of no value to us" (Western Union internal memo, 1876).

"The wireless music box has no imaginable commercial value. Who would pay for a message sent to nobody in particular?" (David Sarnoff's associates in response to his urgings for investment in the radio in the 1920s).

"While theoretically television may be feasible, commercially and financially, I consider it an impossibility, a development of which we need waste little time dreaming" (Lee de Forest, inventor of the cathode ray tube, 1926).

"Who the hell wants to hear actors talk?" (Warner Brothers on the proposal of film with sound, 1927).

"I think there is a world market for about five computers" (Thomas J. Watson, Chairman of the Board of IBM, 1943).

"This is the biggest fool thing we've ever done. The bomb will never go off, and I speak as an expert on explosives" (admiral William Leahy to President Truman, 1945).

"Computers in the future may weigh no more than 1.5 tons" (*Popular Mechanics*, forecasting the relentless march of science, 1949).

"We don't think they will do anything in their market. Guitar groups are on their way out" (a recording company that turned down the Beatles, 1962).

"With over fifteen types of foreign cars already on sale here, the Japanese auto industry isn't likely to carve out a big share of the market for itself" (*Business Week*, 1968).

"But what ... is it good for?" (an engineer at IBM, commenting on the microchip, 1968).

" ... there is no reason anyone would want a computer in their home" (Ken Olson, President, Chairman, and Founder of Digital Equipment, 1977).

"640 K ought to be enough for anybody" (Bill Gates, 1981).

Enlightenment: What Is It?

Autumn 1993

Joe Thomas

In his book, *No Water No Moon: Reflection on Zen*, Bhagwan Shree Rajneesh devotes a chapter to the following poem.

"No Water, No Moon"

The nun Chiyono
studied for years
but was unable to find Enlightenment.

One night,
she was carrying
an old pail filled with water.

As she was walking along,
she was watching the full moon
reflected in the pail of water.

Suddenly, the bamboo strips
that held the pail together
broke, and the pail fell apart.

The water rushed out;
the moon's reflection disappeared –
and Chiyono became Enlightened.

She wrote this verse:

This way and that way
I tried to keep the pail together,
hoping the weak bamboo

would never break.

Suddenly, the bottom fell out.
No more water;
no more moon in the water –
emptiness in my hand.

Enlightenment is always sudden. Everyone has, at one time or another, worked on a problem and given up or had to do another project. I would hate to count the times I worked all day without finding the solution to a problem.

Often, I will be not more than a few blocks from work, walking home, when the answer to a problem comes. Without thinking about it at the time, a solution will appear. Once, I only made it around the corner of the building before that light bulb came on over my head.

Buddhist Enlightenment is like that too. All the studying in the world will not bring Enlightenment. However, the study is necessary. If I do not study the problem, then I will not know the solution when it does come to me.

We cannot plan for Enlightenment. It is not like high school or college, where after passing so many credit hours and certain classes, the student graduates.

Chiyono was a beautiful young woman. The old folks sent her away because they felt that her beauty would distract the other monks. She turned her face so she would be accepted. She studied hard for many years and did not receive Enlightenment. It does not come just because one studies hard or does everything else that is necessary. Enlightenment will not come if one has not prepared. A person must be ready, then Enlightenment will come. It is then we understand all that we know and realize the universe as one.

When the pail broke, Chiyono was Enlightened. She saw what the pail was like and what she held in her mind. It was only an image. The moon did not exist in the pail. Enlightenment did not exist in her mind. Then she understood existence. That was her way of finding Enlightenment.

A person could carry old, rotting buckets of water every night, each with a full moon for the next five hundred years and not find Enlightenment. People must find Enlightenment in their own way. We are all carrying old pails; they are our minds. There is nothing new in there, just old things. The mind is always old. As soon as we know something, it is old. Not only is it old, but it has been colored by what is already in our minds. So, it is neither new nor true.

"Live fully in the moment" may sound trite, and a few weeks ago I would have agreed. How can a person "live fully in the moment," when often we are not following our bliss? How can a person claim to be happy when forced to perform unpleasant tasks? Show me a parent who enjoys changing a diaper, and I will show you a person I do not care to be seated next to at dinner. An intelligent person does not enjoy doing unpleasant tasks. Anyone with enough brains to see something is unpleasant has enough brains not to enjoy doing it.

However, Zen teaches that if we are truly into what we are doing, we will find bliss even in a distasteful task. The point that the task becomes unpleasant is the moment that we conceive it to be unpleasant. When we live in the moment and we conceive the moment to be pleasant, it is just that.

The idea of "momentness" is that only NOW is real. All of our past is clouded by our memory and filtered through our mind. What is in the mind is not real. Our perceptions condition the facts before they are stored in our minds. Any memory starts to spoil, but like wine, some memories improve with age. If we live in the present, we do not allow the past to influence our moment NOW.

Each second is a new experience. Why try to live in the past, if it was unpleasant? Why try to relive the past, if it was pleasant? Reruns are never as good as the first time. Why try to live a lie? Our mind's version of the past is a lie. Remember, "To thy own self be true."

If we live in the moment, let's give it our full attention. Then we will find our bliss. The present task is the most important we have ever undertaken. The present task is our only real task. When we grasp the importance of the present moment, we are able to make the simplest task pleasant. By doing our very best, we will have the personal satisfaction of a job well done. It is human nature to feel good when we do well. Who could perform a personal best and not be happy, proud, and even a little boastful? Do our personal best every moment, and we will follow our bliss.

A good dancer does not live in the past. The good dancer does not dwell on stepping on a partner's toe. Some partners dwell in the past. The good dancer lives in the present. A great dancer is one with the partner, the music, and the floor. All effort flows into the dance, and the moment is beautiful.

During the Olympiad, no gym, no field, no court, or track has athletes living in the past. Good performers do not worry about past failures. They live only in the moment. Nothing else matter but NOW. After winning an event, there is pain on their faces and tears of joy in their eyes.

Somewhere in my life, filtered through my mind, I found the expression. "The past is the crutch of the weak." Living in the moment, I should claim the phrase for myself. Living in the moment, such a well turned phrase gives me bliss. Living in the moment, there could be no plagiarism. The moment is bliss, and I dance with my writing.

Number 11 :: Walker Plank

Proud to Be a Teacher

Summer 2005

Jesse Ugalde

"Where are the heroes of today?" a radio talk show host thundered. He blames society's shortcomings on education. Too many people are looking for heroes in all the wrong places. Movie stars and rock musicians, athletes and models aren't heroes; they're celebrities.

Heroes abound in public schools, a fact that doesn't make the news. There is no precedent for the level of violence, drugs, broken homes, child abuse, and crime in today's America. Education didn't create these problems, but it deals with them every day.

You want heroes? Consider Dave Sanders, the school teacher shot to death while trying to shield his students from two youth on a shooting rampage at Columbine High School in Littleton, Colorado. Sanders gave his life, along with 12 students, and other less heralded heroes survived the Colorado blood bath.

You want heroes? Jane Smith, a Fayetteville, NC, teacher, was moved by the plight of one of her students, a boy dying for want of a kidney transplant. So, this woman told the family of a 14-year-old boy that she would give him one of her kidneys, and she did. When they subsequently appeared together hugging on a national television show, even Katie Couric was near tears.

You want heroes? Doris Dillon dreamed all her life of being a teacher. She not only made it, she was one of those wondrous teachers who could wring the best out of every single child. One of her fellow teachers in San Jose, CA, said, "She could teach a rock to read." Suddenly, she was stricken with Lou Gehrig's Disease, which is always fatal, usually within five years. She asked to stay on job and did. When her voice was affected, she communicated by computer.

Did she go home? Absolutely not! She is running two elementary school libraries! When the disease was diagnosed, she wrote the staff and all the families that she had one last lesson to teach, that dying is part of living. Her colleagues named her "Teacher of the Year."

You want heroes? Bob House, a teacher in Gay, Georgia, tried out for

Who Wants to be a Millionaire. After he won the million dollars, a network film crew wanted to follow up to see how it had impacted his life. New cars? Big new house? Instead, they found both Bob House and his wife still teaching. They explained that it was what they had always wanted to do with their lives and that would not change. The community was both stunned and gratified.

You want heroes? Last year, average school teachers spent $468 of their own money for student necessities: workbooks, pencils, and supplies kids had to have but could not afford.

That's a lot of money from the pockets of the most poorly paid teachers in the industrial world. Schools don't teach values?

The critics are dead wrong. Public education provides more Sunday School teachers than any other profession. The average teacher works more hours in nine months than the average 40 hour employee does in a year.

You want heroes? For millions of kids, the hug they get from a teacher is the only hug they will get that day, because the nation is living through the worst parenting in our history. An Argyle, Texas, kindergarten teacher hugs her little five and six-year-olds so much that both the boys and the girls run up and hug her when they see her in the hall, at the football games, in the malls years later.

A Michigan principal moved me to tears with the story of her attempt to rescue a badly abused little boy who doted on a stuffed animal on her desk, one that said, "I love you." He said he'd never been told that at home. This is a constant in today's society: two million unwanted, unloved, abused children in the public schools, the only institution that takes them all in.

You want heroes? Visit any special education class and watch the miracle of personal interaction, a job so difficult that fellow teachers are awed by the dedication they witness.

There is a sentence from an unnamed source which says, "We have been so anxious to give our children what we didn't have that we have neglected to give them what we did."

What is it that our kids really need? What do they really want? Math, science, history, and social studies are important, but children need love, confidence, encouragement, someone to talk to, someone to listen, and standards to live by. Teachers provide upright examples, the faith and assurance of responsible people.

You want heroes? Then go down to your local school and see our real live heroes, the ones changing lives for the better each and every day!

"Keep Your Head Up, Jack!"

Spring 2001

Drew Urban

I woke up at 6:00 a.m. My knees were shaking, and I couldn't eat my breakfast. It was baseball cut day, and I didn't think I would make it.

I'm not from here. originally; I'm from Shady Springs. I was one of the best players in that town, and everybody knew it. I thought I would make the Fallen Rock baseball team easily, but these players were good, and I didn't practice very well.

Baseball is my life. If I didn't make the team. it would be like losing a part of me. Judgment Day came, and at school, I finally realized the truth.

"Jack, you made it!" Joe, the first person I met here, said.

I was relieved. I didn't know how I would feel without baseball. For me, it was more than just a game; it was a part of me.

You see, my father was a great player, and he always gave me pointers on hitting and pitching, or used to. He died this winter, practically, in my arms.

We were talking about the Shady Springs ball team and the schedule he was going to make for us, when he had a heart attack and died. He always told me to keep my head up, because something good will happen when you least expect it, and you have to be ready for it.

Joe and I walked to the ball yard after school to meet the team. It amazed me how good they were, how they turned two, and how many liners they hit.

"Hey, you," said Coach Darrel.

"Yeah," I said, nervously.

"Grab a bat; you're up next," he said, as he walked to the pitchers.

I grabbed a helmet and walked nervously to the plate. I strode back to the dugout with a puzzled look on my face. The pitcher threw ten fastballs that missed my bat.

"That's it for today," Coach Darrel announced.

"How was it Jack?" Joe asked, happily.

I shrugged and said, "It's going to be a long year."

I walked home with my mind thinking about my dad. Maybe, if he didn't die, I would still be playing for Shady Springs.

"Keep your head up, Jack." The quote was stuck in my head and a good thing, too. I'll probably use it a lot this year.

The first game came against Polmont. I looked at the lineup card and didn't see my name until the bottom.

"Looks like you'll be sitting next to me," Joe exclaimed.

"Unfortunately," I said in a low voice.

I started every game for Shady Springs last year, but this team was no Shady Springs. I practiced a lot better since the first practice after cuts. I hit the ball better, and I fielded very well, I thought, but Buck did it all a lot better. I found myself stuck on the bench the next five games.

The next day, Joe and I walked home after practice.

"I don't understand it. Ever since my dad died, I haven't been able to play the way I used to," I blurted out.

Joe, who was now the backup right fielder, looked up surprisingly. "Where'd that come from?" he questioned.

"I don't know. It's just that at Shady Springs I loved the game, and no pressure was on me. Now, it just seems like I'm miles away from the way I should be playing," I explained.

"Keep your head up, Jack," Joe said.

"Never mind," I replied.

"What?" asked Joe.

"I don't know. It's just that my dad always used to say that to me," I said.

"Jack!" Joe exclaimed, "Just play your game, and don't worry about what others expect of you."

I'm glad Joe said those things to me, because the next day at baseball practice I ripped it up. I hit three over the fence and had a lot of line drives. I fielded okay but not as well as I would've liked. The most important surprise came when Buck came to the ball yard with a sling on his arm. I found out later that he was out for the season because of a broken arm. That meant only one thing. I was the new starting second baseman, the same position I played at Shady Springs.

The next five games I hit .400, had one home run, and fifteen RBI's. The next game was the District final game.

The District game went by fast. The first six innings went by without much action. Then, the good part came. Pat got a single, stole a base, and Luke walked. That brought me up to the plate with a chance to win the game. As I walked up to the plate, my father was on my mind, and my teammates were up and cheering. I looked over to the bench as if to say,

"Yes, I'm going to do it."

The first pitch whizzed by. "Strike one!" the ump yelled.

I took a step back, looked at the signs and dug in. My knees were shaking just like cut hay. I looked in again at the pitcher.

"You can do it, Jack!" Joe screamed.

With that advice, I swung at the next pitch and cracked it. Pat and Luke sprinted around the bases. I looked back to see the ball land between the left and center fielders. I pumped my fist in the air because we had won.

The next week came. We lost at the State Tournament in the first game. Joe and I went see some of my old friends at Shady Springs.

We left after a couple hours for home, but before we did, I went to see my dad's grave. Joe and I slowly walked toward it. We stared at the grave for almost a minute.

"I just want you to know," Joe said, "how proud I am of you, son." I turned, suddenly, but Joe wasn't there anymore. My dad was in his place. I just looked with a blank stare.

"I just love this game, Jack, and I love to watch you play," my dad said gladly. A tear came to my eyes.

"DAD!" I cried, but before I could say anything else, he vanished.

I started crying, not sad tears, but tears of happiness. It was then that I saw the baseball on the ground. A message was written on it.

"I love you, son. Remember to always keep your head up, now, because I'll be watching from above."

The English Dragon
Summer 2005

Arturo Vega

Many people visit foreign countries. They visit tourist areas; they speak some English, and they accept foreign currency. It is a different story when somebody moves to a new country to live and starts from scratch. Imagine if this person cannot communicate, because he can't read or write the language. Learning English is difficult; not only does it have a huge vocabulary, but it is spoken one way and written another.

I came to the United States from Guadalajara, Jalisco, Mexico, at the age of 15. My sister and I had not seen my mother since the ages of 5 and 3. When I saw her for the first time in twelve years, I didn't know what to do. I just stood there while she hugged me and cried. She introduced us to my stepfather and told me we were going to join our oldest sister and younger brother in the U. S. It was hard to accept that I had to leave behind everything I knew: my neighborhood, school, friends, and Grandmother who raised me.

My mother explained English could be a hard language to learn. The first thing I needed to learn was that almost everything is backwards. In Spanish, one says, "La casa blanca," which means "the white house." In English, the descriptive word is written before the noun. In Spanish, every object is feminine or masculine. In English, "the" can be used for both. In English, "El perro" and "La silla" mean "the dog" and "the chair." In English, the double "0" makes a "U" sound. These differences make it hard to learn the language. I didn't have a choice. I had to face my dragon. I couldn't run. I was in the middle of the battlefield.

I enrolled in school, and the English as a Second Language class had a waiting list. I had no choice but to attend regular classes. My work was modified, and I paired up with a student who was bilingual, so I got help if I needed it. I was the only Mexican in choir, and drama class wasn't my cup of tea. I found a program called NJROTC (Naval Junior Reserves Officer Training Corps) that helped me with the language and meeting people.

I was the only freshman ESL student playing varsity football. The reason I tried out was because my English teacher announced there would be "football tryouts" after school. In Spanish, football means soccer (futbol). When I walked into the locker room and they gave me pads and a helmet, I thought I joined the army. Baseball became my favorite sport, because the coach didn't scream like a maniac. He encouraged us to have fun and learn from our mistakes.

Learning English can be difficult, because it has a large vocabulary and is read differently than it is written. We can't sit and wait for it to come to us. I had to acquire it, understand it, and practice it. We learn as we go. I didn't join sports teams because I wanted to be popular. I joined because I needed a routine. I listened and soaked it all in like a sponge. Choir was not fun, but I saw how different people talked to each other: blacks talking to blacks, and Chicanos talking to whites and blacks. ROTC helped me a lot because I learned military terms. I went places and did things; this helped my vocabulary get bigger every day.

Many people come to the United States, but most of them are not successful, because they don't learn English. They may not have had the same chances I did, or it was too hard to learn. It is not about facing the dragon. When individuals understand the way of the dragon, they will be amazed by the things the dragon can do for them.

Freedom

September 1995

Egon Viola

The "Fundament" of The United States of America is built on the doctrine of E Pluribus Unum, "out of many we are one." Not by separation but by unification, we became The United States. Every race, every nationality, and ethnic group contributed to the prosperity of our nation. Separation from each other would split our "Fundament," and we would not be a United States any more. Not the combination of fifty states alone instituted the existence of our nation; the unification of all citizens established the foundation of the United States.

"E Pluribus Unum."

My Little Girl Is Gone

Summer 2002

Pat Vlcan

Over the past several months, it's become apparent to me that my little girl is gone. Each day, I sense that I'm a bit less important in her life and her friends a bit more important. At times, she speaks to me in a voice that I don't recognize. The sparkle in her blue eyes has changed from innocence to independence. I am overwhelmed with the feeling that I am losing her love and what I believe to be the closest relationship of my life.

It's an empty feeling to love someone and not to have that love returned any longer. I never imagined that I would experience this feeling with one of my children. My first reaction was panic. I wasn't ready for this change or willing to accept the fact that this transition was necessary for our relationship to continue to grow. This must be the time when many women buy a cat, so they have something to follow them from room to room and lie on their feet, while they're on the phone. How I miss the little girl who wouldn't give me a moment to myself.

I think I've told her everything, at least twice, and anything that's really important at least three times. I've learned to cherish the time we spend together and to appreciate the time I have alone. I wait, patiently, for the day when my best friend is ready to pick up where we left off.

My Journal Is a Door!

March 1994
Joel Vogts

I've never kept a journal before. Sure, I wrote a lot, but I never wove the pieces together. The words just floated about my room in an unorganized fashion. Never did I imagine that an ordinary book could play such an important role in my daily life. My journal transformed itself into a living, feeling, and breathing creation.

There isn't one word or idea that explains how crucial my journal is to me. This notebook has become my friend, my teacher, and my door to other worlds. This inanimate object developed feelings, emotions, and wisdom. Like a close friend, my journal listens patiently to my stories, problems, and hopes. There is an air of understanding that comforts me.

Though a situation appears hopeless and all roads are blocked, my journal takes my hand and shows me an open path. There is always a shoulder to cry on or open arms to envelop me in a warm hug. I put my tears, ideas, and emotions into our relationship, and the results have been more than satisfying.

My journal is also my teacher. I learn about myself, life and others through the pages of this notebook. There isn't a textbook that can teach me all the valuable things I have learned. I expand my thoughts and ideas on paper, and my journal tells me how many areas I overlook. There are many times when I am reluctant to look at an idea, and my journal gently shows me the truth.

Most of all, my journal is a door. It creates a passage way from my imagination to the paper. This book takes me places I never knew existed. I see memories of the past and dreams of the future. These pages inspire me; it waves the flames of my desire. There isn't a place in the universe or beyond that my journal cannot take me.

This humble notebook that touches my life is what I cannot be to myself. It holds strong feelings and emotions, ideas, miseries, and desires. I alone could not have put meaning into these images I write between its covers. My journal breathed life onto every page. It became a loving friend, teacher, and pathway to my destiny.

To the Heart of the Matter

Summer 1998

David Wallace

Here are some thoughts about how I have experienced reading the four issues of *Fine Lines* that I have seen, including the recent Spring issue.

In the beginning, I felt that it was my duty to read each and every piece from beginning to end, and carefully, lest I dishonor the privilege I have felt at having something of mine printed in *Fine Lines* for others to read.

I have learned that I simply do not turn on to some pieces. Sometimes, I recognize a loser (for me) in the first sentence. I have come to be reasonably OK to simply skip to the next piece and submit that one to my readability test, but I still feel guilty and arrogant when I skip over a piece. I actually get angry with the authors (always strangers to me) who force me to go on to the next piece.

I am surprised again and again at the pieces that inspire me. It is a matter of content and style, of course and it is a matter of how my feelings are touched. Sometimes, it is that the authors are people I least expected to find in such a journal as *Fine Lines*, let alone people who I expected might encourage me to read more.

Occasionally, I find an author whom I know "on the outside" and who I had no idea might be writing things for print. Examples: Barbara Jessing in "Grieving for Trees" and Tom Pappas in "Geezerville." Both pieces are about matters which touch me deeply, but it never occurred to me to write about them. Barb and Tom chose to write, and their writing touched me more deeply than if I tried to write about these topics for myself.

Some pieces go, admirably, right to the heart of the matter and seem not to worry about questions of style or expression or any other delicate issue. They just get right after it. Example: "Laughing Through the Tears" by Jim Wojtkiewicez, a high school senior. I am not intimidated at pronouncing that name. Years ago, one of my daughters was great friends with a member of a family of that name. We attended her wedding. It sounds like "Wock-a-witz," doesn't it?

Still another discovery for me in cruising through *Fine Lines* is that I can understand and even enjoy poetry, if it is written by high school students. One of the earlier issues taught me this, especially. I am one of those geezers who has been "poetry challenged" from high school days 60 years ago. I dared to scan a couple of poems from two issues ago, poems written by high school students, and I finished by reading and liking every one of them in that issue. My judgment is that accomplished poets will do anything they can to obscure or encrypt whatever they are supposedly trying to communicate. The young poets I am reading in *Fine Lines* get right after it, while still writing real poetry.

Finally, I participated in two proof-reading sessions where volunteers read through final drafts of items submitted for *Fine Lines*. I was astonished to read in the current issue several pieces which I proof-read a couple of weeks ago and in which I perhaps marked a few typos. Example: "Fudging and Frogging," by Millie Malone. I read nearly this whole piece today before it came to me that I recently proof-read it in draft form. I have discovered that I see one thing when I am proof-reading a piece for technicalities, and I see something entirely different when I am reading the same piece and trying to commune with the author. This author spoke to me clearly and with deep feeling, using the simplest of symbols. It was a kind of poetry in prose form, and I got it. The typos, if there were any, mattered not.

Black Elk and Jung

Winter 1995

Kathleen Warren

I found Black Elk's Circle to be very interesting. It is much like Carl G. Jung's foundations only using natural symbols. It is logical that the color for the west wind is black, since that is where storms come from. I especially like the idea of the Tree of Life at the center. It is a parallel to the tree of life in the garden from the Hebrew Old Testament. I don't think it is a coincidence that all of the major religions have such similarities.

I am more familiar with the context in which Jung's ideas occur. I can't decide where I fit. My greatest strengths lie in the area of intuition. Close to that is my habit of thinking all of the time. However, even though I try to mask emotional display, I consider myself a very feeling person. I don't know how the senses are supposed to figure in to all of this. I would like to take that test that showed how people fit into the circle. It would be interesting to see where I fit. I know that I have not yet reached a perfect balance in my life. I still think that intuition is my primary foundation. I can't decide what my secondary one is.

I think where a person fits may have something to do with how he or she sees life. It has been said that the maximum good people can achieve on Earth is to know themselves. After all, when you are dead, what good is money or a fancy car? Will you really need all those designer clothes when you are six feet under? You really can't take it with you. What is important is becoming a better person. If we didn't go through hard times or make mistakes, we would all be perfect. I can't imagine a more boring life! Without struggle, there would be no heroes, no truisms, and no art.

Art is colorful. It says something about its creator. If I lived like a work of art, I think I would travel. I would spend all of my days on the highway. I would go everywhere and see everything there is to see on this Earth. I would find beauty in all life (not that I don't now). Another important thing about traveling is the things I will learn. I will find other cultures and learn other ways of living. I won't agree with all of them, but that's okay. Maybe, through this process I will find the Tree of Life and perfect balance.

Poetry as Therapy

Autumn 1997

Dr. Donald Welch

I suspect that one can get well by writing poetry only if one has something good in his well. I also suspect that nothing good can come from nothing good. What evidence I have to believe this comes from reading thousands of poems written by students and adults. I have never deliberately set out to ask people to write poems which could heal them. In fact, I can't imagine very successful poems being written with a poet's health foremost in her mind. This would be a keyhole through which the imagination, at its best, would have a difficult time passing through.

This isn't to say we don't write for our lives. We do. Almost every poem, seriously undertaken, wants to be right. As such, it adds a little rightness to our lives, and over the years, those little rightnesses accumulate and become significant parts of our lives. I am never surprised by how good poems happen. The best poems are little victories, which prove to be remarkably miraculous, and occur in the oddest circumstances. I am going to use two to illustrate how poetry heals and hurts.

I remember asking some fifth graders to write a poem in which they imagined themselves inside something, and then I asked them to describe what it was like inside those things. One boy, sitting right in front of me, refused to write. This was the third day in a week-long residency, and he had not written the two previous days either.

Later, however, in that same period he began to write, then finished, or apparently finished, what he had started. Before I could look over his shoulder and read his poem, his teacher body-blocked me into the wall, whispering, "Kelly wrote. Did you see that, Kelly really wrote?"

Before I could express my puzzlement at being blocked into the wall, the teacher went into the next room, returned with a student teacher, turned the class over to her, and said to me, "Come, we're going to the teacher's lounge to see what Kelly wrote."

Then, the picture cleared up nicely when the elementary principal, a custodian, the school nurse, and I were commanded by Kelly's teacher to take a shot at deciphering what he had written. His handwriting looked like the hieroglyphics on the Egyptian Rosetta Stone.

In time we concluded unanimously this is what Kelly said:

"I am inside my head.

It is a disaster.

It is all falling apart.

There are little green men

Tearing it apart.

I look out my eyes.

I see a sign which says

Do Not Disturb."

It was then that I asked, "Surely someone knows what traumatized this boy into silence?" Whereupon the elementary principal spoke up and told us about Kelly's father coming home drunk one night and throwing the whole family out of the house, including Kelly through the plate glass window of his bedroom on the second floor.

The next day I asked Kelly's class if any of them ever had such a bad day they wanted to put a sign on their noses, saying KEEP OUT! A number of hands went up. Then I asked, "Do your moms and dads have days like this, too?" Then the hands really went up.

I told them one of their classmates had written well about wanting this kind of privacy, and I asked them if they would like me to read his poem. They said they would, so I read them Kelly's poem. Then I looked down at him. He had his head down on his desk, and for a moment, I thought I had blown it. Wanting to show them how well he had written, I had embarrassed or saddened him. I had sent him back into even more silence. But I have taught enough poets to know that almost all of them want others to hear what comes from deep inside them. So, I got down on one knee and looked up into Kelly's face. He was smiling.

This is a rather long story to illustrate how people with good stuff in them can write the bad stuff out. Later in the week, when we were doing another warm-up exercise ("I used to be _____, but now I am _____), Kelly wrote "I used to be an old junk car, but now I am a Trans-Am." Never was advertising and the automotive industry put to better use.

Another student, however, had a very different experience with poetry. Her master's thesis, written under my direction, was entitled "Introducing Myself to My Latest Psychiatrists." Her poetry was brutally frank, raw, and heart-breaking. It had all the hurt and much of the rage we find in the verse of Sylvia Plath. In fact, this young woman may have been influenced by Plath, one of poetry's notable suicides; and if not by Plath, by those currents of self-pity and self-laceration which were sweeping the lives of confessional poets in the 1960s.

In short, this remarkable young woman grew up realizing that writing verse only pulled her more deeply into the black holes of herself. Her poems were an anti-matter which had the opposite effect of healing. Not only wise beyond her years, she was one of the most courageous young people ever to sit in my classes. In addition to acute depression, she had breast and brain tumors, both of which proved non-malignant. She also had an indefatigable will, which she used to fight her way to health. In the process, she learned to stay away from poetry, which was a maelstrom that she barely escaped. She now reads voraciously, but rarely writes verse. Perhaps, although I have no evidence of this, the deliberate choices she makes in her reading are therapeutic.

Almost all writers, however, write because they have to. In the long run, any other reason doesn't amount to much. If they write enough, they write for their lives. By finding a way to write, they find their way in writing, and if they read their own works carefully, they may very well find what I call their underwritings. No writer can write for years without creating a body of underwritings, those tones and beliefs and styles which underlie his work. If you have been writing for as long as I have, some of your nicest surprises come from asking yourself questions about your underwritings.

If you're like me, you don't feel good when you aren't writing. If I'm not writing, time is not necessarily wounded. Writing just makes time better, especially when I've written something passably well and can walk home from my office with a small accomplishment lengthening my bones.

Lest someone conclude that art is more important than life for me, I must say that it isn't. When I'm swinging our granddaughter, the world is utterly and happily wordless. The trick is to live an art-filled life and write a life-filled art. Neither is satisfying without the other.

I think Kelly must have had some great wordless moments. A happy kid deep down, he had a great smile. When he put words to that smile, he became a Trans-Am. I'm all for healing, in big or little ways, and if poetry helps, I couldn't be more pleased. Two things I love are good words and swinging nerve-ends. Brought together they make for whizz-bang people and effervescent moments. I find both therapeutic.

I Am a Writer

Autumn 1999

Laura Werkheiser

I am a writer because I can be. Call me melodramatic, but I think pens and paper are underrated. Strip me of my clothes, take my car, and my credit card. Leave me in a dark room with a broken pencil and a dirty, Village Inn napkin. I'll be fine.

I am a writer because I am meant to be. For some reason, my mind processes thought in a way that even I don't understand. I don't know why I can analyze Greek mythology from an existential standpoint but can't add without a calculator.

I am a writer because I've got that whole pseudo intellectual thing down. I played along with *Jeopardy* on TV, yesterday and beat Roger, the CPA from Radcliffe. I work in a coffee shop, and I know who Slobedan Milosevic is.

I am a writer because the quadratic formula gives me a headache and the Theory of Relativity makes me nauseous. I believe there is science to support my conclusion. They call it neurological preferential behavioral, "supercalifragilisticexpealidocius disorder." I'm sure there's a college scholarship out there for people like me.

I am a writer because I am a reader. The little things inspire me, as do the prolific. I'm influenced by the work of others and motivated by their impact. I see reading not as a hobby but more as a form of exercise and training. Football players pump iron, and writers read.

That's just the way it works.

Poet's Workshop

Autumn 1996

Peggy Wheeler

"one, two: buckle my shoe
Three, four: open the door
...and get out."

(Austin Aufenkamp, told by Brittany Conolly)

I began to search through quote books for words to set an appropriate mood for this article. I looked at what the learned had to say about writing, communication, and specifics of such. I could not find, however, a quote that would convey the same spirit of exuberance as the above quote from my two-year-old nephew (as told to me by my delighted six-year-old niece). Indeed, the flavor of discovery floats upon this clever use of language. That, of course, is one of the reasons we love poetry.

As children, if we are lucky, we are regaled with something called nursery rhymes. Despite the sinister background of some of these (try interpreting "Ring Around the Rosie"), children revel in these games of words. The rhyme, rhythm, and melodic language are pleasing to the child's ear. Indeed, they are pleasing to the adult ear as witnessed by the doggerel that passes for popular music. I'm not a snob; quite the contrary, I admit to enjoying the interplay of rhythm of much popular music. I'm not stupid; however, and I take popular music for what it is: an outlet for pathos, sentiment, everyday emotion, and more importantly, a gateway to more evocative and deeply felt creations of language: poems.

What first catches us about poetry seems to be rhythm. Dame Edith Sitwell said, "Rhythm is one of the principal translators between dream and reality. To the world of sound, rhythm might be described as what light is to the world of sight. It shapes and gives new meaning. Rhythm was described by Schopenhauer as "a melody deprived of its pitch."

In other words, rhythm helps illuminate the meaning of language. Think of how many different ways we can say the phrase, "Nice day, isn't it?" Depending upon the rhythm and inflection of our speech, the phrase can take on several meanings. We humans respond to rhythm. It is one of the cornerstones of our existence. Our blood pulses; our eyelids flutter; we breathe, speak and walk to a rhythm. Our daily life – rising in the morning, eating at regular intervals, sleeping at night – seems to fall into regular rhythms. So important are these rhythms that scientists have discovered that failure to fall into our bodies' natural routines causes physical and mental disorders.

Many other obvious rhythms can be discovered in our lives, if we only look. Seasons, of course, the ebb and flow of one's workload, health, and the list goes on. The importance of rhythm cannot be underplayed. Hypnotists, for example, use rhythmic vocalizations and, occasionally, rhythmic movement of an object to induce hypnosis. Many people involved in meditation use a chant to segue more easily into a meditative or trance state. Rhythm, in these ways, seems to allow the individual to concentrate and gain insight and information more easily. Witness the ease with which youngsters memorize nursery rhymes – and the sometimes-convoluted lyrics of rap music.

What about "melody," then? The words carried along by rhythm? As the paraphrased nursery rhyme shows, we many times use poetry as a teaching device. At the very minimum, rhymes can teach how to count, for example. A second teaching, such as in "Ring Around the Rosie" and also embodied by many epics, is the history of a people.

Almost all other poetry seems to teach basic truths about life and existence. As I try to tell my students each year when I defend the importance of poetry, this art form educates about the real world as opposed to merely preparing one for a career. I believe this form of teaching accounts for the popularity of lyrical music. It "speaks" to the listener of familiar ideas and life episodes. Even at its most banal, music expresses a feeling or idea about some of the great theses in human life: love, death, friendship, and courage.

Why poetry instead of some other form of literature? Indeed, if one were to look at the sales of poetry books as opposed to novels, it would seem that poetry IS NOT the way most people prefer to spend their reading time. I believe this is for the same reasons that much popular music is inane: people don't want to be challenged, and why should they be? Getting through the day with one's ego intact is sometimes challenging enough.

My answer is two-fold. First, while popcorn is a wonderful snack, a steady diet of the same is damaging. In much the same way, a steady diet of popular fiction limits one's abilities to understand and gain the deeper enjoyment available in serious or classic literature. Those who wish to remain dynamic through the years see the inherent danger in such atrophying.

Second, challenging ourselves strengthens us, and we face daily tasks with greater insight. Since poetry is, arguably, the most challenging literature, it would seem to offer the most to the individual. It expands one's mind to wrestle with a novel-full of ideas condensed into a three-line haiku. Poetry forces the reader to rely upon more than the written word; it calls upon a lifetime of resources including previously-gained knowledge, emotion and experience. While this is more demanding than having a story spoon-fed to us, it also engages readers more fully, and I would argue, more satisfyingly, than a novel which only requires passive assimilation of plot, character and dialogue.

Individual experience suggests this to me. I admit a weakness for romance and mystery novels. They are a form of escape, and since I'm used to a stronger diet of literature, I am able to use my imagination and reading abilities to compensate for any flaws I encounter. However, it is rare that a novel engages me for much longer than it takes to read it. Witness the fact that I have been halfway through novels before I realized I'd already read them.

I do not make that mistake with T. S. Eliot or E. E. Cummings. The words of Emily Dickinson and Edna St. Vincent Millay do not pass out the other ear. They become a part of my thought processes, and the phrases come back to me at appropriate times in my life.

From the amusing word games of childhood to the challenging foraging for meaning of the adult exploration of verse, poetry provides a lifetime for the individual to grow. Poetry is not necessary to survive, but it is necessary for life. From the simplistic rhymes of childhood to simple verse learned in adulthood, poems speak to us of experiences, beliefs, reactions, feelings, and odysseys. This simplification sets poetry apart from novels and prose for, as Willa Cather said, to simplify "is very nearly the whole of the higher artistic process ... ."

I am gratified to see the variety of poetic types offered in this publication.

Let's Grow Writers!

Spring 1997
Dr. Leslie Whipp

I think I'm clear about something. That does trouble me. Every time I've ever seen people who were real clear about something, they were on their way to a big mistake. Think of all the Christians in the Crusades killing all the other Christians. They were real clear. So, I don't do much trade with clarity. Now, his sister charity – she's not real clear, but she's a whole lot safer to be around, it looks like to me.

Nevertheless, I'm afraid I'm clear about something. It goes like this:

Schools train teachers to grow writings, not writers, and then hire them to grow writers, not writings. In our workshop, we are trying to grow writers not writings. If you are in the publishing business or in the newspaper business, then you are in the business of growing writings, and you put a lot of emphasis on negative criticism, and you're hyper about grammar and mistakes that could embarrass someone in published discourse. If you are dealing with youngsters or persons who have not yet entered the publishing business and dealing with their use of written discourse, then you are in the business of growing writers, and you want to look for other ways of conducting yourself.

How do writers grow? How does one grow a writer? I am inclined to get confused by that question and to hear it as, "How does one grow a Shakespeare?" I know better. That's not the question. The question is how

221

do I graduate an ordinary person, a contractor, a farmer, and a grocery store operator who are competent and confident in exercising their rights to their written language? This has nothing to do with producing Writers of Literature. This has only to do with not depriving kids of what is natural to them.

In the reading I've done recently in English as a Second Language, frantically grasping after a wee small bit of preparation before going to China, I've been struck by current work in ESL pedagogy. Earl W. Stevick has exerted the strongest influence today on the language teaching profession in attempting to induce teachers to accept what he calls "a new way of seeing." He warns that this is not to be an abandonment of old ways or necessarily the development of new ones, but "something simpler and profoundly more difficult," which he identifies at one point as "a psychodynamic view of teaching." He emphasizes that the personal relationship between students, as well as the personal relationship between the teacher and the students, is of utmost importance; and he says it is vital to place "principles of learning" (looking at the teaching-learning situation from the point of view of the student) before "principles of teaching."

This is precisely true for growing writers. The relationship between student and teacher must take precedence over principles of teaching, principles of the discipline, principles of the curriculum, and all the rest of it. Indeed, if one looks at what happens in ordinary language learning, this is precisely what happens in ordinary language learning. From the earliest times, we acquire those structures that will help us appear to ourselves to be like those persons whom we admire and like and want to be like, and want to like us. I think that has been the experience of every teacher I have ever worked with, and that is their experience in learning their native language. That was my experience in learning spoken English and in learning written English. I am amused, I guess, that so many learned people have worked so hard to ignore that experience in ESL, English Departments, and Curriculum Committees throughout the profession.

What would it be like to take primary emphasis off "principles of teaching" and put it on "principles of learning?" Well, obviously, it means high standards have to be based on a different set of criteria. Principles of learning take us immediately to the teacher-student relationship. Here it seems to me there is no help for it but to be corny. In a nutshell, the basics one needs to grow writers are decency, respect, and courtesy. Not grammar, linguistics, and rhetoric. Decency, respect, and courtesy. Of course, grammar, linguistics, and rhetoric may be useful; I'd be the last person to deny that. It seems clear to me that they're not the basics. Decency, respect, and courtesy are the basics. They don't require much of any negative criticism about language use.

Saturday, the *Lincoln Journal* republished Ann Landers' "Ten Commandments of How to Get Along with People." It looks to me like they're a pretty good set of rules for growing writers, too, for that matter:

Keep skid chains on your tongue. Always say less than you think. How you say it often counts more than what you say.

Make promises sparingly and keep them faithfully, no matter what the cost.

Never let an opportunity pass to say a kind and encouraging word to somebody.

Be interested in others: their pursuits, their work, their homes and their families. Let everyone you meet, however humble, feel that you regard him as a person of importance.

Be cheerful. Remember, everyone is carrying some kind of burden.

Keep an open mind. Discuss, but don't argue. It is a mark of a superior mind to be able to disagree without being disagreeable.

Refuse to talk about the vices of others. Gossip is a waste of valuable time.

Wit at the expense of another is never worth the pain inflicted.

Pay no attention to ill-natured remarks about you. Disordered nerves are a common cause of back-biting.

Do your best and be patient. Forget about yourself and let others "remember." Success is much sweeter that way.

Well, I don't know that the seventh commandment or the last two have much to do with me in my role as a grower of writers, but the others sure do. I would have had much less to overcome as a teacher of writers if I thought and studied more earlier about the role of the relationship in promoting language growth and how one establishes and maintains positive relationships.

I'm sure all of this comes to mind now because I'm concerned about the workshop I am doing. It's clear what we have to do is grow writers, not writings. I'm concerned because it seems to me that I don't know how to encourage people to see they have to lose themselves to save themselves in this business. What we have in this workshop is a greenhouse, a safe environment in which we can try out "a new way of seeing," and new strategies for growing writers. Perhaps, it will come.

Who's Knocking?

Spring 1999

Clark Wisniewski

Life is like a road map. We have many options to get from point A to point B, and life depends on how we read the map. We use our personal experiences to help us navigate the map of life, just as the great explorers did many years ago. It was not until recently that I figured out the direction my life was taking, and even though I now have some idea, I am sure the path will change.

It was not too long ago that I decided to go back to school. I guess people could say that I heard a knock at the door that woke me up. I am grateful that I heard the knocking and answered the door. The problem in life is that we do not always hear the knocking. Many times we choose to ignore it and go back to sleep. It is important that we listen for these knocks in life, so we can better ourselves.

Thomas De Quincey made an excellent point in his essay, "On the Knocking at the Gate in *Macbeth*." The knocking at the gate is a symbol of waking up to life, or in the case of *Macbeth*, death. There are many times in life that we hear a knocking at the gate that wakes us up.

My recent awakening came last year, when I decided to go to school and finish my degree. I quit school thinking I would finish by taking correspondence classes. I was more concerned with obtaining a good job and getting married. Now, I realize I cannot go anywhere without a degree. Since I am closer to graduation, I wish I had gone back sooner. I cannot change the past, only the future.

There could be many unexplained reasons for us to ignore the knocking. One is we do not feel ready to take the challenge. I debated with myself many times about going back to school, but I felt I wasn't ready to dive in. Another reason is people feel it would be easier to ignore the knocking and continue their lives the way they are going.

When a direction has been pointed out to us, it may take several hints for us to notice. This happened to me several times when I was deciding to go back to school. I was happy with my life and did not want to add any more stress. I was afraid that I might fail and make it worse for myself.

Later, I learned I was not happy with the direction my life was going, and I decided the only way to change it would to be to enroll in school. I ignored the obvious signs that going back to school was the right thing to do. A third reason that we choose to ignore the knocking is that we are too busy and do not even hear the knocking. There were many times I felt that my job would interfere with school. It was later I realized I had time to do both well. There are many things that cause us to ignore the knocking and go back to the old way of life.

How can we be sure we answer the knock when it is important? The answer to that question is different for everyone. No one else can decide when I need to wake up and change my life. I am my own best jury that can render the verdict for my life. I have to recognize there is a need to make a change and grow from the experience. Life is a cycle of growing and making our lives better. We can only answer the knocking if the time is right for us to grow. The reason we may not hear the knocking is we are just not ready to make the commitment to change. It is important that we evaluate our own style of recognizing the knocking so we are able to make those changes.

If we chose to ignore the signs of knocking, it could be disastrous. If people forget to set their alarms, they may oversleep and be late for work. If we set alarms in our lives to awaken us to change, then we will be able to better ourselves. The problem is setting the alarm. What do we set it for? Again, this all depends on the individual. The key to successfully setting the alarm is to identify the weaknesses in our lives, and when we hear the knocking, we will wake up. It is important that we set many alarms.

After the clouds clear and the sun comes out, light is shed on our lives. The most important thing about waking up to life is recognizing that our lives are constantly changing. What is important to me now may not be important to me an hour from now or a week from now. If we can recognize that life is constantly changing, then we may be able to hear the knock. A person who does not recognize that life is constantly changing will stagnate and grow weak. If I am not expecting life to change, then I am not going to change my life. It sounds complex, but it is really simple. People will not change if they do not feel they need to be changed. If we answer the knock at the gate, we expect to change our lives.

I am glad I have had many knocks to waken me up to life. I expect I will have many more to come. Life presents us with many challenges. I think I now have the skills to better recognize when there is a knock at the door. Thomas De Quincey had an excellent idea of the explanation of the knocking at the gate in *Macbeth*. I wonder what things were knocking at Shakespeare's door? It is important that we heed the warnings and change life to best suit our needs. I have to go now. I think I hear someone knocking at my door.

Peru :: Laura Neece Baltaro

The Lesson

Spring 2000

Dorothy Apley

I waited in her red velvet chair
and listened to the lesson before me,
Schumann's "Traumerei."
Her blond Pekinese with shiny hair
slept on the sofa.

Two portraits of young women
Hung on her white walls.
Their lips and cheeks were painted in pastel.
I sat on her bench with padded brocade.
The baby grand gleamed shiny and black.
The keys glowed soft white
under dirty fingernails.

I practiced on Grandma's old uprights
yellow, ivory keys.
I would play after supper in our living room.
Gray wallpaper with fading rose peonies,
narrow windows,
Venetian blinds -
I hated to dust the
cream-lace curtains.

She sat in a carved chair beside the piano.
Tight black curls streaked with gray.
Tiny wrinkles spread like cracked glass
over her pink powdery face.
She leafed through my faded books
with gnarled misshapen hands,
too old to play.

We worked on Kuhlau's Sonatina
replaying the phrases together.

227

"Feel, don't think, crescendo-now."
I entered the passage through my fingers,
taking her with me.
"Music is alive. Breathe into it; diminuendo slowly, linger.
The last chord faded into her quiet, white room.

I thanked her
and closed the door, carefully.

Shana :: Walker Plank

Dancer

Winter 1995

Troy Bell

When you were a child,
your mother thought,
as mothers sometimes do,
that you were strong enough,
and sure enough,
to someday be a dancer.

When you were five, or was it six,
or was it nine,
you didn't want to dance.
You couldn't bear to dance,
unless you were dancing in the grass,
and dancing in the mud,
as children often do,
and then your father kicked a ball to you,
and the it was the shape of the whole
wide world to you,
and now if you see green,
you can only think of one thing to do,
and the world slips away from your feet,
and the sky slips down into your arms,
and you are free,
you are free,
you are absolutely free

to be whom you want,
to go where you can,
to be wild, to be loud,
to fly in the mud and run in the rain,
strong enough,
and sure enough,
like a dancer.

Grandma Anna's Shoes

Spring 1996

Alice Blackstone

At fifty,
when her last child
had left the nest,
Grandma took off her
working shoes,
sat down to rest and
read her Swedish Bible.

The streets in Heaven,
she knew were paved
with gold –
There, no more pain,
no more sin –
she always hated sin –
pool-halls, dancing,
particularly the sins of
the flesh –
Sometimes, satisfying
Grandpa's carnal needs
had been a trial,
but since God commanded woman
to obey, be fruitful and
multiply, she submitted.

When Grandpa
finally died, she sold her
home and household goods and
put her meager savings into a
care home where she
shunned people with
worldly ways, listened to
weekly radio sermons,
read her Bible and longed

for the day God would
reach down,
clothe her weary feet in golden
slippers and take her to himself.

London Eye :: David Martin

The Simple, The Profound

Winter 2001

Sheila Boerner

Our technology baffles the untrained mind:
the moon, Mars, no limits to our reach,
yet the greater our horizons expand,
the more constrained we
become at home.

Will we destroy the world in our greed?
We solve questions about the universe
but can't answer problems of our hearts.

Thoreau entered the woods to simplify life.
Whitman and Sandburg extolled
the common man, and Frost
spoke simply of life and death.

Maya enlarges our vision to include
black and white, man and woman.

In my classroom, I strive for this,
to challenge my students to dig deeper,
to search farther for the essence of things,
to find in each other and in the world
the beauty and the wonder of life lived.

Chopper Boy, Rescued Golden

Summer 2002

Mary Bowman

Part I – The Reprieve

In the dead of winter, the old Golden sits
caught in a trap, underside suffering
frostbite, starving, trying to survive.
Lost maybe, dumped perhaps,
he only knows he wants to live.

"Come and get the old Golden, or he'll
be put down." (Business as usual for
the vet towards the rescue group.)

His age? Ten, twelve, fourteen or more?
Adoption papers guess at ten. (Teeth
indicate ten plus years.)

"He may not last a year." (Cautionary
note from my vet.) I don't care.
Chopper's face is tired and worn from
fatigue and fear. We go home together.
He takes a long nap on warm, flannel
sheets. That was two years ago.

Arthritis, cataracts, sheared-off teeth
pulled; skin infections, heart murmur,
ear trouble, cancer twice. (X-rays show
buckshot in hind quarter.) His stamina
is rock solid determination. He just
wants to keep on living.

I loved him at first glance; he is now a
part of my soul forever and ever. He will
never have to worry about survival

again. He snuggles close, his big head resting on my lap, warm, brown eyes meeting mine. I wish he could tell me where he came from. What kind of life did Chopper Boy have before me?

Part II – Adolescent Whippersnapper

Carefully maneuvering the step down to the patio, Chopper Boy is now in a whirlwind of blowing snow. Enemy at one time, the snow brings out a playful, smart-aleck, young pup. Tail up, head erect, he sniffs the air. Prancing now, tail waving, he struts the patio.

"Cold winter, I've beaten you," he woofs to the air. "I'm alive, and I'm happy!"

The snow laughs around him speckling his thick, curly red coat with white. "Life is good!" he's thinking, smashing his head into the nearest snowdrift. He's on his back, all four pitty-patts straight up in the air fighting the attacking snowflakes. He rolls to one side, then to the other, and lies there, smiling a lop-sided, Chopper Boy grin.

Like a helicopter slowly coming to life, his tail starts to flap, then beats the snow covered patio. His legs thrash back and forth and to and fro, as if he's preparing to launch himself up into the swirling clouds above. The snow flies all over the place like a vortex cloud of white, billowing dust, and Chopper diligently begins work on a doggy snow angel.

I know he's my angel sent from above,
and each night before sleep I say,
"Thank you," for having one more day
with this incredible old dog.

Part III – Requiem

Part of me is missing, and I am aware of
it all the time. My bedroom is empty
now; no eighty-five pound curly-red-
coat Golden sleeping (and snoring)
next to my bed.

When I'm working at the table, there no
longer is a big dog constantly sitting
next to me; my free hand has no
Chopper Boy to pet or hug; no thick,
velvet ears to scratch. No big, brown
eyes with white face looking up at me.

It has been six months since Chopper's
passing, and my pain and grief are still
heavy on my heart.

Someone could say, "Why the grief?
You still have two other Goldens."

That may be so; but any animal lover
knows, our pets are never the same.
Their personalities and habits have no
limits. We love them as individuals; we
grieve for them as loved ones, members
of our family.

For me, I have memories, images
stamped in my mind of my beloved
Chopper Boy, and I can draw upon
those images whenever weepy,
melancholy invades my thoughts.

In the meantime, I study with intense interest every Golden that comes into my view. Could Chopper Boy have left a legacy? Somewhere in this country, could there be, "little Choppies" running about? I will always hold out hope; I will always keep on looking; I will always keep his food dish ready in my kitchen.

Waterfall - Meredith, New Hampshire:: David Martin

Vincent's Ravens

Winter 1993

Evetta Brunk

They come
from the dark sky
calling your name
calling, calling
black and low
sending shadows
over gold wheat waving
in the wind.

You shiver
on the lost path
that seems to swallow
your soul.
You sink.
in the shards of doubt
and hear the distant wings
beating, beating.

At Least One Slap in the Face

Autumn 1998

Molly Campbell

Some poetry is like trying to take a drink of water
from a fire hose. It comes in a big surge, and I have
to drop whatever I'm doing to get it all out, to transfer
the swell of emotion from my soul to my fingertips,
through my pencil and onto my paper.

Otherwise, I am in trouble. Once I am done,
I feel a little lighter because whatever it was
that was weighing so heavily on my mind
shifted its burden.

Other kinds are just the opposite. I know there
is something in me that needs to be written down,
but I just can't seem to condense it into words.
The more I try to wrench it free, the more it
seems to coil up and hide inside me.

Poetry usually consists of at least one slap in the face,
with subtlety that pulls back in order to hit me harder.
I am not the same after reading it, and I am not the same
after writing it. Either it drained every last morsel
of creative energy from every cell, or it came so fast and
suddenly and powerfully that I do not really know
what came over me. All I know is that momentary clarity
of thought resulted and was gone just as quickly.

My original thought on this matter still stands.
I can't define poetry, only compare it to other things.
One definition does not include all poetry,
and all poetry cannot possibly fit into one definition.

Great Ideas

Summer 1998
Albert Camus

"Great ideas come into the
world as gently as doves.
Perhaps, then, if we
listen attentively, we shall
hear, amid the uproar of
empires and nations,
a faint flutter of wings,
the gentle stirrings
of life and hope.

Some will say that this hope
lies in a nation, others a man.
I believe, rather,
that it is awakened,
revived, nourished by millions
of solitary individuals."

Union Station – Omaha

Spring 1997

Ardiss Cederholm

I enter the weighty doors once more
only half listen
as a tour guide explains the art deco style
points to its ceilings with gold
and silver leaf trim
cavernous stone walls and terrazzo floors

Again I hear the bustle
the clink of soda fountain dishes
ring of cash registers
loudspeakers booming out arrivals
and departures train whistles
echoing up from the track network below
hundreds of footsteps
coming – going – hurrying
voices calling – greeting – goodbying

And again
I feel the roughness of his khaki uniform
as he holds me close one last time
the name of Omaha
to echo again
some far day

As the Sun Sets, Love Fades

Summer 1997

Unhei Cho

The wind is so calming
leaving the heart to wonder.
Outside in the hazy horizon
the heart beats for someone special.
Peeking of the dawn as the sun rises,
brings warming thoughts
with his gentle touch.

As he follows in his routine,
a single red rose blooms every hour.

Flowers and romantic poems,
a gesture of his faith,
brings smiles and joy
to a once lonely heart.

My love, once so strong,
so full of desire,
fades as the less warming
sun sets off for bed.

He no longer strives for full attention
She knows that dusk has taken over.
The heart now beats a softer beat,
the sun has fallen and now the moon rises.
She no longer has
his gentle touch of comfort,
for night is here and now love is gone.

Gossamer Gown

Winter 2004

Darrel Draper

The winter sun slips 'neath the hill.
Each lonely night grows colder still.
I put on the kettle, and light my briar
And slide some oak into the fire.

Then, growing older, I drink my tea,
Remembering things that used to be.
Dear traveled places, I forget the names.
Perhaps, I'll recall as I stare at the flames,

Which leap and dance and flicker bright.
I remember that magnificent night,
When you danced
by the sea in your gossamer gown,
and the crescent moon smiled,
and the stars gathered round.

The seabirds aloft
watched from their hover,
as you waltzed and smiled at
your make-believe lover.

Unnoticed, I watched
from the high-water dunes,
as you whirled and you sighed
to your fantasy tunes.

You admired your bare finger
and imagined a ring
and dreamt of the joy
you knew it would bring.

I thought, "Venus has risen
and stands on the shore."
Never had I wanted
or desired someone more.

How could I, with my looks so modest,
Ever aspire to the heart of a goddess?
Sadly, slowly, back homeward I crept,
My cheeks awash with the tears I wept.

Look at my fire, just one dying ember,
Long enough for me to remember
That we'd met once in a cafe in town
Before you danced
in your gossamer gown.

Forever, I'll wonder
how might my life be
had I known on that night,
you were dancing with me.

Part II

A cup of tea falls to the floor,
One lonely heart shall beat no more.
The glow has left his final ember
A wisp of smoke meets cold December.
Miles away in a seaside town
Two tiny hands hold a faded gown.

"Was this once yours?"
she asks Aunt Tess.
With misting eyes,
Tess answers, "Yes."

I wore it just once, so long ago,
for a handsome man I used to know.
We met but once in a cafe in town,
The day I bought this gossamer gown.

Alone one night by a moonlit sea,
I pretended that man danced with me.
I looked at my finger, imagined his ring,
I dreamt of the joy it would bring.

He was so dashing, and I was so plain.
I knew I would never see him again.
We met again, in town, and I confessed
of my dance in the gossamer gown.

I'll never forget his look of surprise.
Embarrassed, I fled
with tears in my eyes.
Then, forever,
I avoided that old cafe,
until I had learned
that he'd moved away.

Though, I've thought of him
almost all of my life,
how he probably married
a beautiful wife.

I'll never forget that night
by the sea,
I wore this gossamer gown,
and he was dancing with me.

Genuflections

Summer 2005

Lorraine Duggin

(For Gloria)

She limps across the wide,
lavender-lined driveway, and
tells us we won't be meeting
as a study group next week.
She's having surgery on her knees.

Recycled mother of six,
grandmother besides teaching
Hispanic kids social studies
in junior high, she stumbles
through Spanish with them
to communicate, studies

Monday afternoons
with a priest, two nuns,
a retired widower, and me,
the Czech language
of our ancestors.

Circling her maple kitchen table,
we struggle with flashcards,
translate Bible stories,
as she fidgets at the counter,
pouring juice, serving cupcakes,
a recipe of hospitality
from her grandmother,
orange cat underneath,
rubbing my legs.

Just three years away
from retirement,

but she can barely walk today
after a long day of teaching,
performs a stiff-jointed dance
to reach into the cupboard
for plates.

"I used to spend
a lot of time on my knees,"
she says, as if to explain.

Surrounding dining room walls,
framed family portraits,
a baby apparent every year.
Two in college now,
two graduated and married,
one a professional dancer,
one an artist vagabonding
through Prague.

I try to imagine her past,
young mother,
baby on each hipbone,
stirring pots, chicken stew
cooking atop the stove,
a trite scene, waiting for papa
to come home
with the others from school
or Little League.
I think of her down
on her knees, building
block houses, laughing tots
surrounding, see her kneeling
on the back porch in July,
buckling sandals, tying
sneakers, out in the sand pile,
at the edge of a huge
tractor tire, dredging trucks,
tiny steam shovels,
excavating.

I envision her in the garden
with the brood,
mourning the dead canary,
the kittens, pet dogs,
planting lavender petunias, hostas,
digging in the loam.

Later on horseback,
kneeing the sides
of a pony, fixing the bikes,
pressing the piano pedal,
pivoting in a tennis
match, mowing the lawn,
jogging to the neighborhood
drugstore, down on her knees
searching for lost contact lenses
in the corner of the living room,

picture her gift-wrapping
doodads for Christmas,
selecting tunes on the jukebox
in the basement,
birthday parties,
teaching popeyed-kids
the jitterbug, limbo,
showing them a pirouette,
a polka, how to do the hokey-pokey.

Afterwards down on her knees
scrubbing the floors
every week the kitchen linoleum
the bathroom tiles

cleaning up all those years after
the throwing up, the epidemics,
fevers, accidents

and back to grad school
rapping with teens

the queasy kowtowing
to professors' demands
advanced degrees
getting them through college

all those years,
on her knees,
in prayer.

Boots :: Bradley Martin

A Goodbye

Spring 2005

Joyce Dunn

She sits on the sunny hillside and
lays a blanket of wildflowers over
the tiny grave. Her mind roams back
to that Sunday morning
of fifteen years ago.

Only a few hours ago her world
had been perfect, a two-year-old
at home waiting for his
new brother or sister.

Nothing had prepared her.
No "what if" thoughts had
darkened her mind.
A child's death only
a remote event that had
no place in her world.

Her first memory, the fog of
disembodied voices.
"Your baby is dead."
No! This is a dream!
Her eyes won't open.
More fog, more voices,
one of them hers.
"Is he really dead?
I want to wake up now
and see my son."

When the fog lifts, she sees
his father sitting and weeping.
A glorious sunrise framed
in the window, mocking her
with the promise of a new day.

No one offers to take her
to him, nor does she ask.
Dark memories from her youth
and the shock of her grandma's
body prevent that request.

Only when it's too late
she knows she
should have asked,
should have seen him,
should have said goodbye.

That unsaid goodbye
has left her with fifteen years
of the pain, "if only,"
of dark fantasies that
he is waiting for her to come
get him, of lurking shadows
of regret that she was
not brave enough
to go to him.

Today, finally,
on this quiet hillside
she says her goodbye
and is cloaked with a
gossamer veil of peace.

Reflection

Spring 1997

Mary Filkins

My reflection in the stream
Smiles back at me
A remembered smile
The mountain tops rejoice
As I reach the peak
From the gully below

The path often traveled
Is a familiar journey
But new paths ventured
Reach new horizons
More spectacular views
Seen through new eyes

A fresh, clear outlook
Like the pure stream
Mirroring my smile
Back at me
Reminding me that today
Is but for a moment

And tomorrow's sunrise
Beholds inner truth
I have yet to discover.

A Teacher's Journal

Spring 1999

Thomas Franti

In time, all that remains
will be the words in his journal:

"I taught for many years.
Every waking moment was given to their writing.
My own words were scattered in corners, like yesterday's dirty socks,
while I tended and teased, cajoled and caressed their silent tongues."

In time, a boy who was illiterate
gives voice to fear, a girl heals
with 1,000 words,
anger becomes the black scar on
the virgin page, white spaces
become openings in the heart.
Denial, rage, fear, and joy are
released by the weight of
words in his journal:

"I am grading student's writing by weight.
One and half pounds of paper is an 'A.'
Less than a pound is a 'C,'
an 'F' for words tossed about lightly.
'Weigh your words,' I tell them."

"There is no time
to find myself
when I am the Pied Piper,
piping notes and melodies
of past witnesses, playwrights,
great authors, seers, and true poets
whose questions find voice as
words in my journal."

"Is there wholeness in these words, stark before my eyes,
words that cannot lie, words that make order from disorder,
composure from chaos, saving, setting me free?"

In time, fine lines
from 500 authors
will be published
through his journal.
Every word typed
until fingers lose feeling,
eyes no longer follow
hand-scrawled words
on green paper.
Before the end,
the early authors,
those of the silent tongues,
will return to say,
"What you asked of us
was not so hard. What you gave
to us we remember."
And tears will replace
words in this teacher's journal.

Comets and Onions

Summer 2002

Dr. Reloy Garcia

Smells of grilled burgers and onions
fog the night. We wait to see a
blazing comet show, a burst
of meteors, fireworks in flight.

Northeast, one streaks, Polaris bound,
low height, guests and children gasp,
squeal, long trains of "ohhhh."
Smells of grilled burgers, onions
fog the night.

"A jet!" they cry.
"A head-light!"
"A pen-light!"
"Gold Chinese lanterns in a row!"

A burst of meteors, fireworks in flight.
One spears the moon. A toddler cries,
"Night-light!"

We laugh. Burgers burn. We turn to go.
Smells of grilled burgers, onions
fog the night.

What portents here are told? What
plague or blight? What king will die?
What leader take the blow?

A burst of meteors, fireworks in flight.
Meteors streak, criss-cross without
respite. Is this what shepherds saw,
2,000 years ago?

Smells of grilled burgers, onions
fog the night. A burst of meteors,
fireworks in flight.

Humanoid :: Danyel Engel

Life Is a Metaphor

Autumn 2004

Brett Gilcrist

Life is opportunity and chance,
having the guts to ask that girl to dance.
Life is the courage to succeed at what you do
and trying something new.

Life is taking every risk you can
and the opportunity to travel the land.
Life is doing what you will
and full of tasks we all must fulfill.

Life is being something unique
and dreaming to be someone "magnifique."
Life is telling your girlfriend you love her
and finding a medical cure.

Life is what we make of it, good or bad,
and I'm going to live my life, and be a good dad.

Safe and Whole

Autumn 1995

Cathy Goevert

I am healed, safe and whole.
I am pain-free, guilt-free, and free to make
different choices.
I am a creative author with a valuable message.

I am an artist with a joyous and poignant perspective.
My work heals me, and in doing so,
I have more of myself to give to others.
I am protected and cared for by the universe.

Differences

Spring 1994

Travis Hall

Some will go through life
Never bothering to search for any
Underlying meaning.
These will grow old and die with an
Empty and lost feeling of non-worth.

Others will search all of their lives for
Meaning, but will prove it in vain by
Always looking in the wrong corners.
These will die burned, defeated, and bitter.

A very few shall go
Searching for meaning and shall find it
Under some moss-covered rock.
Inside themselves and others
These shall die satisfied, fulfilled, and enlightened.

I Write

Summer 1997

Judy Haney

I am a writer because it's in my genes.
… because it reveals me.
… because it's relaxing.
… because I want to learn.
… because I put memories on paper.
… because I want to know my ancestors.
… because I like the solitude – the quiet.
… because it makes me think.
… because I feel more deeply.
… because I enjoy re-reading my "stuff."
… because it's like finding a few friend.
… because it expands my imagination.
… because my children all write.
… because I want to keep up with them
… because it's freedom.

I am a writer because, intuitively, I know
that I was meant to write.

How to Live in the Heartland: Planting Trees

Autumn 2004

Twyla Hansen

Humming an old hymn,
I shove my spade deep
and turn over rich earth.
Good soil, good ground for
growing trees that alone
I'm planting this Good Friday.

As did my grandfather, who,
looking over the homestead,
uttered in Dane: Augk! No trees!
and set out to correct the
godless plains. And my young
father planting oak, elm, pine,
cedar, maple, spruce, and
hackberry. I learned those
stories later, worshipped among
the limbs of their labor.

Now these hands and feet
tire, wish they were finished,
yet never quit. Like my
father and grandfather before me,
I pray to the soil, to the sky
for strength, for good planting
weather, to continue.

Each shovelful now a sacrament.
Take, eat, this soil my body
crumbled for your roots; drink
of this water, my blood, shed
for you now, and ever more.

And I sing the hymn
again and again,
knowing there is no end,

knowing there is no end.

> *"It helps to be smart, but I look
> to hire people who have a good
> work ethic and are loyal, honest,
> and show up on time."*
>
> - Warren Buffett

The Blade of Grass

Autumn 1998

Anna Henkens

As I lay prone to the blade of grass
and watched the green tendril
carefully protrude,
I heard a lone bird sing sweetly
a song while thoughtfully wondering
what the tune could conclude.

While watching and wondering
the day continued to pass,
but upon the eve of the evening
I still lay prone on the grass.

As night came, with the yellow eyes
of dark, I strained but could not hear
the lone bird's song,
I squinted but in the darkness
I could not see the blade of grass.
So I waited until morning to see if it was gone.

Morning came and still I lay,
not moving an inch;
again I could see
the tiny green tendril that I
thought had gone
and again I heard
the bird in its place
in the tree.

Not ready to move,
I let the Earth rotate once more.
The new day still brought
the tender tune and tendril,
and I still lay prone on the floor.

But the tune was not the same,
the solo had turned into a duet.
The blade of grass
no longer lived alone,
Where there had been one,
there was now a set.

So as stiff and sore as I might have been,
I stood and stretched away my pain.
I didn't want to be alone anymore,
so I left the place where for two days I had lain.

I could not forget as I left that place,
how happy I felt that they were not alone,
and how much I learned about a blade of grass
and a tuneful bird during the time I spent prone.

Spring Flowers

Spring 2011

David Prinz Hufford

I was thinking about spring flowers,
purple flowers,
when in an instant message
she appeared, saying,
"I just got online,
and there you were."
She likes flowers, so I started thinking
about her and flowers.
She likes yellow flowers.
I like purple.
I planted rows of purple allium
purple tulips,
purple grape hyacinth,
purple crocus,
and, yearly,
purple impatiens.
She wrote that I could use some contrast,
yellow tulips,
yellow crocus,
maybe
yellow alyssum.
She had no comment for why or how
the bad winter killed all the allium
and all but one of the tulips.
I did comment that I like
yellow daffodils,
and they would be nice.
She said that she liked to write to me.

How did we get there from purple?

She thinks my garden has promise.
Perhaps yellow would be nice.

The Problem with Dating a Poet

Autumn 2001

Monica Kershner

Seventy. That's right, seventy love poems
and not one for me. And I suppose
it shouldn't surprise me,
after all we just met and what else
are Midwestern poets to write about
when they're out of corn, angles of geese, and cows.
I understand,
I do - but seventy?

The problem with dating a poet
isn't the love poems, it's not
the way he describes her hair
or the metaphors in her eyes, not
the way he nouns and verbs her,
not even the allegories.

The problem with dating a poet is the women,
but how can I explain that
without sounding jealous?
Not that he's a rock star or anything,
brooding poets don't get groupies,
and it's not even the women.

The problem with dating a poet
is the idea of the women
living forever in ink, the way
their eyes held him, how he loved
every inch of their bodies,
the way their bodies moved
together, how they felt together,
but it's not even the idea of the women.

The problem with dating a poet

is the idea of me, the way his
eyes hold me, how I love every inch
of our bodies, how we feel together,
how I want to amaze him, make him feel
special and different and wonderful
and yet, at times, how I feel little more
than hopelessly ordinary.

*"Sometimes in tragedy, we find
our life's purpose - the eye sheds
a tear to find its focus."*

- Robert Brault

Miracle on the
West Bank of the River

Autumn 2004

William Kloefkorn

—for John Walker

It begins with a guitar's
broken neck,

moves then to its unlikely
replacement, an ancient Stella

found in a farmhouse attic
by a farmer who aware

of our plight
delivers it into our hands,

two of which with new strings,
duct tape, and immaculate patience

perform the delicate and necessary
surgery until—behold !—Stella
clears her throat, hums, begins
to sing, her sound concordant

with the sound the John Deere
made, Johnny-pop-pop-popper

moving heavily from there to here
to bring us tidings of great

joy, for unto us a tune is born
again, the farmer on his tractor

halfway across the continent of stubble
turning to wave, good luck, boys,

good luck, you lovely numbnuts,
in our hearts meanwhile

something ringing—call it, for want
of a better phrase, a melody of love.

Notebook Girl :: Nick Clark

Time

Summer 1998
Andy Koehler

Time is the healer of all wounds.
Shattered bones and deep gashes,
mend themselves with time.

A heart's crushed dream of a companion,
heals with time.

The ecosystem, damaged as it may be,
will repair with time.

Time devours nature's creations.
A still creature, after inhaling its last breath,
will disintegrate and vanish with time.

A mighty mountain, with peaks soaring
through the clouds,
will lay and fester, growing in strength,
only to burst out in time.

Time is a creator.

People will come to recognize and accept
one another's differences, in time.
Thus, time is the creator of peace.

Sacred Woman

Autumn 2002

Judy Leal

Coming home to myself,

The self of new and old layered hurts,
I am she, who has been pierced.
I am she, who now bleeds.
I am she, who has been silenced
in another's life.
I am she, who has been betrayed.
I am she,
who has been dangled around.
I am she, who has questioned.
I am she,
who has doubted her own personhood.
I am she, who has doubted her wisdom.
I am she, who has been needy of that,
which is on the outside of me.
It has made me weak of spirit.

Now,
I've journeyed home to
the Great Alone,
alone inside myself,
aware, ever more aware
of new pain, old heartache.

God of my journey,
reach inside and touch
my needy parts,
with merely the surface of your
Great Spirit breath.
Redeem me into wholeness once again.
Let me be done with groveling,

or so it felt,
when I was dismissed.

I didn't belong; I wasn't heard.
I felt forever lost and alone.
No one is really to be known,
except by you,
Holy One,
Powerful One, Redeemer.

Who and what will I embrace
on this new journey,
this new page?
How will I create new and vibrant
life inside myself?
Who will I include in my journey,
where I am ever alone, yet
truly not?

Sacred Woman,
I am done with sexual secrecy.
All I am is alive and about God inside.
Even the secret parts are hallowed,
sacred spaces of God Being.

All longing can be honored
and expressed through marvelous
creative energy of Sacred Woman.

Embrace yourself.
Create deeper
more compassionate love.

Include any
who come to your heart door
unafraid of powerful energy
deep within.

I wandered and was led
to face the energy force inside of me,
to stare it in the face,
and hold in disbelief and shock.
How quickly it evaporated into a cloud,
blown away by the southwest wind.
Gone.

Particles of this life force
will always reappear.
I'll be happy
for the new clouds of faces
the wind blows in,
for I am inside each and everyone.

Let go once again,
Sacred Woman.

Blessings from the east.
Blessings from the south.
Blessings from the west.
Blessings from the north.

Twirl around, twirl again.
Embrace all the false insecurities.
Let God's wind blow them
beyond the eastern shores.

Feel the fire of the south calling you
to new life.
Light your fire, gently stirring old forgotten embers,
remembering they are only embers,
not the fire,
not the flame.
They will help the burning.

Refresh with water from the west,
washing all as new again and again.
Gently tread upon the northern trails that have brought you

to the south.
Kiss the path with the homage
it deserves.

Be not possessive nor possessed.
Let others in your life go.
Live freely.
They'll come dance again.
I'll accept them, if they come to me.

For I am Sacred Woman,
once locked up,
but now set free.

Always There

Summer 1999
Mary Lewandowski

Be still my heart
do not trespass
the beckoning road
that leads to
darkness,
gloom
and utter despair,
Cast away the shadows,
abandon the agony,
step into
the clearness of light,

Lay hand to heart,
feel the gentle breeze
calm and
soothe away the tears,

See the flowered garden
in grand array of color,
breathe in
the lingering fragrance,

Pause and reflect
as the winding river
flows
in quiet pursuit,

God's world surrounds,
listen,
there is a tapping
on the heart,

Offer praise
in jubilation,
claim
the spirit
of the day.

National Outdoor Leadership School :: Bradley Martin

Gentle Betrayal

Spring 1996

Kathleen Maloney

Unexpectedly, just before dawn,
the last light snow fell,
surprising me early in the morning
when I arose and glanced out of the
bedroom window.
Instead of dew-sparkled grass
and flowering forsythia,
I found a white-dusted green lawn
and frosted hedges
that only yesterday thirstily drank in a
gentle April rain.

Not amused, the ancient maple tree
just outside my window,
that daily measures Nature's moods,
barely maintained its dignity
in this antic joke.
With its white-dressed branches
motionless, its curled new leaves
trembled their exasperation,
affronted by Nature's untimely betrayal.

And then, a cardinal, scarlet
as its scolding song,
fearlessly chiding Nature for
her capricious spirit,
changed its tune from accusatory to
approving, when, without warning,
morning sun rays melted through
spring clouds, dazzled the snow
momentarily, then, erased all traces
of Nature's prank.

Home Plate

Spring 1997
Erin Martin

Erin
is friendly, competitive, and calm.

wishes to be a four-time gold medalist,
dreams of going to Heaven, and
wants to be rich like Bill Gates.

wonders if she will be as tall as Ashley,
fears Chuckie, and
believes in fortune cookies.

plans to be a teacher,
to live on a ranch, and
to become a genius.

loves to eat Chinese food,
to have fun, and
to play softball.

She knows her final destination is
home plate.

Misunderstood Poetry

Summer 1999

Walker Martin

Poetry is often misunderstood! Well, perhaps that is as it should be. One of the more likely complaints or misconceptions surrounds works of modern poetry.

"This stuff can't be poetry. Poems have to rhyme."

My eighth graders insist on this well-known fact to the bitter end. I would like to offer a clarification on the matter, but only, of course, with the plea that no one assume my discussion to be complete. No view of "what poetry is" can ever be complete.

One important distinction within the world of poems is narrative vs. imagery. This separation might also be seen in rough terms as traditional vs. modern poetry. Most of us, when asked to define poetry, think of rhyming and predictable patterns of rhythm. The limerick is an example of both. This is typical of the narrative form. Modern poetry, while having some rhyme and repeating rhythm, doesn't allow either to drive it. Often, no rhyme is present, or the rhythm is difficult to discern. Let us then look closer at these two forms.

The narrative tells a story. It moves the reader through time. The narrative is an ancient form and predates the written word. Its descendants amount to everything from epic ballads, nursery rhymes, and mnemonics (Those cute little memory joggers) to 99.9% of song lyrics. The narrative found its place in our ancestors' lives, because those charged with keeping track of cultural records found it easier to remember information that rhymed and had a specific number of beats in its construction.

The narrative form, then, carries one across time. It is the telling of a story. Imagery, on the other hand, tries to take a slice of time, freeze it, and then "paint the picture." The narrative is the ancient, while imagery is the bent of the modern poet. Understand, the two forms are anything but mutually exclusive. Narrative forms have imagery and vice versa. The differentiation is one of primary purpose.

Imagery can be "painted" with the use of rhyme, but just as likely, if not more so, it is not. Even less likely is the use of a predictable pattern of rhythm. This, however, in no way lets the modern poet "off the hook" in terms of rhythm. All poetry has some element of "flow" to it. This allows comfort on the reader's part. We demand this in sports, movies, art, and so it is with poetry, too. It is just the case that rhythm might not be as readily evident in some modern works.

How does one "paint" imagery? One means is to "freeze" in one's mind an event or scene. The poem is then a description of this frozen moment. All senses are available to play with, as are emotions. For example, what does anger "look" like? The poet's task is then to engage the senses and emotions through words that create visions.

Use of imagery does not preclude telling a story. Any story can be enhanced by the use of imagery. The modern poet would probably view the story as a vehicle for the series of images created in the telling. As readers, we tend to "freeze" scenes from a story anyway. Even the narrative, in the hands of the modern poet, would tend to be a sequence of vividly frozen pictures.

Winter, Bridge, Tree, Snow :: Kim Justus

Let Darkness Come

Summer 2006

Vince McAndrew

Even the brightest stars
are invisible during the day,
yet they shine on,
exploding themselves
moment by moment
until they are no more.

These colossal fiery furnaces
blaze in the heavens all around us,
as we spin through our
own planet's destiny.

Earth bound,
we only glimpse these
distant beacons,
these marvels of physics,
these portals to our past,
at night,
when the light of our own star
has left us.

Though we would design
each day to never end,
to always be in the light,
in yielding to the darkness,

we can,
if we choose,
see the stars
and wonder.

Last Moments

Winter 1996

Larry Munn

The room, dark and dank, like a foxhole –
type O bombs from heaven, shot –
no, slid down the tubes,
leaking life juice into lifelessness.

Pallid gaze from patient to visitor and back,
Pride drained as soiled gown is removed,
naked before nurse and God;
bottomed out in pain.

What pondering transpires inside
a dying brain?
Are memories flying by like
a motion picture,
or are we simply alone,
between sickness and death,
struggling, transfixed
by moving clusters of cancer cells
and an awareness of finality?

Shining brightly, the sun climbs the wall
like a fireball rising to Heaven's gate –
carrying with it his spirit –
free, freeing, freedom.
Love replaces pain:
God's new right-hand man.

(Author's notes: I wrote this because it felt weird to be downtown and hear a kid in the back of a pickup truck holler, "Hey, Geezers!" and when I looked around, I discovered he meant me and my group. I guess I'm getting old.)

Geezerville
Spring 1998

Tom Pappas

No one ever asks directions to Geezerville.
When it's time, you just show up.
It doesn't seem to the younger set
that you could be having much fun,
because you don't willingly go on
the thrill rides any more.

You'll be happy and well fed
when you get there.
Because you carefully select exactly
what you want from the line at
The Old Country Buffet.
Dozens of irate people, trapped behind you,
hope the food doesn't spoil,
because you take so long.

You might show up to a picnic,
in a coat and tie and not notice
or feel the least bit uncomfortable.
You always dress that way,
and it feels natural.

On the way, Tommy Dorsey comes on the
radio, and you reach for the volume knob
to turn it up and keep the kids
from changing it.

You had to pass on the wonderful, hot taco
sauce you can only get in California.
It isn't worth the antagonism it causes
your digestive system.
"Do you have anything that isn't so spicy?
Decaf, please."

You'll get there eventually, but you'll be at
the very end of the line of traffic, because
you stopped and waved to the cars
waiting on the side streets.
Having waited there so many times yourself
makes it seem the right thing to do.

It takes a little longer because
you read the whole text
on the historical markers along the way.

Standing at the mirror getting ready, it's
impossible to see every detail without bifocals,
and you can't do most of what you're there
for with glasses on.
So the result isn't precise.
You look just fine to yourself before you
walk away, then put on your glasses.

You certainly won't be lonely, because you
embarrassed the kids by making conversation with strangers.
You met them in grocery checkout lines and
on airplanes, and every other conceivable place.
You don't seem to understand how cool that isn't.

It takes a little longer to get there because
you are driving slower.
Is it because you're contemplating your
grandchild playing somewhere and
hope and pray she's never hit by a car?
Or your own lifetime of driving and your
good fortune to not hit someone?

No one ever asks directions to Geezerville.
When it's time you just show up.
It may be that you didn't even know that's
where you were heading.
But it will happen.
It's inevitable, and it's not that bad.

One Little Light

Autumn 1992

Lisa Pelto

Through the mundane darkness
You were a flicker for me.
A subtle reminder of
The fun life can be.

A moment, a smile,
A laugh, a tease –
You awakened my spirits
Like the wind in the trees.

Your kiss left me wanting
What I shouldn't desire.
When your eyes touched my hunger
You set me on fire.

That time is over;
The risk is done,
Unaltered exteriors hide
The battle we won.

You may never know
How you've helped me, my friend.
You made me remember
Life's short; it will end.

I'll have more fun now.
Lighten up, if you will.
My life is as it was.
You've simply nudged me uphill.

Perfect Circles

Spring 2005
Stephanie Pluta

Observable perfect circles:
the spherical harvest moons
announcing the newest waves of wheat;
the hearts of the tomatoes full of juices
and dancing a two-step from the soil
on lengths of vine;
the rounded womb,
temple to the hands that feel everyday
for the growing curve of a baby, curled
like the materials forming into soft petals
within the buried Peony seed.

Harvest moons wane
but always return; like the wheat arranged
into a million golden dancers
in summer fields.
Tomato plants are dismantled
their fruits left sitting in place
in a produce bin, by the roadside or in a store;
but the hands that buy and slice them
feed the hungry mouth
so life can go on.

Hands that feel the baby
stretching the womb
to its most complete roundness
soon hold a new life
that uncurls like the touchable shoots and petals
of the Peony flowers, also moving in cycles
as if life's center is a perfect circle.

"Poetry Is ..."
Spring 1998

"A composition in verse with language selected for its beauty and sound, the art of writing stories, poems, and thoughts into verse." -*Webster's Collegiate Dictionary*

everything I cherish and love" (Katie Akers).

a recognized art form in all languages" (Chad Arndt).

a spiritual, eternal aura" (Amanda Arroyo).

a reflection of ourselves (Tim Benson).

being moved enough by something to want to go through a transition" (Molly Campbell).

a tunnel to my soul" (Kitrina Fisher).

given in some way to someone else" (Sarah Gerken).

sprawling my guts in the form of words" (Terra Gillespie).

the astronomer seeking desperately for truth in the darkness" (Andrew Glasser).

ripping my chest open and draining the emotion in my heart onto paper (Matt Handlos).

collecting words from the heart" (James Heimann).

aking a point, fighting for new ground, and my relief" (Sally Hess).

always makes me better, stable, and stronger" (Laura Ingersoll).

feeling so much about a topic that words appear on the page" (Colin Irwin).

pouring out one's soul onto paper" (Carissa Jeffers).

a series of mistakes constantly being corrected" (Nicholas Jones).

felt thought" (Katherine Knott).

life, a science of studying one's inner self" (Adriana Pina).

a subtle tool used to bear a creator's soul" (Chaia Lloyd).

a dichotomy, either the search for truth or the escape from it" (Liz Montag).

writing that puts one's mind at ease and heart at rest" (Tia Nelson).

standing in the laundry room" (James Pandis).

a mystic path into an unknown realm" (Jamie Peery).

the light of truth in a dark world" (Zachary Peterson).

the violence of experiencing emotions bled onto paper" (Luke Smith).

pure feeling put into words" (Noelle Thornburg).

the gateway to the soul, as far as the imagination will take you" (Mark Thorpe).

how I express myself, using all the art of my soul" (Daniel Whelan).
"The world is a poem, and we are verses" (Andrew Glasser).

Fine Lines Campers :: David Martin

Angelic Minds

Spring 1994

Harold Poff

Angelic minds (and where they dwell)
Lie far beyond Man's reaching,
Though often human hearts may swell,
If humans do some teaching.

For as the year begins (or ends?)
And Loving outsmarts Reason,
It's we who tell our angel friends
The wonders of the Season.

Hark, Herald, Sing :: Raleigh Wilkerson

Music Forever

Autumn 2011

Gwen Quill

Singing my heart out
The music comes so easily
My mind opens up, my heart grows wings
And I fly to a world of song

The notes dance on my tongue,
My technique improving every day
My voice getting louder, my lungs growing stronger
Patient teacher beaming with delight

A place where I'm just another face in the crowd
But I can dream for the future to come
I can hope for the successful world of fame
To pick me up and take me away

The room in which I sing is a painted wall of white
Freeing the imagination to soar
Opening up the door to my soul
Slaughtering the feeling of shyness and shame

In a world of dreams I let my voice take me away
Where my heart and song rule all
I attempt to write my name on the unbreakable tablet of fame
I mark my life with song
Here is where I belong

Storm at Night

Spring 2003

Marjorie Saiser

About one in the morning
on Indian Island
the wind wakes me, sucking in
the sides of the tent, sounding in
my ears. The lightning so bright in
the dark that after it is gone,
it remains on the back of my eyelids.
On the back of my eyelids the hoops
and zippers of the inside of the tent.
Thunder close and huge over me.
The rain beating on the tent,
on the purple poppy mallow,
as I imagine it, low against
the ground in the dark.
Talons of the screech owl
grasping the substance of the tree.

When things settle down to
Rain, the surface of the
Platte, as I imagine it,
peppered as if with stones.
I am thinking of my friend who,
when he knew he was going to die,
sat in his yard in the sunshine
with his neighbor. The two of them
sitting on blue lawn chairs drinking
Stroh's. Both of them with their
man-hands rolling cigarettes, making
a trough with the index finger in
squares of white paper, shaking
the tobacco into the trough. Rolling,
licking the papers, trying again.
Both of them not smokers, smoking.

Both of them not talking about illness.

The Platte flowing from its source
around and over gray boulders, flowing
beside Indian Island, beneath thunder,
white for a moment under lightning,
its broad surface wrinkling
like skin. I am thinking of
Crazy Horse, who before he
died, asked for the man who had
pushed the bayonet into the soft
parts of his back. Asked for that
one to stand before him and spoke
to him of pardon. Crazy Horse lying
in his bloody graveclothes.
His mother and father receiving the
body of their light-haired child
to put into the cart.

After rain, not sleeping, thinking.
A wind high in the cottonwoods.
the crickets stroking the dark.
Thinking of my daughter who called
to say she cut her hand with a
knife in her kitchen. My daughter
far down the flow of the Platte,
learning my grandmother's remedy,
using her poultice of sugar and
alcohol. The cut, as I imagine it,
healing. My daughter, her smooth
brown hair, as I imagine it, hanging

above their hands. Young woman's
hands, skin sleek and taut, thin
bark of the slender ash.
Old woman's hands laying the white
cloth of the poultice against
the red line of the scab,
winding strips of cloth,

wrapping the wound.
The Platte from its source
peppered by night rains.
In the sun the water sparkling
like leaves turning in wind.
The Platte wrinkling over its sandbars,
around the smooth white bones
of its cottonwood logs.

Blythe :: Cindy Grady

Aphorisms, Platitudes, Caring

Summer 1999

R. W. Seaman

Being concerned is one thing;
being nosy is quite another.

Weeds choke out the good stuff,
when no one tends the garden.

Where there is little love,
there is but little concern.

It's better to get into the fight
than be shot as an innocent bystander.

If you don't want to get involved,
get out of the way of those who do.

The years may wrinkle the skin,
but indifference wrinkles the soul.

When you remain neutral,
you help and hurt both sides.

Those who see clearly see a lot
they'd as soon not have to look at.

More heartbreak is caused
by people who just don't care
than by those with malice aforethought.

Criminals love those communities where
people don't want to get involved.

A Poet's Wisdom

September 1993

Roxanne Slattery

Simplistic Utopia Does Thoreau Portray
Harmonious tranquility reaches fruition
Find the way through unwavering conviction

Arrogance and Deception Did Crane Inveigh
Gentle war is but the fool's caprice
The true hero crusades for our peace

Emerson Pleas: From Thy Soul Go Not Astray
Contentment to those who but dare to dream
Allow not reliance; Know self-esteem

Of Frost, Conformity Is Peril's Sobriquet
Joyous pleasures once from trees
Always choose the path which frees

Honor and Truth Pope Shall Bewray
Do not remorse those treasures lost
Sacrifice your conscience at no cost

Shackle Thy Genius? Horace Begs, Nay!
Like a waterfall his words cascade
Let knowledge become your palisade

Wordsworth Orates, To Your Faith Belay
Prayer can sorrow always becalm
The wealthy make charity their only psalm

The Bard Bequeaths a Lyrical Bouquet
Omens forewarned by a Delphic sage
Destiny ignored in a blind man's rage

Heed Socrates – Greed Sires Dismay
Havoc lurks waiting in matters unkempt
Of both saints and sinners – feel not contempt

Humbled By Gibran, The Prophetic Émigré
Hatred forever is humanity's bane
Set yourself free – let His love reign

From Bacon, Our Prosperity We Must Repay
Your honorable steps always retrace
Forgive those who fall far from grace

Christ-like Clues Warrant Deductive Play
Suspense, as the woven plots unveil
Many a crime she did curtail

Galaxies and Civilizations Does Asimov Survey
Science, mystery, and legends combined
Fantasy meets reality, to expand the mind

Keating Beckons All to "Seize the Day"
Together, ignorance we will impale
This precious life – so dear, so frail

Of My Mentors' Gifts I Must Convey
To ensure lives be not spent in solitaire
Of the poets' wisdom, may you be the heir

If I Were an Animal

Spring 2005

Grace Solem-Pfeifer

If I were an animal,
I would be a black jaguar.
They're probably my favorite
because they're in the cat family.

They live in the rainforest!
Jaguars are very cool because
they are always mysterious and
secretive animals looming in the shadows.

I also like jaguars because of their split personalities.
Jaguars are fierce hunters stalking their prey,
and the next second, they're a bigger version
of your pussycat curled up in the living room at home.

I love their jet-black fur mostly
because black is my second favorite color.
I like jaguars basically because they're,
in my opinion, the most awesome animals!

The Brown Man's Burden

Summer 1998

Joe Sousa

Take up "the Brown Man's Burden."
Send forth the best ye breed.
Release your sons from exile,
And undo your master's deed.
Lift off that heavy harness,
And go forth through
the towns and wild,
And teach your master's people,
Half devil and half child.

Take up "the Brown Man's Burden."
In patience do abide.
Ignore the threat of terror,
And check their show of pride.
By open speech and simple talk,
A hundred times made plain,
Show together all will profit,
And a future shall be gained.

Take up "the Brown Man's Burden,"
And fight the wars for peace.
Cross the void of ignorance,
And bid the sickness cease,
And when the goal is nearest,
The end for which ye fought,
Watch jealous Pride and ancient Fear
Bring all your hopes to naught.

Take up "the Brown Man's Burden,"
Though dark may be the night.
Follow the spirit of Jah,
For Zion is in sight.
The ports ye shall enter,

The roads ye shall tread,
Go and teach your master's people
Why our kinsman lie dead.
Take up "the Brown Man's Burden."
Seek the ultimate goal,
The battle for Utopia
Is not a deed for a timid soul.
Eden no more will ever be,
Yet, Paradise is what we seek.
To forget what is unobtainable
Is an excuse for the meek.

Take up "the Brown Man's Burden."
Ye dare not stoop to less,
For ye fight for Freedom,
In spite of your weariness.
By all ye cry or whisper,
By all ye think and do,
Our silent, unborn children
Shall weight me and you.

Dragons

Winter 1993

Linda Stevens

Dragons have always been inspiring to me,
their strength, their chemical magic,
the secrets of the cosmos that they keep
locked up and protected in their caves.

Not because
they are evil or greedy, but because they have
been attacked and persecuted.

What they have hidden in their caves is
precious and valuable.
Yes, they are frightening,
but only because they are unknown.

Once they have been invited in
and befriended,

well then,

remember Puff?

Blessings from Me to You

Autumn 2003

Mindy Venditte

May the passions guide you,
When your head holds you back.
May the brightness of the day
Bring the truth to your dreams at night.

May life's little treasures
Dance upon your toes
And make your heart giggle
About the goals you call your own.

May love's ever gentle hand
Hold you when you are weak.
May you always feel protected
By the magic that I speak.

Hold close to the wants
Of the life you call your own.
You have everything inside,
Just turn over the stones.

May the drummer in your heart
Beat the tune that he must drum.
May you never feel alone or blue.
Someone is looking out for you.

An Ode to Mama

Autumn 1995

Mabel Victoria Walter

Mama,
the jewel,
the crown,
the deity,
the center of our universe.
We cry!
Why has she gone,
our beloved Mama?

The fair skin freckled by the sun,
the quick smile that lit up our lives,
her flaming hair turned to auburn
are pictures ever in our minds.
Oh, why?
Why has she been taken away?
She who worked so hard –
had such dreams for her treasured children?

Why – oh, why do we cry?
God give us back our Mama,
but we are too young to understand.
There are four of us,
each so different in our own ways
but bonded by the grief of our terrible loss.

The baby had it hardest of all –
so small and no mama to
soothe and reassure.
"Mama, Mama,"
are the cries in the night.
They go unanswered, and loneliness sets in.

What do we do?
Where do we turn, as we
are torn and separated,
placed here and there?
Oh, woe, we have lost each other, too.

There are no roots,
no place of our own.
We are alone,
nowhere to turn,
each on our own.

Time passed, and we survived.
Even though we are grown
and have families of our own,
we still mourn the loss of
the jewel
the crown
the deity
the center of our universe
our beloved Mama.

Crisis

Summer 1999

Margaret McCann Warren

We who question the ways of man
and the many gods he worships
may choose to live by simpler rules,
leaving our final destinies and such
to the super-wisdom of the Master-Planner,
who seems to have worked the whole thing out
in unbelievable and awesome ways.

What do we do in a time of great distress
when someone whom we deeply love is trapped
in a labyrinth of overwhelming pain, an agony of spirit,
or of body, that will not go away?
In panic, we demand an instant cure
or some relief from this grief and suffering that we must share.
No one has an answer.

We hound our scholars in their ivory towers
and specialists who search through heavy tomes,
even mystic seers, studying the stars.
Each of them offers possible solutions
that might help, and nothing does.

Then, in our anguish, we reach for something more.
Whoever we are, wherever we are, the child in us is
in need of love and comfort and understanding,
a searching and a longing that is universal.
We sink to our knees and pray.

Analysis

Summer 1997

Peggy Wheeler

I have learned many philosophies
I have studied the secrets
of myth and body
the language of women
the manipulations of men
but do I know
any more about that figure
in my rocking chair
that marble made flesh
that lithe slumber
wrapped in wool
in denim in a deep-eyed
pondering
I know nothing of him.

I know nothing of her
who writes recipes like poetry
who comforts the young
with implacable love
like a vein of fire
from her soul surging from
her abdomen through her heart
rushing in her brain
with her lava warmth of
fingertips and timbre.

Man is a fleshy beast
who acts on the merest feather of feeling

and we may
pluck our intellects
and number our reactions
into indexes of attitudes

but we are then
only plucked
like wrench-necked chickens
less attractive than before
more confused than ever.

Dear Muhammad Ali

Summer 2005

Karl White

As a young black man in the world,
I naturally fight.
I fight stereotypes.
I fight peer pressure, and
I constantly fight to win the battle
between success and failure.

Trying to live a life filled
with up's and down's
takes its toll on my nerves
and makes my heart weary.
My decision making is at
an all-time low.

I feel that the world was not made
for a man of my desires.
Sports and relaxation
are all I really need.
Still, I'm forced to be
the city-leading star
that no one likes because
I'm trying, and they're not.

I'm tired of the same city limits
and signs, the exact avenue
of failure is ridden on by me.
Have you ever felt, as if,
even though you succeed
at one level, there are so
many more levels to go through
that your victory is short-lived?

What fun is winning when it's shadowed
by future requirements?
No one ever lets me just win for now.
I always have to conquer more,
but this is the life I lead,
full of distrust
and falsehood because
I only trust myself.

My Rough Draft

Autumn 2004

Sade White

I told you my thoughts, and you
accepted them as your own.
I told you my fears, and you
shielded me as long as you could.

Through stormy nights and
vanilla skies, you said to me
the things I wanted to hear,
instead of the things I needed to hear.

Through rude awakenings and sudden stops,
you held me closely, but you thought of another.
I told you that you were my heart,
and without you I couldn't function.

Now, you are gone, and slowly I shut down.
I ask my Prince Charming, who ever you are,
please come and rescue me from this dark tower
called the world and replace my love that I have no more.

This is how I figure it.
Maybe, this is the rough draft
before the final copy
of my happy ending.

Shadows Behind the Light

Summer 2005

Mary Davey Wilson

A sweetness in daybreak's breath
ladels mist splashes on my face and arms,
slick brushes to moisten parched memories.

Light circles whirl,
bringing forgotten dreams
of dancing candles
on shadowed walls.

Ransacking lips whisper
sophistry, moonlight.

Hedonistic promises
whet momentary delights.

Fantasy sneaks out
the front door, while leaving lies,
emotional bondage, and wasteland.

Solitary circles fade with the dawn,
silent tribute to forgotten candle lights

on shadowed walls.

Excellence

Autumn 1995
Gerri Zerse

Perfection is being right.
Excellence is being willing to be wrong.

Perfection is fear.
Excellence is taking a risk.

Perfection is anger and frustration.
Excellence is powerful.

Perfection is control.
Excellence is spontaneous.

Perfection is judgment.
Excellence is accepting.

Perfection is taking.
Excellence is giving.

Perfection is doubt.
Excellence is confidence.

Perfection is pressure.
Excellence is natural.

Perfection is the destination.
Excellence is the journey.

Kudos from Readers

"Fine Lines is very important in my life, more than anyone knows. I look forward to the first Saturday of each month and the Special Editors' Meetings, as if they were my birthdays."

-Marcia Forecki, Council Bluffs, IA

"When I miss a Fine Lines meeting, I lose my creative boost for the month and the linguistic banter of that day."

-Chris Raabe, 8th grade language arts teacher,
Millard Public Schools

"As a Fine Lines Special Editor, I have my finger on the pulse of creative writers from all over our country and the world. I feel the living creativity in language, and it is alive in this publication."

-David Hufford, retired English professor,
Iowa Western Community College, Council Bluffs, IA

"Fine Lines is so valuable because it connects readers to new voices."

-Sjon Ashby, English professor,
Bellevue University, Bellevue, NE

"When I believe in my dream, to write is just that, a dream, and then I open the pages of Fine Lines and realize that everyone else believes in the same dream. This is what being a writer is about!"

-Mindy Venditte, Cornhusker Driving Academy,
Ft. Calhoun, NE

"Fine Lines stimulates my imagination and encourages the flow of creative ideas. For me, it is the difference between thinking about a book and actually writing one."

-Kim Justus, photographer, Omaha, NE

"Fine Lines is the writing community I wish I had when I was a student. I love the inter-generational collegiality of these members."

-Deborah Ball Derrick, grant writer, Omaha, NE

"Thanks to Fine Lines and all of your editors for encouraging writers like me to keep placing words on paper."

-Linda Hayek, retired mathematics instructor, Omaha, NE

"I would love to share information regarding Fine Lines with anyone and everyone who is interested. Let me tell you my story of the first time I was published in this publication.

I was divorced, alone, sad, and at the Southpointe Mall in Lincoln, NE, shopping for a new shower curtain at Bed Bath and Beyond. It was rainy; the selection of shower curtains was overwhelming, and I really didn't care anyway. So, I went to Barnes and Noble and got a cup of coffee. I walked over to the magazine section, and Fine Lines was sitting there on the shelf, with my name (Dorothy Apley) on the front cover, listed with the other writers whose works were included in that issue.

That was back when the issues were white, and FL had the writers' names listed down the front cover. It instantly made me feel happy and hopeful. I felt like skipping around the room, telling everyone in the bookstore that my name was on the cover of that issue.

This event really did change my outlook on the future. I was too poor to buy more than one copy of that issue and share it with anyone else. Now, I am happily remarried with six grandchildren, but I will never forget that moment. It was like the beginning of all good things.

Thank you for that."

-Dorothy Apley Miller, English teacher, Geneva, NE

"The only positive advance I have been aware of in education in the last 20 years is the advent of Fine Lines. Finally, we have a tool and incentive for students to ignore rote learning and begin to think for themselves. The growing number of contributors worldwide testifies to its success. It well deserves the applause engendered on its twentieth anniversary."

-Raleigh Wilkerson, Meredith, New Hampshire

"We enjoy your Fine Lines publication and so do our patrons."

-Dianne (Children's Librarian),
Lydia Bruun Woods Memorial Library, Falls City, NE

"I really enjoy the Fine Lines journals. I use them for my adult learners at Creighton University's EOC outreach program."

-Carol Hipp, retired history teacher
and chair at Central High School, Omaha, NE

"I can't tell you how pleased I am to watch the continuing growth of Fine Lines. It is such a credit to you and all who encourage good prose."

-Edie Goodwin, Council Bluffs, IA

"Fine Lines is a great outlet for writers and artists of all ages and abilities. David and his co-editors do an amazing job of putting together a quality publication that is a treat for both the eyes and the mind. I'm proud to be one of those published in it."

-Carol Wessling, Bellevue NE

"Fine Lines is that inviting body of water where writers of all ages and backgrounds have been launching their craft; a short story, a poem, a memoir, for the sheer joy of the journey of recognition. The breeze that drives across its pages is the human spirit, the main ingredient that gives its defining character and longevity. The title itself, Fine Lines, conjures up the expression seamen use in appraising a sailing vessel's potential, "Aye, she has fine lines!"

-Gerald Schnitzer, Laguna Woods, CA

"Fine Lines is a literary journal that welcomes work from people of all backgrounds. What is special about it is the diversity of writers that readers get to know. Fine Lines is not only a literary journal but also a medium of connecting people with a universal passion. To be a part of Fine Lines is not only an honor but something that weaves a common thread to everyone involved. Through the art of writing and the love of reading, Fine Lines unites people from all walks of life."

-Salma Mohamed-Smith, Omaha, NE

"I'd love more information about being a Fine Lines representative. It sounds pretty awesome. I told my classmates to submit their work; and you actually published my friend Christine's poem in your fall issue. I'll definitely sign up for a subscription. I think it will be a little easier than having to steal Fine Line's copies from my teacher's desk. -Lizzie, Martha's Vineyard Regional High School, MA

"I received my first edition of Fine Lines with my story in it. I can't tell you how pleased I am. I'm very impressed. Thanks for all of your work in making such an outstanding publication."

-Jason Garrett, Kailua, HI

"Fine Lines is a literary journal that began modestly as a high school class newsletter in 1990 and has since become an internationally circulated quarterly. The journal's purpose is to validate writing and to validate writers. It is a journal for the people, for all people who care enough to invest in their writing. Fine Lines is an extracurricular pedagogical gift, and I have personally witnessed many of our own students in jubilation over seeing their work appear between its covers."

-Dr. Robert Darcy, English Department Chair,
the University of Nebraska at Omaha

"You have no idea how good it is to be involved with your Fine Lines writing group. I look forward to it."

-Portia Love, Omaha, NE

"Happy Anniversary to Fine Lines! Congratulations! Bravo! To you and to all who have made this journal possible! As we writing teachers know, it is an honor to encourage our students to write the truth, as they know it and be a part of their writing journey. As an educator I know that we all need to hear voices which capture and tell as many truths as possible.

Our writing community, our lives, all continue to intertwine, just as our love of writing continues beyond the boundaries of semesters and the borders of countries. I will continue to encourage students and members of the writing community whose paths cross mine to submit their works to Fine Lines. I do this because I know the editorial needs and expectations and that well-written pieces will be carefully read.

My heart sings joyful songs today for Fine Lines and for the master editors of this world-class journal. Encore! For years and years to come!

With my very best wishes,

-Nancy Genevieve Perkins, Associate Professor of English, Past Chair, 2003-2005, English Department, University of Illinois at Springfield

"Thank you Fine Lines for always encouraging me to write. I created space in my schedule to write, today. I just plugged it into my 'holy time,' and I always look forward to your feedback."

-Monika Lukasiewicz, occupational therapist, Lincoln, NE

"I greatly appreciate the challenging and unique writing by people of so many diverse backgrounds in each issue of Fine Lines. It is exciting when you publish my students' work and when they receive feedback from others who have read it."

-Sheila Boerner, English teacher, North Platte, NE

"It is so nice to read a quality literary magazine that offers a voice for young writers. It's hard for new writers to break into the creative writing community. Many get discouraged along the way and give up. Publication in *Fine Lines* is a gift, one that I am grateful for."

-Karen O'Leary, West Fargo, ND

"Our students are excited when they have a story or poem published in Fine Lines. You are doing a great job with the publication. We display the copies we receive in our library, so students and teachers can enjoy the writings. I will continue to encourage our teachers to submit writings. Keep up the good work."

**-Linda Severin, Gifted Student Coordinator,
Alice Buffett Magnet Middle School, Omaha, NE**

"Thank you for publishing my writing. I respect your Fine Lines mission statement, and I look forward to working with you in achieving that goal."

**-Julie Temple, student,
Minnesota State University at Moorhead**

"I use Fine Lines in the classroom with my honor's students and appreciate the opportunity to submit their work. Thank you for this publication."

**-Sharon Oakman, language arts teacher,
Morton Magnet Middle School, Omaha, NE**

"I use Fine Lines in my classroom every Friday, during the school year. We call it 'Fine Lines Friday.' The kids love our creative writing day."

**-Paula Anderson,
high school English teacher, Louisville, NE**

"I was pleased and surprised to find my article in a recent issue of Fine Lines. Thank you for giving me more confidence in my writing ability."

**-Jeanie Boll,
a Metropolitan Community College student, Blair, NE**

"Fine Lines is a well-respected, national creative writing journal. It serves as a fantastic outlet for many of our beginning writers' productions. I cannot tell you how many times my students have confided in me that they write poetry or short fiction but do not know whether it is any good. Invariably, I pull out a copy of Fine Lines from my bookshelf and suggest they send their work to Fine Lines. A number of students have published their work in Fine Lines, and I know being included in its pages means the world to them. It gives our students a real-life objective to shoot for with their writing."

**-Dr. Charles Johanningsmeier, Professor of American Literature,
the University of Nebraska at Omaha**

Author's Biographical Notes

Kathryn Aagesen was a student in New York City at the Academy of American Arts and Drama. She looked forward to becoming an actress in Hollywood.

Alina Banasyak was a senior at Omaha Central High School, was born in Ukraine, and came to this country two years before.

Josh Bieber was a Central High School junior in Omaha, NE.

Kay Bret was the University of Nebraska at Omaha English Department secretary and wrote in a journal to bring sanity and love to her world.

Carolyn Bullard was a tenth grade student at Omaha Central High School. The following summer she traveled to Abidjan, Ivory Coast, Africa, to be a summer exchange student, and she hopes to increase her fluency in the French language. Upon graduation, she will enroll at Davidson College, North Carolina, as an English major.

Stu Burns works for an insurance company and uses his free time to study religious history.

Ray Dewaele was a special education teacher at Omaha Central High School.

Rachel Danford was a junior at Central High School in Omaha, NE.

Deb Derrick was the Editor and Communications Specialist in the College of Engineering and Technology at the University of Nebraska at Lincoln.

Mike Dropinski was a student at Metropolitan Community College in Omaha, NE.

Nicole Dubas was a sophomore at Omaha Central High School.

Rebecca Fahrlander, PhD, has an educational background in sociology, social psychology, and philosophy. She taught at UNO, UNL, and Creighton

University. She also has experience in research, management, and consulting.

Mary Filkins was a secretary for Sterling Software in Bellevue, NE, and was working on a business degree at Metropolitan Community College.

Kirsten Furlong was an artist and student at the University of Nebraska at Omaha. She used her journal to slay many dragons that tried to prevent her from realizing her artistic goals.

Stephen Gehring is an Omaha, NE, attorney.

Lawrence J. (Larry) Geisler was an English teacher and department chairman in Marshalltown, Iowa, for many years. He is now retired but continues to write every day.

Dinah Gomez was a sales manager for Lite 96 FM Radio in Omaha, NE.

Gregory L. "Woody" Gruber is a graduate of the University of Nebraska and works for the Omaha Public Schools.

Robert Hamm, an English teacher and also an assistant principal in the West Linn School District of Portland, Oregon, submitted this list of book "truths" with which all serious readers will surely agree.

Mindy Hauptman was a student at UNO, a lover of butterflies, an observer of all traffic lights, and learned many things by studying metaphors of all kinds.

Anna Henkens-Schmidt lived in Chadron, NE, and was a newspaper reporter and free-lance writer.

Mindy Hightower was a registered nurse and the Omaha manager of Concentra Managed Care, one of the largest personal care providers in the country.

Hanna Hinchman wrote *A Life in Hand: Creating the Illuminated Journal*, which was sent to Lisa Pelto prior to Journalathon I and is printed with her permission and the author's. Hinchman's book is published by Gibbs-Smith in Layton, Utah (ISBN number 0-68549-558-2).

Analisa Jacob was a senior at Omaha Central High School.

Yoshi Kardell was a graduate of Omaha Central High School.

Jon Kathol was a UNL architecture student and Renaissance man.

Kip Kippley was a computer systems manager for Sitel Corporation

Richard Koelling is a retired businessman and lives in Omaha, NE.

Penny Koenig was a UNO student.

Hilary Kyler was a junior at Omaha Central High School.

Tina Labellarte quit her day job in Topeka, KS, to become a writer and a student of literature at the University of Kansas. She has an Italian father and an American mother, two grown children, one small grandchild, and plenty of family scattered from Chicago to Rome. She writes fiction drawn from impressions of her real-life adventures.

Lori Leuthje graduated from high school in Holdrege, NE, and began college at Concordia College in Bronxville, NY. She hopes to become a writer.

Chaia Lea Lloyd was a junior at Omaha Central High School.

Dr. John Mackiel is the Superintendent of the Omaha Public Schools.

David Mainelli was a UNO student and the manager of Julio's Restaurant at 123 street and West Center Road in Omaha, NE.

Dr. Stan Maliszewski was the Chairman of the Counseling Department at the University of Arizona at Tucson. "I started volunteering last Friday morning at 6 a.m. This was a training run for me. I volunteered to drive the water truck to some of the water stations in the desert on Sunday mornings. We go to church at the reservation mission on Saturday night. Most people are in church on Sunday, so someone is needed to fill the water stations. Can you believe that 1,500 migrants leave Altar, Mexico, each day in an attempt to cross the desert? The water supplies need to be checked daily."

Kathleen Maloney was *Fine Lines'* Book Review Editor and taught English at Omaha Central High School.

Brad Martin was a senior at the University of Nebraska at Lincoln, worked for the Outdoor Venture Center on campus, and led wilderness tours all over the nation.

David Martin is the creator and managing editor of *Fine Lines*.

Erin Martin was then a freshman at Nebraska Wesleyan University in Lincoln, NE.

Dr. John J. McKenna is a retired English professor from the University of Nebraska at Omaha.

Mary Binder Misfeldt was a regular columnist for the Douglas County Post-Gazette.

Deborah McGinn taught creative writing at Lincoln High School in Lincoln, NE.

Jane Meehan was an English instructor at the University of Nebraska at Omaha. "How delighted I was last fall when Omaha City Council President Lee Terry proposed an ordinance that would strengthen the city's response to neighborhood complaints about people who hold frequent garage sales. It reminded me of a poignant journal entry I wrote over a decade ago."

Jacquelyn Morgan was an English major at the University of Nebraska at Omaha.

Hilary Moshman was a senior at Omaha Westside High School. She went to India on a foreign exchange trip her junior year in high school for nine months. Her teacher was Doug Pierson.

G. Lynn Nelson is the Director of the Phoenix, AZ, Writing Project and a Professor in the English Department at Arizona State University.

Jill Parker was a roving correspondent for *Fine Lines*. She lived and studied in Bangkok, Thailand. Her dream was to travel the world, and she promised to write about her adventures for our readers.

Dr. Karl Paulnack, pianist and director of the music division at The Boston Conservatory, gave this fantastic welcome address to the parents of incoming students on September 1, 2004.

Irv Peckham was the Director of Writing and a professor of English at UNO.

Marty Pierson is a retired teacher and writes to celebrate her past memories in the classroom.

Donald F. Prince was a retired physician and lived in Minden, NE.

Kathleen Pugel was an education student at UNO.

Armando Salgado, a native of Mexico, was a junior at Central High School in Omaha, NE.

Patricia Schicker was a *Fine Lines* Advisory Board member and retired speech pathologist.

Jayne Schlosser lives in Omaha, NE.

Madelon Shaw was a social critic and writer in Omaha.

Bill Schock, retired-publisher of *The Falls City Journal*, was a bomber pilot during WWII. After his airplane was shot down, he became a prisoner of war.

Jan Shoemaker, for years an English teacher at Jackson Preparatory School in Jackson, MS, and Director of the Mississippi Writing Project, was working on her PhD in English at Louisiana State University in Baton Rouge, LA.

Roxanne Slattery was an undergraduate psychology and English major at the University of Nebraska at Omaha.

Michael Strauss, a graduate of Yale University with a degree in English Literature, is a professional musician and lived in Cedar Rapids, IA. His musical specialty is the viola.

Mary K. Stillwell was a teaching assistant at UNO and Resident Artist with the Nebraska Arts Council, grades 4-12. She studied with Erica Jong, attended school at UMKC and NYU. Her poetry has been printed in a dozen or more poetry reviews and several anthologies. In the next issue of *Fine Lines*, we will share some of her poems with our readers.

William Tarbox worked in the computer department at Boystown, NE, and was a senior at the University of Nebraska Omaha.

Ted Theisen was a student at UNO.

Joe Thomas was a UNO graduate and studied Zen for many years.

The author of the following article is unknown. It was submitted by Jesse Ugalde, a *Fine Lines* member in San Diego, CA. He thought many "unsung" educators would like to know they are appreciated more than they realize.

Drew Urban was a sophomore at Seward, NE, High School.

Arturo Vega was a Metropolitan Community College student.

Egon Viola is an artist specializing in designer mosaic murals. The words above form the caption placed below a huge mural inside the front door of the Elkhorn Valley Campus building of Metropolitan Community College, Elkhorn, NE.

Pat Vlcan recently retired from the Omaha Mutual Insurance Company, is the mother of a teenage girl and writes to release the pain of everyday living.

Joel Vogts (Eveleth) writes in her journal with much love and discipline. She remarried recently and moved from Omaha to Caldwell, Idaho. One of the first items she packed was her journal.

David Wallace was a retired architect.

Kathleen Warren was student teaching this semester in an English classroom in District 66. She will graduate this semester from the University of Nebraska-Omaha.

Dr. Donald Welch, professor of English Emeritus from the University of Nebraska at Kearney, shares his all consuming love of poetry.

Laura Werkheiser was an Omaha Central High School senior.

Dr. Leslie Whipp was an English professor at the University of Nebraska at Lincoln.

Clark Wisniewski was an undergraduate student at the University of Nebraska at Omaha.

Poet's Biographical Notes

Dorothy Apley is an English instructor at Geneva High School, renamed Fillmore Central High School. This writing is based on an occurrence that took place in 1959.

Troy Bell was a junior at Central High School in Omaha and thought about either entering the business world or the Army upon graduation.

Alice Blackstone started writing poetry in her 60s, because she loved the compaction of the language, its pictures, and the emotional feelings. She continued to write into her 90s. "I like looking back in time, because there is value, even in the bad times. That is an achievement. I believe in doing today what I am thinking of tomorrow. I am grateful for my friends, young and old. I keep active. People do a lot of nice things for me, and I let them. I get pleasure from doing things for others. I received more blessings than not. I focus on the positive, but I am not really a 'Pollyanna!' "

Sheila Boerner teaches English at St. Patrick's Catholic High School in North Platte, NE.

Mary Bowman lives in Lincoln, NE.

Evetta Brunk was a student at the University of Nebraska at Omaha in the Fine Arts College's Writer's Workshop. She was a professional model, rode thoroughbred horses, kept a serious journal, and wrote to understand reality.

Molly Campbell was a junior at Omaha Central High School.

Albert Camus (1913 - 1960) was a French author, journalist, and philosopher. He was awarded the 1957 Nobel Prize for Literature. "His clear-sighted earnestness illuminated the problems of the human conscience in our times." The second-youngest recipient of the Nobel Prize in Literature, after Rudyard Kipling, and the first African-born writer to receive the award, he is the shortest-lived of any Nobel literature laureate to date, having died in an automobile accident just over two years after receiving the award.

Ardiss Cederholm was a retired teacher from Lincoln, NE, and is an active member in the Chaparral Poetry Society.

Unhei Cho was a senior at Papillion-Lavista High School and enjoyed writing poems and short stories.

Darrel Draper is an historical re-enactor and lives in Omaha, NE.

Lorraine Duggin is an ESL instructor at Metropolitan Community College and a published poet.

Joyce Dunn passed away in 2011. She published two books and was a nurse.

Mary Filkins now works for TDAmeritrade. She has been writing in her journal religiously since she was in high school.

Dr. Thomas Franti is a professor at the University of Nebraska at Lincoln. He is a published author and a member of the Chaparral Poetry Society in Lincoln.

Dr. Reloy Garcia is an English professor at Creighton University in Omaha, NE.

Brett Gilcrist was a freshman at Missouri Western State College, St. Joseph, MO.

Cathy Goevert was selected the Angela Trimmer Golden Merit Award Winner for her poetry and was the only Nebraskan chosen to be included in the Anthology of National Library Poetry Contest the year this poem was published in *Fine Lines*.

Travis Hall was a senior at Omaha Central High School.

Judy Haney was a nurse for almost 30 years. She now volunteers for CASA, a program for abused and neglected children.

Twyla Hansen lives in Lincoln, NE.

Anna Henkens was a freshman at Chadron State College in Nebraska.

David Prinz Hufford is a retired English professor. For more than 35 years, he taught at Iowa Western Community College in Council Bluffs, IA.

Monica Kershner was a Presidential Fellow in English at the University of Nebraska at Omaha and was a PhD student at the University of Arizona.

William Kloefkorn (1932 – 2011) was a poet and educator based in Lincoln, NE. He was the author of twelve collections of poetry, two short story collections, a collection of children's Christmas stories, and four memoirs. Additionally, Kloefkorn was professor emeritus of English at Nebraska Wesleyan University. In 1982, Kloefkorn was appointed State Poet of Nebraska. In addition to his literary honors, Kloefkorn boasted that he won first place in the 1978 Nebraska Hog-Calling Championship.

Andy Koehler lives in the American heartland and is a lover of quotations. His favorite is from Euripides: "God gave man two ears and one mouth, so he may listen twice as much as he speaks."

Sister Judy Leal was a nun in the Order of Saint Francis. She now lives in Denver, CO.

Mary Lewandowski was an 83-year-old great grandmother who lived in Omaha. She was published often during her lifetime, notably in the *Blackberry Press Anthology*.

Kathleen Maloney was an English teacher at Central High School

Erin Martin was a fifth grade student at Oakdale Elementary School in District 66, Omaha, NE.

Walker Martin taught eighth grade English at McMillan Middle School in Omaha.

Vince McAndrew rises early in the morning at 4 a.m. every day to write poetry before he goes to work.

Larry Munn taught English at Falls City, NE, High School.

Tom Pappas was an English teacher in Lincoln, NE, at Lincoln High School.

Lisa Pelto graduated from the University of Nebraska at Omaha and became the Production Manager at HMJ & Associates in Omaha, NE.

Stephanie Pluta was a student at Metropolitan Community College.

Harold Poff, a public relations executive for 40 years, the presidential campaign manager for Senator Kerr of Oklahoma, a professional copy writer for TV, radio, and print advertisers, concentrated on rhyme, meter, and satire in his compositions.

Gwen Quill has been writing since she was in fourth grade. Her favorite subjects to write about include poetry, fantasy, and fiction. If she could sum up her life in two words it would be "writing music."

Marjorie Saiser lives in Lincoln, NE, and the following poem is from her book, *Wellsprings*.

R. W. Seaman is a retired minister living in New Castle, Delaware.

Roxanne Slattery is an English and psychology major at UNO. Reading her writing is like visiting an "all you can eat buffet."

Grace Solem-Pfeifer goes to Willa Cather Elementary School.

Joe Sousa wrote this poem in the eleventh grade at Omaha South High School.

Linda Stevens, a UNO student, writes poetry for many reasons. It connects with the unconscious. It heals. It speaks the truth. It reveals.

Mindy Venditte lives in Ft. Calhoun, NE.

Mabel Victoria Walter is a retired accountant, artist, sculptor, and long time journal writer from Ulysses, Kansas.

Margaret McCann Warren lived in Omaha and filled her column with years of wisdom.

Peggy Wheeler was an English teacher at Omaha Central High School.

Karl White was a student at the University of Illinois, Chicago.

Sade White was a creative writing student at Omaha Central High School.

Mary Davey Wilson teaches English at Omaha North High School.

Geri Zerse submitted this poem of wisdom. A retired teacher and counselor, she is now a realtor in Omaha, NE.

Artist's Biographical Notes

Laura Neece Baltaro is a contributor to *Fine Lines*

Eddith Buis is an inveterate "cheerleader for art." Eddith is best known for directing public art projects for the Omaha Metro area. After learning the process for community projects through managing grants for the Omaha Public Schools, she moved on to direct the J. Doe Project, the Lewis & Clark Icon Project for the Riverfront, five years of summer sculpture installations at Leahy Mall for the Summer Arts Festival, benchmarks for artist-painted MAT bus benches, and exhibits at both Fontenelle Forest and Lauritzen Gardens. Over the years, Eddith has taught art to all ages of students through Joslyn Art Museum, the Boys and Girls Clubs, and UNO's gifted student and adult continuing education programs. As a 34-year veteran of teaching, Eddith Buis holds a B.S., and M.A. and a Specialist Degree in art education. She is currently an adjunct instructor at Metropolitan Community College's Fort Omaha Campus.

Wipanan Chaichanta was born in Chiang Rai, Thailand, and graduated from Sukhothai Thammathirat Open University. She now lives in Houston, TX.

Nick Clark was a student at Andrson Middle School in Millard, NE.

Dana Damewood was an Omaha Central High School student.

Danyel Engel was an art student at Metropolitan Community College in Elkhorn, NE.

1st Lt. Jacob N. Fritz, 25, of Verdon, NE, graduated from the US Military Academy at West Point and was captured on January 20 in Karbala, Iraq. He was abducted by insurgents and was later shot and killed. He was assigned to the 2nd Battalion, 377th Parachute Field Artillery Regiment, 4th Brigade Combat Team, 25th Infantry Division, Fort Richardson, Alaska. One of Fritz's younger brothers followed him to West Point as a member of the class of 2008.

Cindy Grady spends her days managing a book publishing company in Omaha, NE

Kim Justus is a poet and photographer and lives in Omaha, NE. Her work is available at kimotofoto.com

Jasmine Kitchen was an art student at Omaha Northwest High School.

Stan Maliszewski is a Professor of Counseling Education at the University of Arizona.

David Martin is the creator and managing editor of *Fine Lines*.

Yolie Martin is a school counselor in Omaha, NE and volunteers at the *Fine Lines* Writing Camp

Deborah McGinn is a retired English teacher in Lincoln, NE.

Shari Morehead is an amateur photographer and lives in Salem, NE.

Walker Plank is an Omaha, NE artist who graduated with a BFA from Indiana University. He taught K-12 art at a private school for three years, after which he joined active duty military as an avionics technician. His art pursuits continued throughout his six years of service, and he began displaying his work in public after separating from the military in 2009. That same year Walker completed his MSA in Human Resources from Central Michigan University, and he intends to explore that career field while working on his art.

Jimmy Reistad loves his dog, Chase, who is a four-year-old Golden Doodle. Jimmy was entering fifth grade at Highlands Elementary School in Edina, Minnesota, when he took this photo.

Anna Henkens Schmidt is a graduate of Chadron State College in Chadron, NE. She Now lives and works in North Carolina.

Raleigh Wilkerson is a retired, professional artist and lives in Meredith, NH.

Jay Worden taught for many years at West High School in Bellevue, NE. He is now retired and spends a great deal of time traveling the world.

Fine Lines Membership

Membership with *Fine Lines* includes four perfect bound journals delivered to your front door. Frequently, we send an e-letter with *Fine Lines* news, upcoming events, and the inside scoop on special issues.

In addition, we provide hundreds of copies to students who have no means to buy subscriptions. Your membership will help provide copies for young writers who cannot purchase *Fine Lines* for themselves.

We offer two methods of payment for your *Fine Lines* donations.

- U.S. residents should make checks payable to *Fine Lines* for $50. Schools and libraries in the U.S. should send $40. Those living outside the U.S. must send their checks for U.S. $60. Please include your name, address, and e-mail with your payment and send to:

  Fine Lines Journal
  PO Box 241713
  Omaha, NE 68124

- We also accept credit card payments via PayPal on the *Fine Lines* Web Site: www.finelines.org

Submissions

We accept e-mail, file attachments, CDs formatted in MS Word for PCs, and laser-printed hard copies.

No overt abuse, sexuality, profanity, alcohol, drugs, or violent articles are reviewed. Editors reply when writing is accepted for publication, if a stamped, self-addressed envelope or e-mail address is provided.

Address changes and correspondence should be sent to *Fine Lines*, PO Box 241713, Omaha, NE 68124.

Do not send "whole class projects." Teachers may copy *Fine Lines* content for classes and submit student work for publication when they act as sponsors.

Kathleen K. Maloney
designs

The Deem Corporation
P.O. Box 451117 • Omaha, NE 68145 • USA
Tel: (402) 895-5748 • Fax: (402) 895-2306

kathmalo@cox.net

Dan Botos, AAMS®
Financial Advisor

Edward Jones
MAKING SENSE OF INVESTING

8424 West Center Road
Suite 200
Omaha, NE 68124
Bus. 402-391-2100   Fax 888-224-8764
TF. 888-391-2112
dan.botos@edwardjones.com
www.edwardjones.com

Epilepsy Affiliate of Nebraska
Epilepsy Foundation of North Central Illinois, Iowa, Nebraska
Laura Neece-Baltaro
Volunteer

9315 Pauline Street
Omaha, NE 68124-3836

(402) 827-7080
(402) 319-4744
QKRLaura@aol.com
www.epilepsyheartland.org

MARK G. SMITH, D.D.S.
KARRY K. WHITTEN, D.D.S.

2936 S. 86th CIRCLE
OMAHA, NE 68124
Phone (402) 393-2484
Fax (402) 393-2490
www.gotsmileomaha.com

System Integrators

Sebastian Arul
Communication Systems Engineer
14513 South 25 Avenue Circle
Bellevue, NE 68123

402-614-6996   sebastian.arul@cox.net

TAX AND BUSINESS CONSULTANTS
"Your Tax Specialists"

Tom Tomasek
Tax Consultant

229 So. 17th St.
P.O. Box 390
Blair, NE 68008
(402) 426-4144
Fax: (402) 426-4156

2816 North Main, Ste A
P.O. Box 815
Elkhorn, NE 68022
(402) 289-5756

E-mail: tomt@rvrco.net

Dangerous Songs, Banned Books & Censored Movies

Come celebrate the First Amendment:
your freedom of speech and expression
with music by the Academy of Rock.
Thursday, October 1
6:00pm-8:30pm
Duffy's Tavern, 1412 O Street, Lincoln

A Lincoln Calling Event

From 2001 to 2008, American libraries were faced with 3,736 challenges.

- 1,225 challenges due to "sexually explicit" material;
- 1,008 challenges due to "offensive language;"
- 720 challenges due to material deemed "unsuited to age group;"
- 458 challenges due to "violence"
- 269 challenges due to "homosexuality;" and
- 103 materials were challenged because they were "anti-family," and an additional 233 were challenged because of their "religious viewpoints."

Banned Book Week, from September 26 to October 3, calls attention to the wealth of creative expression that is stifled when books, music or film can be forbidden to the public. Advances against censorship and in the defense of privacy can only be accomplished when individuals are vigilant and speak out to protect their rights. We encourage you to mark Banned Books Week by celebrating great works of art that someone once thought were too dangerous for you to experience.

Sponsored by: ACLU Nebraska, Academic Freedom Coalition of Nebraska,
Nebraska Library Association Intellectual Freedom Committee &
The Academy of Rock-Northeast Family Center

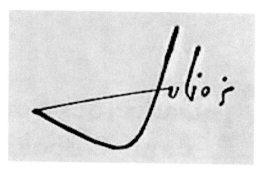

Julio's Restaurant
is proud to
support *Fine Lines* and the
hard working people who
produce these wonderful
works of the human spirit.
Thanks to all who make this
publication another great
"Omaha Original!"

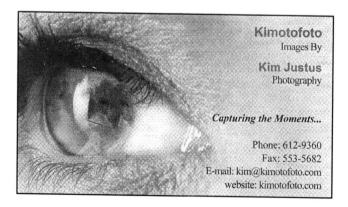

WRITE ABOUT LIFE

---

www.WriteLife.com

Whether you want to write a novel, a biography, or even a "how to" book, our web site has been developed with you in mind, and we offer numerous advantages to those interested in collaborative publishing.

NELAC

Nebraska Language Arts Council (NELAC) is a statewide professional volunteer association of language arts educators who join together to network through conferences, meetings, journals and conversation. NELAC is Nebraska's official state affiliate with the Nebraska's Council of Teachers of English and membership is open to all educators of language arts kindergarten through college level.

NELAC Promotes:

- Excellence in Student Magazines
- Young Writers' Programs
- Achievement in Writing Awards
- Promising Young Teacher Award
- The Nebraska English Journal
- The Nebraska Stdent Journal
- Nebraska Literary Map
- Guide to Nebraska Authors
- Annual Nebraska Poetry Month
- Annual High School Quiz Bowl
- Plum Creek Children's Festival
- SLATE (Support for the Learning and Teaching of English)
- AFCON (Academic Freedom Coalition of Nebraska
- Nebraska Center for the Book

Join NELAC this year!

Send $10 to:

**NELAC
PO Box 83944
Lincoln, NE 68501-3944**

Contact:

Clark Kolterman
Ckolte00@connectseward.org

AFCON

Academic Freedom Coalition of Nebraska promotes academic freedom, defined as intellectual freedom in educational and research contexts. This includes freedoms of belief and expression and access to information and ideas.

As a Member, you can help us:

- Support applications of the First Amendment in academic contexts, including elementary and secondary schools, colleges, universities, and libraries.

- Educate Nebraskans about the meaning and value of intellectual freedom, intellectual diversity, mutual respect, open communication, and uninhibited pursuit of knowledge, including the role of these ideas in academic contexts and in democratic self-government.

- Assist students, teachers, librarians, and researchers confronted with censorship, indoctrination, or suppression of ideas.

- Act as a liaison among groups in Nebraska that support academic freedom issues.

To become a Member:

Send dues, organization or individual name, address and phone number to

Cathi McCurtry
15 N. Thomas Ave.
Oakland, NE 68045

AFCONebr.org

Facing the Blank Page

by David Martin

"In his collection of personal essays, Martin gives us no less than a series of prescriptions for how to conduct an examined life."
Dr. J.J. McKenna

"These essays are an interesting journey from introspective curiosity about what makes Martin's soul tick to excellent narratives about motivating one to write."
Richard Koelling

"I am delighted to see the essays I have read through the years in one book where I can turn the pages, taste the ideas, and savor!"
Colleen Aagesen

"Martin is devoted to his calling and is an inspiration to fledgling writers and diehards in the field."
Mary Bannister

Facing the Blank Page

A Collection of Essays and Poems
from the First Ten Years of *Fine Lines*,
a Literary Journal, 1992-2001

David Martin

Available at:

Now Available:

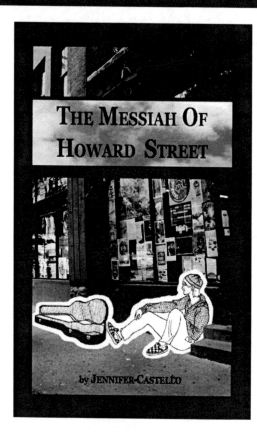

Available at:

www.WriteLife.com

www.Amazon.com

www.Amazon.co.uk

www.BooksAMillion.com

www.AbeBooks.com

www.Alibris.com

www.BarnesAndNoble.com

In *The Messiah of Howard Street*, Hayden Bell has successfully evaded University of Nebraska at Lincoln by employing himself as a street performer in the Old Market. Kelly Erickson is watching her mother die of cancer, and Janie Harris is watching her best friend march off to Iraq. Frank Kuzchenitsh is stuck in a dead end job, Ryan Fairfield just filed for divorce, and Thomas Stall is successfully making his escape via an impromptu Colorado road trip.

Through Jennifer Castello's small portraits of those who have found themselves on the threshold of change and monotony, the city of Omaha comes to life in a story of growing up, standing up, and taking chances.

ISBN: 978-1-60808-013-7

BOXES

The Secret Life of Howard Hughes

Eva McLelland was good at keeping secrets, and she had a big one. Sworn to secrecy for thirty-one years until the death of her husband, Eva was at last able to come forward and share a story that turns twentieth century history on its head and fills in puzzling blanks in the mysterious life of the tycoon Howard Hughes.

How could Hughes appear to witnesses as an emaciated, long finger-nailed, mental incompetent, yet fly a jet aircraft four months later? How could a doctor describe him as looking like a "prisoner of war," when at the same time investment bankers, politicians, and diplomats who met him said he was articulate and well-groomed? The answer is a perfect example of the brilliance of the elusive billionaire. He simply found a mentally incompetent man to impersonate him, drawing the attention of the Internal Revenue Service and an army of lawyers who pursued him, while he conducted his business in peace from Panama with his new wife, Eva McLelland. Sound fantastic? It is. However, after seven years of research and verification, Eva's story produces the final pieces in the mysterious puzzle that was Howard Hughes.

ISBN: 978-1-60808-017-5

BOXES

The Secret Life of Howard Hughes

DOUGLAS WELLMAN

Available at:

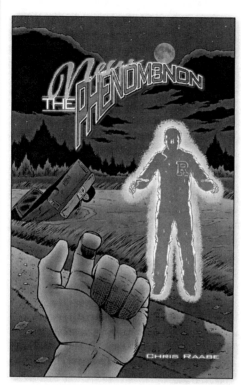

CPSIA information can be obtained at www.ICGtesting.com
Printed in the USA
LVOW090032030212

266787LV00002B/3/P